New Technology and Mediated Chinese Tourists

This book aims to curate a collection of articles to showcase the latest work and biggest trends shaping the global tourism industry in the past two decades – new technology and the Chinese tourists.

While the emergence of new technology continues to propel the evolution of the tourism industry, Chinese tourists as a dominating market have won increasing attention across worldwide destinations. On one hand, the vast advancement of technology has fundamentally shifted the way Chinese tourists travel. On the other hand, the arrival of technologically savvy Chinese tourists has provoked tourism providers and destinations to adopt innovative technology (e.g., mobile payment). Standing on the edge of the third decade of the twenty-first century, the tourism industry and scholarly community are facing unprecedented challenges amidst exciting opportunities. Particularly, this line of research is perhaps timelier than ever, with the pandemic physically distancing people whilst augmenting technology's function in mediating social interactions and connecting lives beyond geographic boundaries.

New Technology and Mediated Chinese Tourists will be a great resource for researchers and students of Tourism and Hospitality including those interested to understand how innovation and technology are embedded in the tourism industry. This book was originally published as a special issue of the *Journal of China Tourism Research*.

Han Shen is Professor of Tourism at Fudan University, Shanghai, China.

Alei Fan is Assistant Professor in White Lodging-J.W. Marriott, Jr. School of Hospitality and Tourism Management at Purdue University, USA.

Laurie Wu is Associate Professor and Arthur F. McGonigle Research Fellow in the Department of Tourism and Hospitality Management at Temple University, USA.

T0321357

New Technology and Mediated Chinese Tourists

Edited by
Han Shen, Alei Fan and Laurie Wu

Routledge
Taylor & Francis Group

LONDON AND NEW YORK

First published 2023
by Routledge
4 Park Square, Milton Park, Abingdon, Oxon OX14 4RN

and by Routledge
605 Third Avenue, New York, NY 10158

Routledge is an imprint of the Taylor & Francis Group, an informa business

Introduction, Chapters 1–7 © 2023 Taylor & Francis

British Library Cataloguing in Publication Data
A catalogue record for this book is available from the British Library

ISBN13: 978-1-032-49148-6 (hbk)
ISBN13: 978-1-032-49149-3 (pbk)
ISBN13: 978-1-003-39234-7 (ebk)

DOI: 10.4324/9781003392347

Typeset in Minion Pro
by Newgen Publishing UK

Publisher's Note
The publisher accepts responsibility for any inconsistencies that may have arisen during the conversion of this book from journal articles to book chapters, namely the inclusion of journal terminology.

Disclaimer
Every effort has been made to contact copyright holders for their permission to reprint material in this book. The publishers would be grateful to hear from any copyright holder who is not here acknowledged and will undertake to rectify any errors or omissions in future editions of this book.

Contents

Citation Information   vi

Notes on Contributors   viii

Introduction—Embracing the Future: New Technology and Mediated
Chinese Tourists   1
Laurie Wu, Alei Fan and Han Shen

1   Impact of High-speed Rail on Destination Accessibility: A Case Study of China   8
    Jin Weng, Xiaolin Zhu and Xin Li

2   Hong Kong Millennials' Intention to Visit Local Hotel Spas   24
    Lok Yan Jessie Lam and Yixing (Lisa) Gao

3   Leisure Mobility of Chinese Millennials   41
    Jieyu (Jade) Shi, Alei Fan and Liping A. Cai

4   Corporate Social Responsibility Communications on Social Media and
    Consumers' Brand Engagement: A Case Study of Hotels in Hong Kong   61
    Cheukhei Danny Chung, Yixing (Lisa) Gao and Daniel Leung

5   Channeling Life Satisfaction to Tourist Satisfaction: New Conceptualization
    and Evidence   80
    Yong Chen

6   Relationship between Hotels' Website Quality and Consumers' Booking
    Intentions with Internet Experience as Moderator   99
    Liang Wang and Rob Law

7   Social Media Comments about Hotel Robots   120
    Hio Nam Io and Chang Boon Lee

Index   140

Citation Information

The chapters in this book were originally published in the *Journal of China Tourism Research*, volume 16, issue 4 (2020). When citing this material, please use the original page numbering for each article, as follows:

Introduction

Embracing the Future: New Technology and Mediated Chinese Tourists
Laurie Wu, Alei Fan and Han Shen
Journal of China Tourism Research, volume 16, issue 4 (2020), pp. 487–493

Chapter 1

Impact of High-speed Rail on Destination Accessibility: A Case Study of China
Jin Weng, Xiaolin Zhu and Xin Li
Journal of China Tourism Research, volume 16, issue 4 (2020), pp. 494–509

Chapter 2

Hong Kong Millennials' Intention to Visit Local Hotel Spas
Lok Yan Jessie Lam and Yixing (Lisa) Gao
Journal of China Tourism Research, volume 16, issue 4 (2020), pp. 510–526

Chapter 3

Leisure Mobility of Chinese Millennials
Jieyu (Jade) Shi, Alei Fan and Liping A. Cai
Journal of China Tourism Research, volume 16, issue 4 (2020), pp. 527–546

Chapter 4

Corporate Social Responsibility Communications on Social Media and Consumers' Brand Engagement: A Case Study of Hotels in Hong Kong
Cheukhei Danny Chung, Lisa Gao and Daniel Leung
Journal of China Tourism Research, volume 16, issue 4 (2020), pp. 547–565

Chapter 5

Channeling Life Satisfaction to Tourist Satisfaction: New Conceptualization and Evidence
Yong Chen
Journal of China Tourism Research, volume 16, issue 4 (2020), pp. 566–584

Chapter 6

Relationship between Hotels' Website Quality and Consumers' Booking Intentions with Internet Experience as Moderator

Liang Wang and Rob Law

Journal of China Tourism Research, volume 16, issue 4 (2020), pp. 585–605

Chapter 7

Social Media Comments about Hotel Robots

Hio Nam Io and Chang Boon Lee

Journal of China Tourism Research, volume 16, issue 4 (2020), pp. 606–625

For any permission-related enquiries please visit:
www.tandfonline.com/page/help/permissions

Notes on Contributors

Liping A. Cai is Professor and Director of Purdue Tourism and Hospitality Research Center in School of Hospitality and Tourism Management at Purdue University, USA. His research interests include hospitality principles and consumer experiences in travel and tourism.

Yong Chen, PhD, is Assistant Professor at Ecole hôtelière de Lausanne (EHL), Switzerland, where he lectures on tourism and hospitality economics. Dr Chen's research interests include tourist behavior, tourism demand, the sharing economy, and Chinese outbound tourism.

Cheukhei Danny Chung is BSc (Hons) student in Hotel Management in the School of Hotel and Tourism Management at The Hong Kong Polytechnic University, Hong Kong SAR, China.

Alei Fan is Assistant Professor in White Lodging-J.W. Marriott, Jr. School of Hospitality and Tourism Management at Purdue University, USA. Her research interests include service innovation, consumer behavior, and cross-cultural study.

Yixing (Lisa) Gao is Assistant Professor in the School of Hotel and Tourism Management at The Hong Kong Polytechnic University, Hong Kong SAR, China. She holds a PhD in hospitality management from the Pennsylvania State University. Her research focuses on corporate social responsibility issues and consumer behavior.

Hio Nam Io is PhD candidate in the Faculty of Business Administration at the University of Macau, Macau SAR, China. His research interests include human–robot interactions, social media mining, and e-commerce technology.

Lok Yan Jessie Lam is a BSc (Hons) student in Hotel Management in the School of Hotel and Tourism Management at The Hong Kong Polytechnic University, Hong Kong SAR, China.

Rob Law is Professor in School of Hotel and Tourism Management at The Hong Kong Polytechnic University, Kowloon, Hong Kong SAR, China. His research interests include information technology, internet, and e-commerce.

Chang Boon Lee is Associate Professor of Business Information Systems in the Faculty of Business Administration at the University of Macau, Macau SAR, China. His research interests include e-commerce management and applications of technology in the gaming and hospitality industry.

Daniel Leung is Assistant Professor in the School of Hotel and Tourism Management at The Hong Kong Polytechnic University, Hong Kong SAR, China. He has authored/coauthored a number of research articles in first-tier academic journals. His research interests are in the areas of electronic word-of-mouth, electronic marketing as well as hotel and tourism website evaluation.

Xin Li is a graduate student in the Department of Tourism at Fudan University, Shanghai, China. His research interests are in regional economics and tourism destination development.

Han Shen is Professor of Tourism at Fudan University, Shanghai, China.

Jieyu (Jade) Shi is a doctoral student in School of Hospitality and Tourism Management at Purdue University, USA. Her research interests include tourism and quality of life, China market, and intercultural learning in higher education.

Liang Wang is Lecturer in School of Management at Zhejiang University, Hangzhou, China. Her research interests include online marketing and structural equation modeling (SEM) applications in the tourism and hospitality area.

Jin Weng is Associate Professor in the Department of Tourism at Fudan University, Shanghai, China. His research interests are in tourism economics and tourism destination development.

Laurie Wu is Associate Professor and Arthur F. McGonigle Research Fellow in the Department of Tourism and Hospitality Management at Temple University, USA.

Xiaolin Zhu is a graduate student in the Department of Tourism at Fudan University, Shanghai, China. Her research interests are in tourism destination development and tourism geography.

Introduction—Embracing the Future: New Technology and Mediated Chinese Tourists

Reflecting upon the biggest trends shaping the global tourism industry in the past two decades, two keywords shall not be missed: new technology (He et al., 2018; Tussyadiah, 2020; Wang et al., 2016) and Chinese tourists (Chen & Huang, 2018; Fu et al., 2017; Hsu et al., 2010; Li et al., 2011). While the emergence of new technology continues to propel the evolution of the global tourism industry, Chinese tourists as a dominating market have won global attention across worldwide destinations. As one of the largest source markets, Chinese outbound travelers have skyrocketed from 4.5 million in 2000 to 170 million in 2019 (China Daily, 2020). During this time, new technology devices, platforms, systems, and infrastructure have continued to shape industry landscapes, stimulating tourism development at an unprecedented rate. On the one hand, the vast advancement of technology has fundamentally shifted the way Chinese tourists travel around the globe. On the other hand, the arrival of technologically savvy Chinese tourists has provoked service providers and destinations to adopt innovative technology (e.g., mobile payment). Interactively and over time, these two forces have changed tourism practices, promoted infrastructural development, and energized an unrivaled round of disruptive innovation, which has transformed connectivity and travel experience for visitors in a global community.

A growing body of literature

As a reflection of technology being an essential and indispensable reality, the last two decades have witnessed a rapid increase of scholarly work on this grand phenomenon. A review of literature indexed by the keywords of 'Technology' and 'Chinese Tourists' in six leading journals (i.e., *Annals of Tourism Research, Tourism Management, Journal of Travel Research, Journal of Hospitality and Tourism Research, Journal of Travel and Tourism Marketing*, and *Journal of China Tourism Research*) has revealed an exponential growth of scholarly enthusiasm in this realm (Figure 1).

A further analysis of the reviewed literature uncovered an exciting, enriched, and enlightening network of scholarly forays into the front edge of technology and tourism. Based on the same sample of journals, Figure 2 demonstrates research themes and subject networks in seven interconnected clusters of topics: technology, use, travel, marketing, tourism, perceptions, and (Chinese) tourists. As further showcased in Table 1, the integration between the two streams of literature (i.e., 'Technology' and 'Chinese Tourists') mainly comes in three forms. First, there is a school of literature focused on how technology empowers the Chinese tourists and enriches their travel experiences both at home and abroad as they navigate through the pre-, during, and post-travel stages. In that regard,

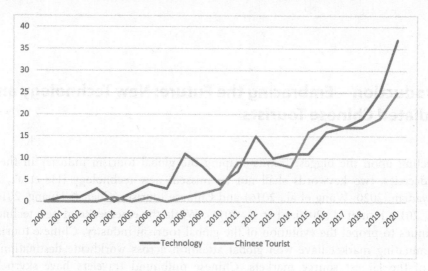

Figure 1. 'Technology' and 'Chinese tourists' research (2000–2020).

O'Regan and Chang (2015) studied how smartphone adoption influences travel experience amongst the Chinese youth. Second, there is a group of studies adopting Chinese tourists as subjects to inform theory-driven research. With the rapid and pervasive infusion of technology in contemporary Chinese society, Chinese tourists are perhaps one of the most tech-savvy group of individuals around the globe and hence have become an ideal group of subjects for technology-related research. For instance, Fong et al. (2017) studied the impact of locus of control and intentions to reuse mobile apps for making hotel reservations based on Chinese participants. Third, the technology-empowered new information infrastructure (e.g., social media platforms) have provided an extra set of methodological lens for scholars to examine the emerging dynamics and processes in the tourism industry, addressing both Chinese tourists' domestic and international travel as well as inbound tourists' experience in China. For example, Sun et al. (2015) utilized data from Chinese travel blogs to examine perceived destination image of New Zealand. Wu and Pearce (2017) took a netnographic and comparative approach to examining Chinese tourists' needs and preferences in regard to recreational vehicle tour experiences.

This special issue: New technology and mediated Chinese tourists

Inspired by this collective scholarly inquiry, the current special issue attempts to curate a collection of articles to showcase the latest work in the examination of new technology and the mediated Chinese tourists. This special issue compiles a diverse group of empirical work intersecting the two fascinating themes and encompassing its broader impacts on the global tourism industry and society.

The special issue opens with a documentation of an infrastructural technology wonder developed hand in hand with the proliferation of Chinese tourism: the massive construction of high-speed rail (HSR). Weng et al. (2020) examined the impact of HSR's construction on tourists' transportation choice and the resulted improvement in the accessibility of destinations. Utilizing ArcGIS network analysis, their research revealed that HSR has

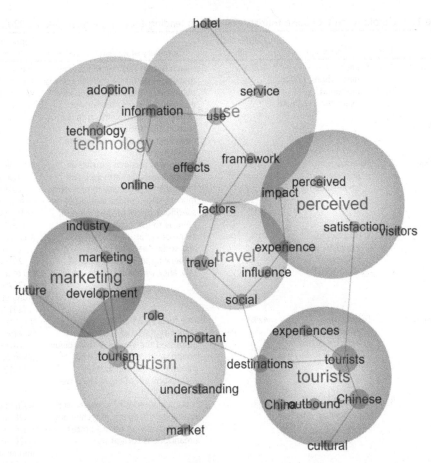

Figure 2. Research themes and subject networks on 'technology' and 'Chinese tourists' (2000–2020).

greatly improved the market potential of Chinese cities, particularly the small- and medium-sized ones.

The notion of mobile technology function affecting tourist behaviors is not new. Yet, how mobile technology affects tourists' recreational behaviors in a spa context awaits exploration. Lam and Gao (2019) fulfilled this gap in the literature. Focused on the technology generation of the millennials, Lam and Gao (2019) surveyed Hong Kong millennials' behavioral intention toward local hotel spas. Most excitingly, this work revealed how mobile device usage moderates the impact of spa attributes on visit intentions. To that end, this research showcases how the mediation of technology reshapes tourists' values and preferences in consumption contexts, which provide ample implications for relevant business practitioners.

Continuing this line of inquiry, Shi et al. (2020) examine how the adoption of mobile technology impacts Chinese millennials' leisure travel experience and continuous engagement with mobile technology. Addressing the pressing topic of optimizing mobile app development, their study revealed that it is mainly the utilitarian and social functions of mobile apps that influence Chinese millennials' leisure travel experience. Further, this work showcases a virtuous circle between

Table 1. 'Technology' and 'Chinese tourists' research in leading tourism journals (2000–2020).

Theme	Hits	Concept	Connectivity %	Summary of Research Focus	Representative Research
Tourists	627	Tourists, Chinese, destinations, China, outbound, experiences, cultural	100%	Research hitting this theme examines tourists, in particular Chinese tourists' behaviors, preferences, destination experiences and culture-driven behavioral patterns. The empirical examination focused on both outbound and domestic tourism experiences.	Li et al. (2011) Ji et al. (2016) Wu and Pearce (2017)
Tourism	532	Tourism, market, important, role, understanding	50%	This school of research focused on examining market structure and interactional processes to provide a more in-depth understanding of one specific segment of the important Chinese tourism market.	O'Regan and Chang (2015) Qi et al. (2008) Zhang et al. (2016)
Travel	419	Travel, factors, experience, social, influence	44%	This line of literature revealed individual and social relational factors influencing travel experience in relevance with technology use.	Anaya and Lehto (2020) Cai et al. (2020) Wong et al. (2019)
Technology	372	Technology, information, industry, online, adoption	42%	Mostly focused on individual travelers, technology related literature addressed the impact of technology adoption, in particular that of information communication technology adoption, in the travel industry.	He et al. (2018) Oh et al. (2016) Wang et al. (2016)
Use	436	Use, service, framework, effects, hotel	40%	This particular series of scholarly work examined the effects of technology use in optimizing service processes in organizations such as hotels.	A. Chan et al. (2015) E. S. Chan et al. (2018) Shin et al. (2019)
Perceptions	225	perceptions, satisfaction, impact, visitors	22%	With perceptions being a core focus of study in the tourism literature, this cluster of literature examines visitors' perceived experience, satisfaction in relevance with technology use.	Araña et al. (2016) Kim et al. (2006) Yasami et al. (2020)
Marketing	184	marketing, development, future	15%	The impact of technology development in propelling the marketing practices of tourism organizations is another theme in the past research.	Jin et al. (2019) Prayag and Soscia (2016) Zhang and Murphy (2009)

mobile technology engagement and leisure travel experience, explicating how an optimized mobile app experience during leisure travel can further contribute to one's continuous mobile technology engagement.

One of the most awing ways technology impacts contemporary business is how its adoption shapes our way of thinking, our shared values and essentially our shared goals as an industry. It has both practical and social values to examine what important societal roles new technologies can play. To answer such a research call, researchers start paying increasing attentions on how the prevalent social media platforms function as a uniting community connecting consumers and businesses in Corporate Social Responsibility (CSR) Communications. Adopting a mixed-method design, Chung et al. (2019) found that the disclosure of CSR efforts, in particular societal CSR efforts, on Facebook has a strong explanatory power of consumer brand engagement, unveiling how technology facilitates value transformation and industry advancement at the forefront of social responsibility practices.

With technology becoming further infused into our everyday life, the connection between daily life and travel is tighter than ever. In reflection of such notions, Chen (2019) examined the possibility of life satisfaction channeling to tourist satisfaction via destination experiences. Based on empirical evidence collected in a large-scale survey, Chen (2019) showed that the technology savvy Chinese tourists as well as tourists from seven other countries share a common experience: their life satisfaction at home can be channeled to their subsequent destinations through experience-based affect and destination image, which eventually affects tourist satisfaction.

Concluding remarks

Altogether, this special issue hopes to inspire more research on (or at) the intersection of technology and Chinese tourists. On the basis of this collection, we would like to call for future scholarly work to further advance the literature on technology and Chinese tourism. With technology-empowered innovation continuing to evolve along with the industry both at home and beyond, the subject interfacing new technology and the technology-mediated Chinese tourists will continue to thrive.

Standing on the edge of the third decade of the twenty-first century, the global tourism industry and the global scholarly community are currently facing unprecedented challenges amidst exciting opportunities. Nevertheless, the development of new technology and tourism activating an increasingly globalized civil society will remain to be a constant theme, to which the Chinese tourism industry and scholarly community could continue to contribute. The constant emergence of new technology in the tourism landscape will also persist to challenge our existing knowledge and propel for new research priorities. Intriguingly, this line of research is perhaps more timely than ever, with the pandemic physically distancing individuals whilst augmenting technology's function in mediating social interactions and connecting lives beyond geographic boundaries.

Last but not least, we want to express our sincere gratitude to the contributing authors to this special issue, without whom this collective work will not be able to come to fruition. We are also thankful for the contributions of the manuscript reviewers for this special issue, who were extremely professional and constructive. Every day, we are deeply inspired by the splendid work our scholarly community produces. Humbled by this service opportunity advocating for innovation, we are honored to be part of our scholarly community's joint force in envisioning a better tomorrow for the global tourism industry. The future is here and now, and may the future be always with us.

Disclosure statement

No potential conflict of interest was reported by the authors.

References

Anaya, G. J., & Lehto, X. (2020). Traveler-facing technology in the tourism experience: A historical perspective. *Journal of Travel & Tourism Marketing, 37*(3), 317–331. https://doi.org/10.1080/10548408.2020.1757561

Araña, J. E., León, C. J., Carballo, M. M., & Moreno Gil, S. (2016). Designing tourist information offices: The role of the human factor. *Journal of Travel Research, 55*(6), 764–773. https://doi.org/10.1177/0047287515587113

Cai, W., McKenna, B., & Waizenegger, L. (2020). Turning it off: Emotions in digital-free travel. *Journal of Travel Research, 59*(5), 909–927. https://doi.org/10.1177/0047287519868314

Chan, A., Hsu, C. H., & Baum, T. (2015). The impact of tour service performance on tourist satisfaction and behavioral intentions: A study of Chinese tourists in Hong Kong. *Journal of Travel & Tourism Marketing, 32*(1–2), 18–33. https://doi.org/10.1080/10548408.2014.986010

Chan, E. S., Okumus, F., & Chan, W. (2018). Barriers to environmental technology adoption in hotels. *Journal of Hospitality & Tourism Research, 42*(5), 829–852. https://doi.org/10.1177/1096348015614959

Chen, G., & Huang, S. (2018). Understanding Chinese cultural tourists: Typology and profile. *Journal of Travel & Tourism Marketing, 35*(2), 162–177. https://doi.org/10.1080/10548408.2017.1350253

Chen, Y. (2019). Channeling life satisfaction to tourist satisfaction: New conceptualization and evidence. *Journal of China Tourism Research*, 1–19. https://doi.org/10.1080/19388160.2019.1631926.

Chung, C. D., Gao, L., & Leung, D. (2019). Corporate social responsibility communications on social media and consumers' brand engagement: A case study of hotels in Hong Kong. *Journal of China Tourism Research*, 1–19. https://doi.org/10.1080/19388160.2019.1643434.

Fong, L. H. N., Lam, L. W., & Law, R. (2017). How locus of control shapes intention to reuse mobile apps for making hotel reservations: Evidence from Chinese consumers. *Tourism Management, 61*, 331–342. https://doi.org/10.1016/j.tourman.2017.03.002

Fu, X., Cai, L., & Lehto, X. (2017). Framing Chinese tourist motivations through the lenses of Confucianism. *Journal of Travel & Tourism Marketing, 34*(2), 149–170. https://doi.org/10.1080/10548408.2016.1141156

He, Z., Wu, L., & Li, X. R. (2018). When art meets tech: The role of augmented reality in enhancing museum experiences and purchase intentions. *Tourism Management, 68*, 127–139. https://doi.org/10.1016/j.tourman.2018.03.003

Hsu, C. H., Cai, L. A., & Li, M. (2010). Expectation, motivation, and attitude: A tourist behavioral model. *Journal of Travel Research, 49*(3), 282–296. https://doi.org/10.1177/0047287509349266

Ji, M., Li, M., & Hsu, C. H. (2016). Emotional encounters of Chinese tourists to Japan. *Journal of Travel & Tourism Marketing, 33*(5), 645–657. https://doi.org/10.1080/10548408.2016.1167353

Jin, X. C., Qu, M., & Bao, J. (2019). Impact of crisis events on Chinese outbound tourist flow: A framework for post-events growth. *Tourism Management, 74*, 334–344. https://doi.org/10.1016/j.tourman.2019.04.011

Kim, W. G., Ma, X., & Kim, D. J. (2006). Determinants of Chinese hotel customers' e-satisfaction and purchase intentions. *Tourism Management, 27*(5), 890–900. https://doi.org/10.1016/j.tourman.2005.05.010

Lam, L. Y. J., & Gao, Y. (2019). Hong Kong millennials' intention to visit local hotel spas. *Journal of China Tourism Research*, 1–17. https://doi.org/10.1080/19388160.2019.1597800.

Li, X. R., Lai, C., Harrill, R., Kline, S., & Wang, L. (2011). When east meets west: An exploratory study on Chinese outbound tourists' travel expectations. *Tourism Management, 32*(4), 741–749. https://doi.org/10.1016/j.tourman.2010.06.009

O'Regan, M., & Chang, H. (2015). Smartphone adoption amongst Chinese youth during leisure-based tourism: Challenges and opportunities. *Journal of China Tourism Research, 11*(3), 238–254. https://doi.org/10.1080/19388160.2015.1077181

Oh, H., Jeong, M., Lee, S., & Warnick, R. (2016). Attitudinal and situational determinants of self-service technology use. *Journal of Hospitality & Tourism Research*, *40*(2), 236–265. https://doi.org/10.1177/1096348013491598

Prayag, G., & Soscia, I. (2016). Guilt-decreasing marketing appeals: The efficacy of vacation advertising on Chinese tourists. *Journal of Travel & Tourism Marketing*, *33*(4), 551–565. https://doi.org/10.1080/10548408.2015.1065214

Qi, S., Law, R., & Buhalis, D. (2008). Usability of Chinese destination management organization websites. *Journal of Travel & Tourism Marketing*, *25*(2), 182–198. https://doi.org/10.1080/10548400802402933

Shi, J., Fan, A., & Cai, L. A. (2019). Leisure mobility of Chinese millennials. *Journal of China Tourism Research*, 1–20. https://doi.org/10.1080/19388160.2019.1687060.

Shin, H., Perdue, R. R., & Kang, J. (2019). Front desk technology innovation in hotels: A managerial perspective. *Tourism Management*, *74*, 310–318. https://doi.org/10.1016/j.tourman.2019.04.004

Sun, M., Ryan, C., & Pan, S. (2015). Using Chinese travel blogs to examine perceived destination image: The case of New Zealand. *Journal of Travel Research*, *54*(4), 543–555. https://doi.org/10.1177/0047287514522882

Tussyadiah, I. (2020). A review of research into automation in tourism: Launching the *annals of tourism research* curated collection on artificial intelligence and robotics in tourism. *Annals of Tourism Research*, *81*, 102883. https://doi.org/10.1016/j.annals.2020.102883

Wang, D., Xiang, Z., & Fesenmaier, D. R. (2016). Smartphone use in everyday life and travel. *Journal of Travel Research*, *55*(1), 52–63. https://doi.org/10.1177/0047287514535847

Weng, J., Zhu, X., & Li, X. (2020). Impact of high-speed rail on destination accessibility: A case study of China. *Journal of China Tourism Research*, 1–16. https://doi.org/10.1080/19388160.2019.1709937.

Wong, I. A., Liu, D., Li, N., Wu, S., Lu, L., & Law, R. (2019). Foodstagramming in the travel encounter. *Tourism Management*, *71*, 99–115. https://doi.org/10.1016/j.tourman.2018.08.020

Wu, M. Y., & Pearce, P. L. (2017). Understanding Chinese overseas recreational vehicle tourists: A netnographic and comparative approach. *Journal of Hospitality & Tourism Research*, *41*(6), 696–718. https://doi.org/10.1177/1096348014550869

Yasami, M., Promsivapallop, P., & Kannaovakun, P. (2020). Food image and loyalty intentions: Chinese tourists' destination food satisfaction. *Journal of China Tourism Research*, 1–21. https://doi.org/10.1080/19388160.2020.1784814.

Zhang, C., Singh, A. J., & Yu, L. (2016). Does it matter? Examining the impact of China's vacation policies on domestic tourism demand. *Journal of Hospitality & Tourism Research*, *40*(5), 527–556. https://doi.org/10.1177/1096348013503993

Zhang, Y., & Murphy, P. (2009). Supply-chain considerations in marketing underdeveloped regional destinations: A case study of Chinese tourism to the goldfields region of Victoria. *Tourism Management*, *30*(2), 278–287.

Laurie Wu

Alei Fan

Han Shen

✉ shen_han@fudan.edu.cn

Impact of High-speed Rail on Destination Accessibility: A Case Study of China

Jin Weng, Xiaolin Zhu and Xin Li

ABSTRACT

The massive construction of high-speed rail (HSR) in China has changed tourists' choice for transportation and shortened travel time, thus improving the accessibility of destinations. The principal goal of this paper is to investigate the impact of HSR on accessibility. With the ArcGIS network analysis toolkit, this paper calculates the market potential of destination cities, using 336 prefecture level municipalities in China as samples. It then measures the impact of HSR on accessibility to these cities, giving consideration to multiple modes of transportation, namely: aviation, high-speed rail and expressway. The study finds that HSR has become the top priority of transport in the context of short and medium-range travel distance for tourists. Meanwhile, thanks to HSR, the market potential of all cities in China has increased by 12.8%, the improvement being more significant for small- and medium-sized cities especially. In addition, HSR also strengthens the centrality of city with the hub airport. Lastly, regional differences in accessibility are expanded by HSR at a national level.

高铁对目的地可达性的影响:以中国为例

摘要

中国高铁的大规模建设改变了旅游者对交通方式的选择, 新的交通方式或交通方式组合缩短了旅游者的旅行时间, 从而提高了目的地的可达性。本文以中国336个地级行政区和直辖市为样本, 综合考虑了航空, 高速公路和高铁多种交通方式, 利用ArcGIS网络分析方法计算了目的地城市的市场潜能, 以测度高铁对目的地城市可达性的影响。研究发现, 高铁改变了旅游者对交通方式的选择, 中短程距离内高铁成为主要方式。高铁使全国所有城市的市场潜能提高了12.8%, 中小城市的提高更为显著。高铁也强化了航空枢纽城市的中心性。从全国尺度看, 高铁扩大了可达性的区域差异。

Introduction

The development of the tourism industry is influenced by transport facilities (Khadaroo & Seetanah, 2008; Prideaux, 2000). The implementation of railway, aviation and expressways has contributed dramatically to the development of the tourism industry. With the development of high-speed rail (HSR), the impacts of HSR on the tourism industry are gaining increasing attention from researchers. The main issues of current research include the impacts of HSR on destination accessibility (Cao, Liu, Wang, & Li, 2013; Gutiérrez, 2001; Gutiérrez, González, & Gómez, 1996; Monzon, Lopez, & Ortega, 2019; Moyano, Martínez, & Coronado, 2018; Wu, Liang, & Wu, 2016), the impacts of HSR on tourism spatial structure (Masson & Petiot, 2009; Wang, Niu, & Qian, 2018a), the impacts of HSR on tourist behavior (Chan & Yuan, 2017; Shyr, Chao, & Huang, 2015) and so on. This paper aims to discuss the impact of high-speed rail on the fastest travel transportation mode and the accessibility of tourism destinations. Unlike previous studies, the sample of this study includes all 336 prefecture-level cities with high-speed rail access and cities where high-speed rail is not accessible. Tourists can choose direct or intermodal transportation through aviation, high-speed rail and expressway. This setting is more realistic, but it also adds difficulty in calculation. In the case of various modes of transportation, the first research question of accessibility is transportation mode choice. The newly constructed high-speed rail system has provided new options of transportation, and shortened the travel time of tourists by changing the choice of tourists regarding transportation. Finally, it improved the accessibility of destination cities.

Existing studies on tourist destination choice have indicated variables that influence tourist destination choice. These include the characteristics of tourists, such as gender, age, occupation, income, educational level, etc. (Woodside & Lysonski, 1989), and variables related to destination such as product, price, channel (Woodside & Lysonski, 1989) and accessibility (Sun, Zhang, & Xue, 2011). Furthermore, relationship variables between origins and destinations, such as cultural distance (Liu, Li, Cárdenas, & Yang, 2018), and trade connection (Sun et al., 2011), exert impacts on tourist destination choice as well. Empirical studies have shown that accessibility is a significant variable of tourist destination choice (Tóth & Dávid, 2010; Woodside & Lysonski, 1989). Accessibility is traditionally the potential for opportunities for interaction (Hansen, 1959), now it is a critical indicator in transport geography such as transport network analysis, transport planning and land-use (Jiao, Wang, Jin, & Dunford, 2014). Accessibility indicators are frequently used to measure the impact of HSR (Cao et al., 2013; Gutiérrez, 2001; Masson & Petiot, 2009; Vickerman, 1997). Higher accessibility indicates lower travel time cost, while lower travel cost affects the destination choice of tourists. Therefore, the construction of HSR will not only influence tourists' option for travel transportation mode, but also ultimately affect their choice of destination city.

This study intends to select the fastest transportation mode for travelers under the condition of the preliminary formation of the HSR network. The market potential approach is then utilized to evaluate the change in accessibility of 336 national prefecture-level administrative units in 2014 in China (excluding the cities of Sansha and Danzhou in the province of Hainan). The study not only directly reflects the impact of HSR on tourists' fastest travel transportation mode, but also indirectly reflects the influence of HSR on tourists' choice of destination city. Our calculation is based on ArcGIS 10.2.

The next section of this paper reviews the impacts and measurement of HSR on accessibility of the destination city. The third section illustrates the method and data of this research. The result is given in the fourth section while the five section is the discussion. The final part is limitations and future research.

Literature review

Quantitative methods have been widely used in analyzing the influence of HSR on destination city accessibility. Existing literature focuses on the impact on different countries and regions. At present, Europe and China, with a large geographic scale, are used as research cases. From the papers that can be obtained, early work began with a study of the European case. Bruinsma and Rietveld (1993) used the market potential index to discuss the impacts of road, rail and aviation network on accessibility of 42 major cities in Europe. They found that among three modes of transportation, HSR had the most significant impact on accessibility. Gutiérrez et al. (1996) combined the 2010 European HSR program with a weighted average distance indicator to estimate the impact of HSR on accessibility of the destination city. They came to the conclusion that HSR would increase imbalances between central cities and marginal areas. However, the connectivity between the core and periphery would be strengthened. Gutiérrez (2001) used the Madrid–Barcelona–French border high-speed line as an example to discuss the relationship between HSR and accessibility. The author indicated that disparity of accessibility is widening at the national level while narrowing at a European level. Later, in 2010, Gutiérrez measured spatial spillovers of investment in transport infra- structures by market potential. In addition, Bonnafous (1987) investigated the influence of the TGV from Paris to Lyon. Sánchez-Mateos and Givoni (2012) paid attention to a newly built HSR line in UK, while Ortega, López, and Monzón (2012) set Spain as case study. More research on a European scale include works by Vickerman, Spiekermann, and Wegener (1999), Masson and Petiot (2009) and Ureña, Menerault, and Garmendia (2009). Levinson (2012) took the United States as an example to review the HSR planning. There are also articles analyzing Korean HSR's impact on Seoul metropolitan area (Chang & Lee, 2008).

Recently, with the rapid development of China's High-Speed Rail Network construc- tion, an increasing amount of research on HSR has emerged. As a country with a large geographic scale, China is an ideal case for research of HSR and accessibility. There are two main types of research currently. The first is based on national-scale research and the second is about the impact of HSR on a specific region.

In a national-scale study, Chen (2012) analyzed the reshaping effect of HSR on Chinese spatial development strategies. Cao et al. (2013) introduced quantifying indica- tors such as weighted average travel times and travel costs, contour measures, and potential accessibility to estimate accessibility in 49 major cities in China. By comparing and analyzing two different travel transportation ways: ordinary rail and aviation, they found that the role of central-eastern cities was reinforced and the Beijing–Shanghai axis as well as Pearl River Delta Region gained high accessibility with HSR. Shaw, Fang, Lu, and Tao (2014) took a timetable-based accessibility evaluation approach to analyze the changes in travel time, travel cost and distance accessibility in different stages on HSR development in China. Jiao et al. (2014) used three indices as WATT (Weighted Average Travel Time), DA (Daily Accessibility) and PV (Potential Values) to explore the acces- sibility impact. They found an increase in nodal accessibility and enlarged inequality. Wu et al. (2016) calculated accessibility changes of all counties in China with the approach of market potential. The results showed that with only consideration of rail transportation, the construction of high-speed rail has strengthened the polarization effect. Wang, Liu,

Mao, and Sun (2018b) did similar research. They evaluated the potential impacts of HSR on ground transportation accessibility in 2030 by two indicators: the weighted average travel time and daily accessibility. Wang et al. (2018a) used the method of intensity model to study the influence of HSR on the evolution of urban tourism spatial structure with a sample of 338 national prefecture-level administrative units. The conclusion was that HSR strengthened tourism links between cities and the high-accessibility areas showed the characteristics of "corridor" distribution.

There are also researchers focusing on the impact of HSR on a specific region in China. Wang, Liu, Sun, and Liu (2016) studied the accessibility impact of the HSR network in Jiangsu province from 2010 to 2030. Jiangsu Province is an economically developed region and one of the most important origins of tourism in China. Their research found that accessibility in Jiangsu Province would improve by 9.6% while the regional imbalance in accessibility would reduce by 25.7%.

Researchers have also pointed out topics requiring further discussion and improvements, such as the accessibility of tourism destination (Cao et al., 2013), and accessibility under various modes of travel transportation mode, such as aviation (Wang et al., 2018a). This is also where the current research needs to be improved. Tourists have to transfer a lot when traveling. For example, they will transfer from expressway to aviation, from trunk airline to branch airline, from HSR to aviation, etc. Therefore, once the accessibility of a tourist destination is considered, it is unavoidable to face the problem of multiple transport combinations. The opening of HSR directly increases the transportation modes available to tourists. So the calculation of the fastest mode of transportation between two places has become the primary task of the measurement of accessibility.

Methodology

Case setting

China is taken as an example in this study, as it is the fastest-growing country in HSR construction and is also the country with the longest HSR rail network. Since the first HSR came into operation in 2008, the operating HSR mileage reached over 22,000 kilometers by the end of 2016,[1] accounting for 65% of the global HSR operating mileage. As a country with a large geographic scale, China provides an excellent sample for observing the impact of HSR on the fastest travel transportation mode and the impact of HSR on accessibility change of destination city. Newly published research related to HSR takes China as a case study as well.

Measurement of accessibility

Existing measurements of accessibility include WATT (weighted average travel times), Market potential, Daily accessibility, Contour measure and so on (Cao et al., 2013; Gutiérrez, 2001; Vickerman, 1974; Wu et al., 2016). WATT measures average travel time weighted by population. The shorter is the average travel time, the greater is the accessibility. In comparison, market potential measures the scale of demand weighted by travel time. It is the algebraic sum of the weighted scale of demand. These two indicators both reflect the location condition of a certain place, while daily accessibility and contour measure pay attention to the reachable area within a certain time, which is the special case of market potential. In the study, we use market potential as an indicator of accessibility, because it can intuitively reflect the size of demand in the city's market and depicts the spatial relationship between the supplier and the demander. Market potential methods are widely applied in research in the field of spatial economics, urban economics, industry economics, international trade, etc. (Fujita, Krugman, & Venables, 2001; Hanson, 2005; Head & Mayer, 2004; Liu & Meissner, 2015). The greater the market potential, the greater the possibility for certain economic activities, such as production, retailing, tourism, etc. The market potential approach is also applied in measuring the impacts of HSR on accessibility (Cao et al., 2013; Gutiérrez, 2001; Wang et al., 2016; Wu et al., 2016). With time–space compression by HSR, travel time between the origin and the destination is shortened, and the possibility of arriving at a certain destination is increased. Namely, the tourism demand of a destination is expanded. The market potential indicator can directly reflect such a change.

The market potential formula is as follows:

$$MP_i = \sum_{\substack{j=1 \\ j \neq i}}^{n} \frac{Y_j^{\alpha}}{(d_{ij})^{\beta}} + \frac{Y_i^{\alpha}}{(d_{ii})^{\beta}} \tag{1}$$

where MP_i stands for the market potential of place i, Y_j is the market size of place j, Y_i is the market size of place i, d_{ij} indicates the distance between places i and j, d_{ii} indicates the inner distance of place i, using the formula $\frac{2}{3}\sqrt{\frac{S_i}{\pi}}$ to calculate it (Redding & Venables, 2004). Meanwhile, S_i is the area of place i. According to the previous study, α is set as 1 (Bruinsma & Rietveld, 1993; Cao et al., 2013; Gutiérrez, 2001) and β has three settings, i. e. 2/3, 1 and 2, which reflects the sensitivity of Market potential to distance.

The size of the tourism market is reflected by GDP, which reflects population and income per capita. The availability and reliability of GDP data in national prefecture-level cities is strong. Distance is measured by travel time. Many current studies have converted spatial distance into time distance (Bruinsma & Rietveld, 1993; Gutiérrez et al., 1996; Prideaux, 2000; Vickerman, 1974; Wang et al., 2018a; Wu et al., 2016). This approach reflects a basic fact that tourists are more sensitive to time than money. Time is the major constraint for tourists.

In the calculation of travel time, parameters are set as follows. The speed of HSR is 250 km/h, with data derived from the average speed of six HSR lines, Beijing–Shanghai, Beijing–Guangzhou, Wuhan–Guangzhou, Harbin–Dalian, Shanghai–Kunming, and Guiyang–Guangzhou. The speed of aviation is 600 km/h while the speed of the express-way is 120 km/h. The speed of ordinary roads is given as 60 km/h. In addition, the study takes waiting time and transfer time into consideration. In comparison with aviation, the waiting time for HSR and expressway is significantly shortened. For tourists whose travel distance is different, traveling time, which is similar to fixed cost, is an important factor affecting the choice of transportation mode. As a result, referring to suggestions given by airport, HSR stations and airline companies, we set the waiting time for an airplane as 1.5 h, the waiting time for HSR as 0.25 h, transfer time for an airplane as 2 h, transfer time from aviation to expressway as 2 h. In addition, we take the average flight delay time[2] as

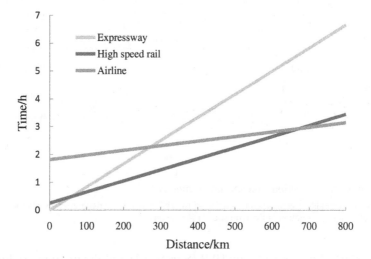

Figure 1. Time consumption for different transportation modes.

19 min into consideration. As shown in Figure 1, in terms of traveling time, the express-way has advantages for short-distance travel while an airplane is more popular for long-distance travel. There is no formal definition of the English language words motorway, freeway, and expressway. In most cases, they are defined by local standards. In this paper, expressway means a controlled-access highway, which can also be called a national highway in some countries. In China, the average speed of expressway is 120 km/h.

Data

Cities are important tourism destinations as well as major transportation nodes. So we take all 336 prefecture-level administrative units of China as samples, containing 332 prefecture-level cities and four municipalities directly under the central government. Taking all nationwide cities as samples, it is easier to figure out the difference in accessibility in different types of cities affected by HSR. Among all 336 cities, there are 178 cities with aviation, 39 cities with a hub airport and 139 cities with a regional airport.[3] There are 163 HSR access cities[4] and 314[5] cities with an expressway. Based on the above data, we draw the vector map of aviation, HSR and expressway in ArcGIS 10.2 to get relevant spatial data. GDP data comes from the 2014 Statistics Bulletin of the National Economic and Social Development of the People's Republic of China and the area of cities comes from the government portal website of the municipal city.

When it comes to transportation mode selection among aviation, HSR and express-way, tourists can choose one of the modes of transportation or a combination of multiple modes of transportation based on the principles of shortest travel time, such as from expressway to aviation, from trunk airline to branch airline, or from expressway to HSR. This makes calculation extremely complicated. As indicated in Figure 2, there are seven combinations available for travelers. Among them, aviation includes direct flight and air transit. Similarly, HSR consists of direct line and transit line. And others are in the form of intermodal transport.

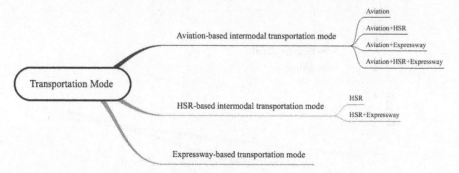

Figure 2. Combination of various transportation modes.

Scenario 1 represents condition without consideration of the HSR network, Scenario 2 represents the condition in the context of the preliminary formation of the high-speed rail network.

In the context of not considering HSR (Scenario 1) and the preliminary formation of the HSR network (Scenario 2), this study uses the network analysis toolkit in ArcGIS to build a network, allowing that all 336 cities can be interconnected through aviation, HSR and expressway transportation modes. It then introduces transit time by setting traffic impedance between different layers. The OD cost matrix tool of ArcGIS is used to select the fastest path between two cities in all possible traffic combinations and to calculate time distance. Specific work includes four steps, as follows. First, acquiring geographic layer data, including the line shapefile as the Aviation Line, the HSR Line and the Expressway Line in 2014; and the point shapefile for city center, HSR Station, Hub airport, and Branch airport. Second, connecting different layers to form an interconnected network. At the same time, the speed of various vehicles is set. Third, using the Network Analysis function of ArcGIS to construct a traffic network dataset. Fourth, using the function of the "OD Cost Matrix" to get the shortest travel time distance. The calculation loads the Origins and Destinations and sets the time impedance of the point layers to describe the waiting time (for train and aviation) and transit time. In this way, the shortest time distance between two cities can be calculated.

Results

Change in choice for transportation mode

The implementation of HSR has dramatically altered tourists' choice of transportation mode. In the Scenario without consideration of HSR, aviation-based transportation mode accounts for 77.3% of city pairs while expressway-based transportation takes up 22.7% of city pairs (see Table 1). Under the preliminary formation of the HSR network, the proportion of the HSR-based transportation mode reaches 18.6% of all pairs of cities. By contrast, aviation-based transportation decreases to 68.5% of pairs of city. Meanwhile, the number of two cities connected by expressways drops to 12.9% (see Table 1). The result shows that the major trend of an aviation-based intermodal transportation mode doesn't change since China is a country with a large geographic scale. The aviation-based traffic pattern has not changed in the case of only 163 cities with HSR access. The result, however, demonstrates HSR has an evident substitution effect on aviation.

Table 1. The fastest transportation mode between any two cities (city pairs).

Transportation mode		Scenario 1		Scenario 2	
		Percentage	Sum	Percentage	Sum
Aviation-based	Aviation	24.2%	77.3%	22.6%	68.5%
	Aviation+Expressway	53.1%		24.1%	
	Aviation+HSR	/		15.7%	
	Aviation+HSR+Expressway	/		6.1%	
HSR-based	HSR	/	/	14.3%	18.6%
	HSR+Expressway	/		4.3%	
Expressway-based	Expressway	22.7%	22.7%	12.9%	12.9%

Scenario 1 represents condition without consideration of HSR network, Scenario 2 represents condition in the context of the preliminary formation of the high-speed rail network.

Table 2. Ratio of city pairs using aviation, HSR or expressway to connect at least once.

	Scenario 1	Scenario 2
Aviation	77.3%	68.5%
HSR	/	40.5%
Expressway	75.8%	47.4%

Scenario 1 represents the condition without consideration of the HSR network, Scenario 2 represents the condition in the context of the preliminary formation of the high-speed rail network.

In terms of fastest combinations of transportation modes, about 40% of city pairs depend on high-speed rail at least once in transportation (see Table 2). Hence, HSR has become an important means of inter-city transportation for tourists. However, the proportion of aviation-dependent city pairs is still as high as 68.5% while 47.4% of city pairs take advantage of an expressway at least once (See Table 2). The frequency of using aviation and expressways is still higher than that of high-speed rail, which can be explained as, in this study, the sample cities with HSR access number 163 rather than all prefecture-level cities in China.

If only 163 cities with HSR access are considered, the percentage of taking HSR as the main transportation mode between city pairs will increase tremendously. According to Table 3, in the ranges of within 50 km, 50–700 km, over 700 km, the proportion of HSR-based transportation has increased significantly. Within 50 km, 47.1% of city pairs depend on HSR as the main inter-city transportation mode. The proportion rises to 96.8% in the range of 50–700 km. As for a distance of more than 700 km, the percentage is 64.7%.

Table 3. The fastest transportation mode between any cities (city pairs) with HSR access.

Transportation mode		Within 50 km	50–700 km	Over 700 km
Aviation-based	Aviation	0	0.9%	12.6%
	Aviation+Expressway	0	0	0.8%
	Aviation+HSR	0	0	20.3%
	Aviation+HSR+Expressway	0	0	0.4%
HSR-based	HSR	47.1%	96.8%	64.7%
	HSR+Expressway	0	0	0
Expressway-based	Expressway	52.9%	2.3%	1.2%

Only 163 cities with HSR access are included in the statistics, travel distance refers to the mileage of HSR.

Change in market potential

The first column of Figure 3 depicts the market potential of the destination city without considering the high-speed rail network (Scenario 1), and the second column describes the market potential for the destination city in the context of the preliminary formation of the high-speed rail network (Scenario 2). In general, the distribution of market potential gradually decreases from east to west, and gradually decreases from the middle of the coastline to the north and the south directions. The market potential in the eastern

Scenario1   Scenario2

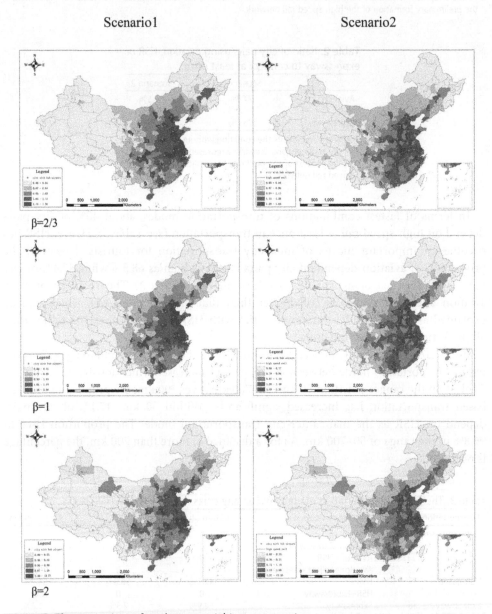

$\beta=2/3$

$\beta=1$

$\beta=2$

Figure 3. The comparison of market potential in two scenarios.
β is 1 in the formula.

region is high, especially in cities along the coastline, while the market potential in the west, northeast and south China is low. The eastern region, especially the Yangtze River Delta Region, has obvious location advantages (see Figure 3).

Second, under the influence of high-speed rail, the distribution of market potential gradually changed from an island structure to a network structure. This is the evident difference in the two scenarios. As shown in the first column of Figure 3, in the context of not considering high-speed rail, the market potential distribution shows an obvious island structure, that is, high-market potential areas are like isolated islands while the market potential of the surrounding is rather low. These high market potential areas are capital cities and cities with hub airports. As shown in the second column of Figure 3, in the context of the preliminary formation of the high-speed rail network, the highest market potential areas are concentrated in areas along the high-speed rail line, which presents a network structure. The regions with the largest changes in market potential are located along the two vertical high-speed rail lines in central and eastern China (Beijing–Guangzhou HSR Line and Beijing–Shanghai HSR Line) as well as the coastal regions from Zhejiang to Guangdong (see Figure 4), with a change ratio range from 16% to 28%. The change indicates that aviation-based intermodal transportation is characterized by the point-to-point link between the origins and the destinations. Large cities are often cities with hub airports, so big cities are the beneficiaries of aviation networks. In contrast, high-speed rail changes the accessibility of all cities along its network, including both large cities and small/medium-sized ones (see Figure 4). Since small/medium-sized cities are often cities with a regional airport or cities without an airport, small and medium-sized cities are the biggest beneficiaries of HSR construction (see Table 4).

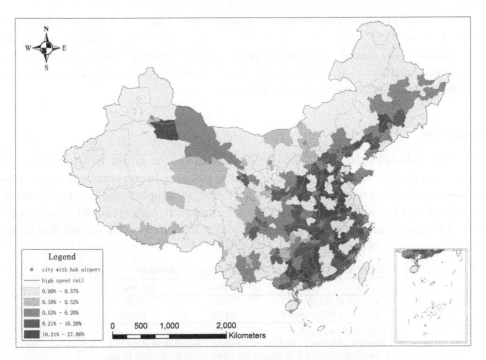

Figure 4. Areas with a significant increase after the construction of HSR.

Table 4. Mean value change of market potential in different types of cities.

	Cities with HSR access		Cities without HSR access	
	Number of cities	Change rate in mean value	Number of cities	Change rate in mean value
Cities with hub airport	35	5.3%	4	0.5%
Cities with regional airport	45	11.9%	94	0.4%
Cities without airport	83	18.4%	75	0.6%

β is 1 in the formula.

The β value reflects the sensitivity of market potential to the effects of time-distance. The larger the value of β, the greater will be the effect of time-distance, while the smaller the value of β, the smaller the effect of time-distance. From the three cases of $\beta = 2/3$, 1 and 2, the characteristic of market potential distribution, that is, the trend from an island structure to a network structure and a decrease from east to west, has not changed.

Variation in change of accessibility

The accessibility of all destination cities has been improved, even the cities without HSR have benefited from the construction of the HSR network. However, the increase in market potential varies. In all cities in China, the average market potential increases by 12.8% while in cities with HSR access, average market potential increases by 22.4%, which is much higher than the national average. The coefficient of variation (CV) of market potential of all 336 cities increases from 29.7% to 34.9% (see Table 5). This indicates a 'Polarization' trend of the market potential of the destination cities on a national scale, which can be explained as accessibility is rising faster in high accessibility areas.

However, in the sample of cities with HSR access, the coefficient of variation decreases from 24.7% to 23.5% (see Table 5). At present, high-speed rail in China is mainly concentrated in the central and eastern regions. The construction of high-speed railways has reduced variation of accessibility between cities in the central and eastern regions, thus the connectivity between cities is enhanced.

Discussion

This study calculates the impact of high-speed rail on the fastest transportation for tourists and the accessibility of destination cities. Different from previous research, this study takes all 336 prefecture-level cities in China as samples, and comprehensively considers various modes of transportation, such as aviation, high-speed rail and express-ways, and their coordinated transport. This makes measurement of accessibility more

Table 5. Change rate of the coefficient of variation.

	Scenario 1	Scenario 2
All cities in China	29.7%	34.9%
Cities with HSR access	24.7%	23.5%

β is 1 in the formula.
Scenario 1 represents the condition without consideration of the HSR network, Scenario 2 represents the condition in the context of the preliminary formation of the high-speed rail network.

realistic (Wang et al., 2018a), and reveals overall changes. Through large-scale geo-calculation and analysis of the results, the following conclusions can be obtained.

First, high speed rail has tremendously changed the choice of tourists' modes for transportation. In the short and medium distance of 50–700 km, high-speed rail has overwhelming advantages. In the 56,280 city pairs of China, 6859 of the city pairs are within the 50–700 km range of distance, which accounts for 12.19%.[6] Furthermore, these cities are mainly located in densely populated areas of China. Taking waiting time into account, 700 km basically covers a travel time distance of 3 hours. This means that HSR will become the best choice for urban residents who spend 2 days on the short and medium distance tour.

Second, high-speed rail has improved the accessibility of all destination cities as a whole, but the improvement of accessibility of small and medium-sized cities is the most significant. In all sample cities, once the high-speed rail has been opened in a city without an airport, the increase in accessibility is remarkable (see Table 4). This is of great value to the development of tourism. A great number of natural and cultural tourism resources with development value are located in small and medium-sized cities. The improvement of accessibility has greatly increased the value for development. High-speed rail promotes the matching of tourism resources and accessibility, meanwhile, it enables a large number of small and medium-sized cities to become important tourist destinations. The construction of a high-speed rail network will reshape China's tourism geography.

Third, high-speed rail has promoted easier connection of small- and medium-sized cities to aviation network cities and has strengthened the centrality of cities with a hub airport. The number of passengers in small- and medium-sized cities has increased significantly through air–rail transportation to destination cities. Among the 163 cities with access to HSR, tourists in 128 cities transfer to cities with a hub airport through high-speed rail. Among these cities, there are 83 without airports and 45 with regional airports. The HSR enhances the connectivity between the aviation hub city and its surrounding small- and medium-sized cities, which expands the geographic market of cities with an airport and strengthens the radiation effect of a city with a hub airport. This also means that the relationship between high-speed rail and aviation is not only competitive and substitutable, but also cooperative and reciprocal.

Fourth, cities in densely populated areas, the east of the Heihe-Tengchong Line, are the biggest beneficiaries of the construction of high-speed rail networks. For the sake of profitability, high-speed rail lines are constructed over densely populated areas, which are high market potential areas before the construction of the high-speed rail network. Figure 5 is a scatter plot based on market potential and market potential growth rate. It can be seen from the figure that cities with a dramatic increase in accessibility brought by HSR are precisely those cities whose market potential is higher than the average value before the construction of the high-speed rail network. These cities are mainly located in the central and eastern regions, which is the eastern part of the Heihe-Tengchong Line, an important geographical boundary of China. Therefore, the construction of high-speed rail has made the accessibility of Chinese cities appear to show the polarization effect of "the stronger, the stronger". High-speed rail is of greater significance to densely populated areas in the central and eastern regions.

Fifth, the regional differences of change in accessibility are influenced by the scale of samples. Does high-speed rail enhance regional differences in accessibility? This is a common concern in existing papers. Our research finds that from the perspective of all

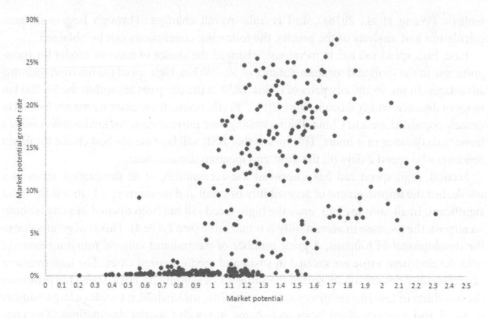

Figure 5. Scatter plot of market potential and market potential growth rate.
Value "1" is the average value of market potential of all sample cities after standardization.

cities, high-speed rail has expanded regional differences in accessibility. This is similar to the conclusions of Wu et al. (2016) and Wang et al. (2018b). The reason was explained in the fourth conclusion. However, for some sample cities, that is all cities with high-speed rail access, the regional differences in accessibility have narrowed. This conclusion is similar to the findings of Gutiérrez (2001) and Wang et al. (2018a). Their research suggests that high-speed rail narrows the accessibility of cities along the railroad. Different conclusions also indicate that although research based on all sample cities is more difficult, such research is necessary.

Limitations and future research

The limitation of this paper is that this study attempts to measure more accurately the impact of high-speed rail on tourists' choice of transportation mode and on destination city accessibility. However, the selection of parameters is a difficult task. For example, the speed of each high-speed rail line varies, and even the speed on different parts of the same line varies. It is difficult to give a perfectly accurate parameter for high-speed rail speeds. The average speed is used in this study, which causes the market potential of some cities to be overestimated (such as the area along the Hangzhou–Shenzhen HSR Line), and of some cities to be underestimated (such as the area along the Beijing–Shanghai HSR Line). Using big data and GIS for more accurate measurement is the direction for future research. Travel time, market potential and accessibility can also be used as explanatory variables to carry out related research, such as the substitute effect of high-speed rail on aviation, the impact of high-speed rail on tourism investment and so on. In the future, the road system can be refined to county-level cities, which means deeper detailed research.

Notes

1. China HSR website (http://news.gaotie.cn/yunying/2017-08-15/414584.html).
2. Civil Aviation Administration of China. (2015). *Statistical Bulletin of Civil Aviation Industry Development in 2014*. Retrieved from website: http://www.caac.gov.cn/en/HYYJ/NDBG/201602/t20160216_28397.html.
3. Civil Aviation Administration of China. (2015). *Statistical Bulletin of Civil Aviation Industry Development in 2014*. Retrieved from website: http://www.caac.gov.cn/en/HYYJ/NDBG/201602/t20160216_28397.html.
4. China General Railway Company. (2015). *China Railway Yearbook 2015*. Beijing: CGRC.
5. Ministry of Transport of People's Republic of China. (2015). *China Highway Atlas 2015*. Beijing: China Communications Press.
6. It is measured according to the mileage of the expressway.

Disclosure statement

No potential conflict of interest was reported by the authors.

Funding

This work was supported by the National Natural Science Foundation of China [41001068].

References

Bonnafous, A. (1987). The regional impact of the TGV. *Transportation, 14*(2), 127–137.

Bruinsma, F., & Rietveld, P. (1993). Urban agglomerations in European infrastructure networks. *Urban Studies, 30*(6), 919–934.

Cao, J., Liu, X. C., Wang, Y., & Li, Q. (2013). Accessibility impacts of China's high-speed rail network. *Journal of Transport Geography, 28*, 12–21.

Chan, C.-S., & Yuan, J. (2017). Changing travel behaviour of high-speed rail passengers in China. *Asia Pacific Journal of Tourism Research, 22*(12), 1221–1237.

Chang, J. S., & Lee, J. H. (2008). Accessibility analysis of Korean high-speed rail: A case study of the Seoul metropolitan area. *Transport Reviews: A Transnational Transdisciplinary Journal, 28*(1), 87–103.

Chen, C.-L. (2012). Reshaping Chinese space-economy through high-speed trains: Opportunities and challenges. *Journal of Transport Geography, 22*, 312–316.

Fujita, M., Krugman, P., & Venables, A. J. (2001). The spatial economy: Cities, regions, and international trade. Cambridge, MA: MIT Press.

Gutiérrez, J. (2001). Location, economic potential and daily accessibility: An analysis of the accessibility impact of the high-speed line Madrid-Barcelona-French border. *Journal of Transport Geography*, *9*(4), 229–242.

Gutiérrez, J., González, R., & Gómez, G. (1996). The European high-speed train network: Predicted effects on accessibility patterns. *Journal of Transport Geography*, *4*(4), 227–238.

Hansen, W. G. (1959). How accessibility shapes land use. *Journal of the American Institute of Planners*, *25*(2), 73–76.

Hanson, G. H. (2005). Market potential, increasing returns and geographic concentration. *Journal of International Economics*, *67*(1), 1–24.

Head, K., & Mayer, T. (2004). Market potential and the location of Japanese investment in the European Union. *The Review of Economics & Statistics*, *86*(4), 959–972.

Jiao, J., Wang, J., Jin, F., & Dunford, M. (2014). Impacts on accessibility of China's present and future HSR network. *Journal of Transport Geography*, *40*, 123–132.

Khadaroo, J., & Seetanah, B. (2008). The role of transport infrastructure in international tourism development: A gravity model approach. *Tourism Management*, *29*(5), 831–840.

Levinson, D. M. (2012). Accessibility impacts of high-speed rail. *Journal of Transport Geography*, *22*(5), 288–291.

Liu, D., & Meissner, C. M. (2015). Market potential and the rise of US productivity leadership. *Journal of International Economics*, *96*(1), 72–87.

Liu, H., Li, X. (Robert), Cárdenas, D. A., & Yang, Y. (2018). Perceived cultural distance and international destination choice: The role of destination familiarity, geographic distance, and cultural motivation. *Journal of Destination Marketing & Management*, *9*(2018), 300–309.

Masson, S., & Petiot, R. (2009). Can the high speed rail reinforce tourism attractiveness? The case of the high speed rail between Perpignan (France) and Barcelona (Spain). *Technovation*, *29*(9), 611–617.

Monzon, A., Lopez, E., & Ortega, E. (2019). Has HSR improved territorial cohesion in Spain? An accessibility analysis of the first 25 years: 1990–2015. *European Planning Studies*, *27*(3), 513–532.

Moyano, A., Martínez, H. S., & Coronado, J. M. (2018). From network to services: A comparative accessibility analysis of the Spanish high-speed rail system. *Transport Policy*, *63*, 51–60.

Ortega, E., López, E., & Monzón, A. (2012). Territorial cohesion impacts of high-speed rail at different planning levels. *Journal of Transport Geography*, *24*, 130–141.

Prideaux, B. (2000). The role of the transport system in destination development. *Tourism Management*, *21*(1), 53–63.

Redding, S., & Venables, A. J. (2004). Economic geography and international inequality. *Journal of International Economics*, *62*(1), 53–82.

Sánchez-Mateos, H. S. M., & Givoni, M. (2012). The accessibility impact of a new high-speed rail line in the UK – A preliminary analysis of winners and losers. *Journal of Transport Geography*, *25*, 105–114.

Shaw, S. L., Fang, Z., Lu, S., & Tao, R. (2014). Impacts of high speed rail on railroad network accessibility in China. *Journal of Transport Geography*, *40*, 112–122.

Shyr, O. F., Chao, C. W., & Huang, C. K. (2015). Impacts of new transportation systems on tourism behavior: The experience of high-speed rail. *International Journal of Transport Economics*, *42*(1), 89–110.

Sun, G. N., Zhang, Y., & Xue, J. (2011). Scenery attraction, location accessibility and trade connection: Three factors and their influences on destination choice of Japanese tourists (in Chinese). *Geographical Research*, *30*(6), 24–28.

Tóth, G., & Dávid, L. (2010). Tourism and accessibility: An integrated approach. *Applied Geography*, *30*(4), 666–677.

Ureña, J. M., Menerault, P., & Garmendia, M. (2009). The high-speed rail challenge for big intermediate cities: A national, regional and local perspective. *Cities*, *26*(5), 266–279.

Vickerman, R. (1974). Accessibility, attraction, and potential: A review of some concepts and their use in determining mobility. *Environment and Planning A*, *6*(6), 675–691.

Vickerman, R. W. (1997). High-speed rail in Europe: Experience and issues for future development. *The Annual of Regional Sciences, 31*, 21–38.

Vickerman, R. W., Spiekermann, K., & Wegener, M. (1999). Accessibility and economic development in Europe. *Regional Studies, 33*(1), 1–15.

Wang, D., Niu, Y., & Qian, J. (2018a). Evolution and optimization of China's urban tourism spatial structure: A high speed rail perspective. *Tourism Management, 64*, 218–232.

Wang, L., Liu, Y., Mao, L., & Sun, C. (2018b). Potential impacts of China 2030 high-speed rail network on ground transportation accessibility. *Sustainability, 10*(4), 1270.

Wang, L., Liu, Y., Sun, C., & Liu, Y. (2016). Accessibility impact of the present and future high-speed rail network: A case study of Jiangsu province, China. *Journal of Transport Geography, 54* (2016), 161–172.

Woodside, A. G., & Lysonski, S. (1989). A general model of traveler destination choice. *Journal of Travel Research, 27*(4), 8–14.

Wu, W., Liang, Y., & Wu, D. (2016). Evaluating the impact of China's rail network expansions on local accessibility: A market potential approach. *Sustainability, 8*(6), 512.

Hong Kong Millennials' Intention to Visit Local Hotel Spas

Lok Yan Jessie Lam and Yixing (Lisa) Gao (ID)

ABSTRACT

Visiting spas has become a popular activity in Hong Kong. Particularly, millennials are increasingly prone to visiting spas, it is essential for spa managers to understand their characteristics and utilize resources in attracting them. This study aims to understand Hong Kong millennials' behavioral intention towards local hotel spas. An online questionnaire was distributed to collect data from 250 participants. The preliminary results indicate that of the seven spa attributes examined, 'price' was rated as the most important, followed by 'therapists.' Moreover, 'price,' 'location,' 'product,' and 'promotion' were the four factors with significant impacts on millennials' booking intention. In addition, mobile device usage was found to moderate the impact of spa attributes on millennials' visiting intentions. Managerial implications are discussed.

香港千禧一代对当地酒店水疗的访问意向

摘要

在香港, 水疗已成为一项很受欢迎的活动。尤其是千禧一代越来越倾向于去温泉, 因此, 了解他们的特点和利用资源来吸引他们很重要。本研究旨在了解香港千禧一代对本地酒店水疗的行为意向。通过发放在线问卷, 本研究收集了250名参与者的数据。结果显示, 在七项水疗属性中, '价格'被评为最重要的, 其次是'治疗师'。此外, '价格'、'地点'、'产品'和'促销'是对千禧一代预订意向有显著影响的四个因素。此研究还发现移动设备的使用可以调节水疗属性对千禧一代访问意愿的影响。本文对水疗管理提出了管理建议。

Introduction

Visiting spas has become a healthy option for urban residents who wish to relieve stress and maintain their well-being (Furrer, 2010). Spa activities are a fashionable and relaxing method for individuals to unwind and reduce stress levels (Furrer, 2010). Hotel or resort spas have become a rapidly growing segment in the hospitality and tourism industry (Keri, Ottenbacher, & Harrington, 2007; McNeil & Ragins, 2005). Spa therapy took off in Asia countries beginning in the mid-1990s, and its rapid development can be attributed to the rapid expansion of the lodging industry within the region (Tang, 2014). In Hong Kong, hotel spas account for 30% of the total spa industry (Yung, 2010). Among 124 registered members of the Hong Kong Hotels Association (HKHA), 25 offer hotel spa treatments

(Tang, 2014). Hong Kong hotel spas have been recognized as 'quite outstanding' and five hotels made the 'Top 150 World-Class Spas' list of *Spa Asia Magazine*, namely the Four Seasons Hotel, the Grand Hyatt, the Intercontinental, the Landmark Mandarin Oriental, and the Peninsula (Kucukusta, Pang, & Chui, 2013).

However, although Hong Kong was among the world's top 20 largest spa-going cities in terms of revenue (Global Spa and Wellness Summit, 2008), only approximately 2% of overnight hotel visitors wanted spa services in 2010 (Hong Kong Tourism Board, 2010). This relatively low demand from overnight hotel visitors suggests that hotel spas should devote resources to attracting local day visitors, further developing the spa market in Hong Kong. In addition, hotel spas that focus on local consumers appear to maintain their business performance better than hotels that focus on travelers (Tabacchi, 2010). Spa treatments to relieve stress surprisingly grew in demand during weak economic periods, due to the 'lipstick effect' (Tabacchi, 2010). This phenomenon suggests that consumers will continue spending on small luxury goods during an economic down-turn, even when they reduce their expenditure in other areas, such as travel. Thus, local spa consumption may not necessarily decline in difficult circumstances, and instead spa-goers may simply select lower price treatments. This result implies that attracting local consumers would provide more stable customer-flow and revenue for hotel spas.

The stereotype of female, and wealthy, spa-goers dominating the usage of hotel spas has shifted in recent decades. Several research studies have found that the spa market is experiencing a generational shift, from a predominance of baby boomer customers to an emerging trend of millennials (Mak, Wong, & Chang, 2009; Panchal, 2012). Hence, it is crucial for hotel managers to understand the characteristics of these young customers. For example, millennials make extensive use of the Internet for background research, and thus managers must establish online marketing strategies instead of traditional promotional methods such as spa magazine advertisements.

The majority of current spa-related research focuses on customers' expectations of service quality and preferences (e.g. Gonzalez & Brea, 2005; Lo & Wu, 2014; Lo, Wu, & Tsai, 2015; McNeil & Ragins, 2005; Sherman, Clemenz, & Philipp, 2007). However, few studies have investigated Hong Kong consumers' decision-making processes in selecting hotel spas, and even fewer have examined the topic from the perspective of millennial spa-goers. To promote Hong Kong hotel spa facilities among millennials, this study aims to understand local millennials' behavioral intention in visiting hotel spas. The results will allow spa managers to allocate resources more effectively to meet and satisfy the needs of millennials, the sector of the local population targeted in this study.

Literature review

Hotel spas

The word 'spa' derives from the Latin phrase 'sanus per aquam,' meaning 'health through water' (Puczkó & Bachvarov, 2006). According to the International Spa Association (2017), spas in the 21st century provide professional services promoting the renewal of patrons' mind, body, and spirit, to enhance their overall well-being. However, the term 'spa' has gradually gained many different meanings as almost all health service providers call themselves spas (Puczkó & Bachvarov, 2006).

Spas can be classified into seven categories: day spa, resort or hotel spa, medical spa, club spa, destination spa, mineral spring spa, and cruise ship spa (Frost, 2004). Hotel spas, the focus of this study, refers to spas owned by or situated within resorts or hotels. In particular, these professional spa services integrate components of fitness and wellness such as nutrition (Langvinienė, 2011). They also enhance individuals' all-round well-being by offering a diversity of high-touch services such as body massage and treatments such as body scrubs and manicures (Kucukusta et al., 2013). Skin care products and herbal supplements are also promoted to rejuvenate clients' body and spirit. Unlike other types of spas, urban hotel spas target at customers who are local residents living within metropolitan areas, who usually patronize spa services without using hotel accommodations (Tsai, Suh, & Fong, 2012).

The core of a spa service is providing captivating experiences to awaken all five senses. The pressure of the massage, the smell of the incense stick, the taste of refreshing tea, the sound of soothing music, and the sight of tranquil and calming decorations all contribute to the sensory experience (Wuttke & Cohen, 2008). Rather than being confined to the treatment experience, as Remedios (2008) has explained, a spa experience can be considered 'a series of individual moments [that] when accumulated together…shape a complete and enthralling experience.' The five moments of truth of a spa experience include the initial arrival experience, reception experience, flowing facilities experience, core treatment experience, and post-treatment experience (Ely, 2009). Previous studies have discussed the experience of the spa environment. However, it is important to understand local millennials' characteristics, to cater their needs more effectively. Several researchers have studied the attributes of spa-goers. Key spa attributes identified in previous research are summarized in Table 1.

Table 1. A summary of attributes used in selecting hotel spas.

Spa Attribute	Items	References
Product	• Branded spa products • Diversification of products • Uniqueness of products • Signature treatments • Range of treatments • Diversification of treatments • Traditional treatments	Ellis (2008); Kucukusta et al. (2013); Tabacchi (2010)
Promotions	• Package • Discounts • Value added/Upgrade • Loyalty program	Kucukusta et al. (2013)
Therapists	• Certificate of therapists • Professional skills • Knowledge of products and service • Courtesy • Grooming	Kucukusta and Guillet (2014); Lo, Qu, and Wetprasit (2013); Lo et al. (2015)
Ambience	• Sense of privacy • Sense of tranquility • Aroma • Theme/Decoration • Color usage	Guillet and Kucukusta (2016); Kucukusta and Guillet (2014); Wakefield and Blodgett (1994)
Facilities	• Range of facilities • Type of treatment room • Size of treatment room • Size of bed • Quality of linen • Cleanliness of facilities	Ellis (2008); Lo et al. (2013)

Products

Spa products can be categorized as either branded or generic (Ellis, 2008; Tabacchi, 2010). Up-scale spas tend to use branded products as a competitive edge to differentiate themselves from other spas. Branded products also ensure quality and minimize the risks of skin problems. However, providing spa customers with branded products is a recent direction in the spa industry. Branded products are usually linked with quality and further impact treatments' ability to meet individual needs. Park and Reisinger (2009) also emphasized that brand products are usually preferred by Asians, and luxury consumption is a way of projecting a high social status. It is thus common for luxury spas to adopt branded spa products in positioning and differentiating themselves from competitors. Aside from spa product brands, hotel brand names such as Four Seasons and spa outlet brands such as Angsana symbolize high quality and value (Biswas, 1992). Consumers may therefore gain confidence from the brand name, which encourages their purchase (Herbig & Milewicz, 1995). Regarding spa treatments, millennials place stronger emphasis on signature treatments, leading to a diversification of treatment types compared to older generations (Kucukusta et al., 2013).

Promotion

Females in general are more enthusiastic about value-added services than males, indicating that spa managers could offer value-added services by increasing the quality of products used or bundling special treatments in spa packages (Kucukusta et al., 2013). All-inclusive spa packages consisting of massages, facials, and spot treatments are attractive and could provide added value. In addition, because frequent spa-visitors tend to spend more on treatments, loyalty programs should be launched to motivate their return and generate repeat business (Kucukusta et al., 2013). It is also important to train spa staff with better merchandizing and promotional skills to maximize opportunities for financial gain.

Therapists

The qualifications and experience of therapists are considered more important than price by Chinese visitors, including Mainland Chinese, Hong Kongers, and Taiwanese (Kucukusta & Guillet, 2014). The likely explanation is the perceived importance of expertise in Traditional Chinese Medicine (TCM), including cupping, acupuncture, and herbal medicine. However, Terry (2007) reported that a shortage of certified therapists is one of the challenges of today's spa industry, and Hong Kong is not an exception, given that some spas employ therapists who are skillful and well-trained but lack professional certification. Research also indicated that spa-goers who visited spas with one or more companions pay extra attention to therapists' qualifications compared with individual spa-goers. Spa consumers who favor traditional massages and treatments are keen to select their preferred therapists (Kucukusta & Guillet, 2014). Day spa consumers also concentrate more on therapist qualifications than hotel spa-goers, due to the perception that hotels (especially branded hotels) employ qualified therapists (Kucukusta & Guillet, 2014). It is likely that infrequent spa visitors would be unfamiliar with spa etiquette or the procedures of spa treatments; therefore, they are more likely to rely on information from therapists (Lo et al., 2013). Aside from therapists' qualifications, their courtesy level allows guests to wholeheartedly enjoy the spa experience and therefore has a positive effect on spa visitors' emotions (Lo et al., 2015).

Ambience

Altogether, privacy, price, and therapist qualifications account for more than 80% of the factors affecting spa-goers' decision to visit a spa (Kucukusta & Guillet, 2014). This statistic suggests that spa professionals should provide privacy for guests during treatments and in common areas, such as the lobby and single-sex changing rooms (Guillet & Kucukusta, 2016). Level of privacy is also believed to alter visitors' sense of relaxation, which is significant because relaxation and tranquility are top motivations for visiting a spa. In addition, women and youth are believed to pay more attention to the theme and decoration of the spa. Themes such as 'Green,' 'Ocean,' 'Feng Shui,' 'Fusion,' or 'Oriental' can directly influence the overall spa experience of these core spa-goers. Wakefield and Blodgett (1994) also showed that the design and décor of spa facilities are vital to creating excitement among customers.

Facilities

Basic spa facilities means the treatment rooms alone, while the full range of facilities refers to the treatment rooms, pools, jacuzzis, steam rooms, saunas, etc. (Ellis, 2008). Although spas generally cultivate an image of safety, some customers are concerned about cleanliness. This concern is reasonable because facilities such as saunas or whirlpools could be an avenue for infectious diseases. Thus, frequent cleaning and maintenance of facilities is necessary (Lo et al., 2013). One survey showed that poor cleanliness influences customers' choice of spa (Trihas & Konstantarou, 2016).

Millennial consumers

A generation or generational cohort is characterized by a specific time span during which a group of people experience similar external events (Benckendorff, Moscardo, & Pendergast, 2010). Each generation has its unique experience that shapes its common traits (Bannon, Ford, & Meltzer, 2011; Lewis, 2015). However, there is much disagreement as to how to classify generations. According to the United States Census Bureau, the millennial generation is those are born in late 1980s to early 2000s. Despite the diverse definitions, this study will (following a number of others) define millennials as people born between 1981 to 2000, i.e. aged between 18 and 37 in 2018 (Beekman, 2011; Cekada, 2012). Millennials have commonly been classified as Generation Y (Ng, Schweitzer, & Lyons, 2010). Post-80s and Post-90s are other nicknames used to describe millennials in Chinese society (Ordun, 2015).

Millennials account for more than 81 million people in the US, a figure that recently surpassed the 76 million baby boomers (Kardes, Cronley, & Cline, 2015). However, millennials have distinctive views of the world compared with previous generations (Balda & Mora, 2011). What an older hotel guest may consider attentive and responsible customer service, a millennial may find boring and worthless. Consequently, hoteliers face huge challenges in building close and durable relationships with them (Lazarevic, 2012). More millennials are expected to graduate from university and enter the workforce, and their earning power of approximately 170 billion dollars will make them a coveted group of consumers (Cui, Trent, Sullivan, & Matiru, 2003; Lassere, 2012). Fashion, food, jewelry, and health and beauty products are their major focuses of consumption (Valentine & Powers, 2013). Many millennials have grown up in a prosperous economy with two working parents. This environment provides more opportunities for consumer spending and means that they are more involved in family decisions than their predecessors (Phelps, 1999). Bakewell, Mitchell, and Rothwell (2006) explained that millennials live in a materialistic society and therefore are more likely to engage in status-seeking consumption to display their wealth and purchasing power (Eastman & Liu, 2012; O'Cass & Frost, 2002). Noble, Haytko, and Phillips (2009) agree that this group of consumers is brand-conscious, owing to a higher discretionary income than previous consumers of the same age. Several studies have reported that millennials prefer products that match their identity and lifestyle (Phillips, 2007). Furthermore, millennials' fickle loyalties make them more challenging for service providers to attract and retain (Reisenwitz & Iyer, 2009).

Recent research on spa suggests that spa attributes such as therapists' qualification, price, and treatment significantly influence spa goer's booking intention (e.g. Guillet & Kucukusta, 2019; Kucukusta & Guillet, 2014; Kucukusta et al., 2013). Therefore, we argue that these findings will hold for millennial consumers given that they care about quality, convenience, and value for money (Eastman, Iyer, & Thomas, 2013).

H1: There is a positive relationship between hotel spa attributes and millennials' intention to visit local hotel spas.

The role of technology

Millennials are a 'digital generation' and 'technologically savvy,' as the majority have grown up with digital technology (Martin, 2005). Almost 90% of millennials use their mobile phones to send and receive messages, compared to 77% and 51% of Gen Xers and Boomers, respectively. Three-fourths of millennials have created a social network profile, while only one-half of Gen Xers and less than one-third of boomers have opened an account on a social networking site (Ordun, 2015).

Because they are heavily invested in technology, millennials' purchase decision process typically involves the Internet (Ordun, 2015). Apart from online shopping, millennials commonly conduct primary research into products and services online (Moriarty, 2004; Wolburg & Pokrywczunski, 2001). Doing so allows them to be more aware and cautious of marketing campaigns compared to previous generations (Lissitsa & Kol, 2016). A report by Deloitte also suggested that 47% of millennials pay close attention to social media when shopping and making purchase decisions (Roesler, 2015). Instead of heeding brand advertising, millennials listen to their peers about which products and services to purchase (Rohampton, 2017).

Social media influences have a stronger impact for goods such as baby products, home furnishings, automobiles, and health and wellness services (Rohampton, 2017). Thus, businesses should utilize technology to leverage their relationship with millennials. A few studies have found that almost three-fourths of spa-goers used the Internet in the background research stage, compared to around one-third who purchased and read spa-related magazines (MedSci Communications & Consulting Co, 2006). Joppe (2010) also reported that over 80% of spa participants considered websearches the most common tool for research, compared to slightly over one-third who used the Internet in

1999. Hotel spa-goers specifically obtained spa and pricing information through the Internet. Therefore, it is clear that hotels should continuously update their spa websites, to stay connected to potential spa consumers and compete in the market (Okech, 2014; Ozdipciner, 2010). That said, recreational spa consumers engage in less extensive online information searches than heavy and frequent spa consumers.

The influence of the Internet cannot be underestimated, even though there is currently no research revealing how millennial spa-goers use the Internet in the pre-purchase stage. That said, the Internet plays a crucial role in travelers' planning and booking (Kucukusta, Law, Besbes, & Legohérel, 2015). Hong Kongers are no exception (Nielsen, 2010), with 31.8% of them visiting more than one travel website from 2007 to 2009, and 17.6% of them purchasing products from travel websites (Cheung & Law, 2009). Online platforms provide rich qualitative information that enables customers to compare diverse products and facilitates communication between suppliers and customers, and thus aids customers' decision-making process (Ip, Leung, & Law, 2011; Ruiz-Mafé, Sanz-Blas, & Aldás-Manzano, 2009). Chu (2001) stated that a user-friendly website should be attractive, informative, and interactive. To conclude, hotel day spas should use their websites to effectively communicate with potential spa-goers (Kucukusta & Guillet, 2014). Given the importance of the Internet, the following hypothesis will be proposed to understand whether the use of technology during the information search process affects millennials' intention to visit spas.

Therefore, we argue that the effect of spa attributes will be more influential to heavy mobile device users who are exposed to internet information, online search, and social media. Thus, we propose that,

H2: Mobile device usage moderates the relationship between spa attributes and millennials' intention to visit local hotel spas.

Methodology

This study uses a quantitative method to provide statistical evidence regarding the relationship between spa attributes, mobile usage, and the intention of millennials to visit local Hong Kong hotel spas.

After a review of the literature, a questionnaire comprising four parts was devised. The first section aimed to measure the usage of mobile technology (e.g. 'I am confident in using mobile devices.') on a 7-point Likert scale (1 – strongly disagree to 7 – strongly agree) (Zhang, Abound Omran, & Cobanoglu, 2017). The second section was designed to measure the importance of selective attributes of millennials in selecting local hotel spas (Kucukusta et al., 2013). Respondents were asked to indicate the importance on 7-point Likert scale (1 – not at all important to 7 – extremely important). The third part measured respondents' behavioral intention to visit a hotel spa by asking if they agreed with statements such as 'I am likely to visit a hotel spa sometime soon' (Lee, 2015). The final section focused on the socio-demographic characteristics of the respondents, such as age, gender, and educational level. The questionnaire was constructed bilingually (i.e. in Chinese and English). Back-to-back translation was performed to ensure consistency between the two versions. To assure the linguistic accuracy and clarity of the content, one professor and a group of 10 students were invited as a pilot group to review the questionnaire before it was administered to a larger sample. 294 questionnaires were collected and analyzed using the Statistical Package for Social Sciences (SPSS). A convenience sampling method was adopted. Target sample were approached by one researcher's contacts. Electronic questionnaires were distributed via Qualtrics. A screening process was performed to ensure only the target population was analyzed. Two hundred and fifty valid responses out of 294 in total (85%) were finally obtained.

Results

Descriptive analysis

A descriptive statistics analysis was conducted to illustrate the demographic profile (Table 2). Of the 294 participants, 55.6% were female and 44.1% were male. It should be noted that almost all respondents (98.3%) were born in Hong Kong. Over one-fourth (27.9%) belonged to the age group 23 to 27, followed by 23.8% aged 18 to 22; 15.3% aged 28 to 32; 18.0% aged 33 to 37; and 15.0% aged 37 or above. Almost 40% of respondents were single, while 60.3% of respondents were either partnered or married. In terms of education, over 50% were degree holders, followed by those (23.1%) who completed vocational school or a sub-degree. One-fifth had obtained a secondary school qualification or below, while slightly less than 5% had a Master's degree. A quarter of respondents were students, and the administrative and managerial occupational group contributed 20.2% of the results. Only 49 individuals (16.7%) had hotel-related experience in areas such as guest relations and spas. With reference to monthly household

Table 2. Demographic Profile of Respondents.

	N	%		N	%
Gender			**Education**		
Male	130	44.1	Secondary or lower	60	20.4
Female	164	55.6	Vocational school/sub-degree	68	23.1
Place of Origin			Bachelor's degree	149	50.7
Hong Kong	289	98.3	Master's degree	14	4.8
China	3	1.0	Doctoral degree	0	0
Taiwan	1	0.3	Other	3	1.0
Other	1	0.3	**Occupation**		
Age			Student	72	24.5
18 or below	0	0	Administrative/Clerical	62	21.1
18–22	70	23.8	Labor	31	10.5
23–27	82	27.9	Management level/Professional	62	21.1
28–32	45	15.3	Retired	3	1.0
33–37	53	18.0	Self-employed	23	7.8
37 or above	44	15.0	Unemployed	5	1.7
Marital Status			Other	36	12.2
Single	112	38.0	**Monthly household income (HK$)**		
With partner	77	26.1	$20,000 or below	49	16.7
Married without children	37	12.5	$20,000 – $39,999	102	34.7
Married with children	64	21.7	$40,000 – $59,999	75	25.5
Separated/Divorced	4	1.4	$60,000 – $79,999	40	13.6
Widowed	0	0	$80,000 – $99,999	10	3.4
Experience in hotel industry			$100,000 or above	18	6.1
Yes	49	16.7			
No	245	83.3			

income, 34.7% earned between $20,000 and $39,999, while the group earning $40,000 to $59,999 was next largest, at 25.5%. Slightly over 9% of respondents had a monthly household income of more than $80,000.

Given that previous research has established the dimensions of these attributes (e.g. Guillet & Kucukusta, 2019; Kucukusta et al., 2013), a reliability test shows that the Cronbach's alpha values of the scales range from 0.765 to 0.915, suggesting good internal consistency for each dimension. The means of the attributes indicate that price (M = 5.88), therapists (M = 5.69), and ambience (M = 5.57) are the most important attributes of a spa for millennials (see Table 3).

Hypotheses testing

To test H1, we ran a multiple linear regression with intention to visit as a dependent variable and the seven attributes as independent variables. Assumptions checks were performed before the analysis. The variance inflation factors (VIF) are all below 3 indicating there is no multicollinearity issue. The model was significant (F $(7, 242)$ = 8.858, p = 0.000). However, the results revealed that 'product' (t (250) = 2.108, p < 0.05), 'promotion' (t (250) = 2.479, p < 0.05), 'location' (t (250) = 2.489, p < 0.05), and 'price' (t (250) = −2.716, p < 0.01) were significant attributes predicting millennials' intention to visit. Therefore, only these attributes were included in further analysis.

Table 3. Descriptive Analysis of the Attributes.

Dimensions	Mean	SD	Cronbach's α
Product	*5.03*		
P1: Product uniqueness	4.98	1.238	0.847
P2: Signature treatment	5.06	1.211	
P3: Treatment diversity	5.04	1.190	
Promotion	*5.10*		
PR1: Discount	5.71	1.244	0.765
PR2: Upgrade/value-added	4.96	1.336	
PR3: Loyalty program	4.62	1.484	
Therapists	*5.69*		
TH1: Therapists' certificate	5.69	1.234	0.811
TH2: Therapists' reputation and professional skills	5.86	1.0478	
TH3: Therapists' courtesy	5.77	1.068	
TH4: Therapists' grooming	5.22	1.260	
TH5: Therapists' product and service knowledge	5.89	1.012	
Ambience	*5.57*		
A1: Aroma	5.39	1.133	0.849
A2: Sense of privacy	6.21	0.976	
A3: Sense of tranquility	5.93	1.007	
A4: Lighting/color	5.26	1.113	
A5: Theme/décor	5.04	1.197	
Facilities	*5.28*		
F1: Type of treatment rooms: e.g. single/couple	5.24	1.258	0.819
F2: Size of treatment rooms	5.17	1.170	
F3: Size of bed	5.20	1.265	
F4: Quality of linen	5.49	1.306	
Intention	*4.09*		
IN1: In the future, I intend to become a frequent customer of local hotel spas	3.88	1.461	0.915
IN2: I am likely to visit a local hotel spa soon	3.86	1.538	
IN3: I believe I will enjoy a local hotel spa in the near future	4.52	1.330	
IN4: I will strongly recommend that others visit local hotel spas	4.09	1.341	
Location	*5.21*	*1.294*	n.a.
Price	*5.88*	*1.097*	n.a.

To test H2, PROCESS Model One was used, with intention to visit as the dependent variable (Hayes & Montoya, 2017). Regressing intention to visit on these spa attributes, mobile usage, and their interaction revealed a significant interaction (t (250) = 2.36, p < 0.05) (see Table 4). To decompose this interaction, we used the Johnson-Neyman technique of floodlight analysis to identify point of mobile usage for which the effect of the spa attributes was significant. This analysis revealed that there was a significant positive effect of perceived importance of the spa attributes on intention to visit for mobile usage greater than 3.47 (B = 0.27, SE = 0.14., p = 0.05), but not for mobile usage less than 3.47 (See Figure 1).

Discussion

Spa attributes

Consistent with the findings of previous research (e.g. Kucukusta & Guillet, 2014; Kucukusta et al., 2013), price and therapists were ranked as the top two most important dimensions among millennials. First, this result suggests that millennials are price-sensitive when making hedonic services purchases. Therefore, more dynamic pricing and promotion strategies are needed to attract millennial spa customers, given the growing purchasing power of millennials (Cui et al., 2003; Farris, Chong, & Dunning, 2002; Lassere, 2012). The

Table 4. Process Output.

	b	se	t	p	LLCI	ULCI
Constant	4.9548	1.7110	2.8958	0.0041	1.5847	8.3250
Attributes	−.1976	0.3231	−0.6117	0.5413	−0.8340	0.4387
Mobile Use	−0.7013	0.3114	−2.2520	0.0252	−1.3146	−.0879
Attributes * Mobile Use	0.1375	0.0581	2.3659	0.0188	0.0230	0.2519

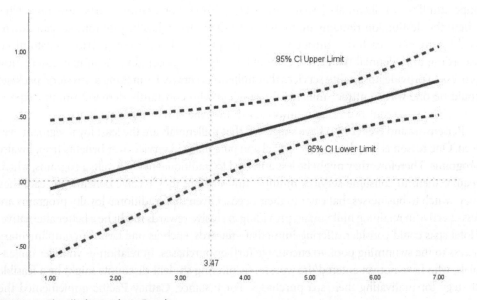

Figure 1. Floodlight Analysis Result.

lower demand for hotel spas could also be attributed to the high price; as the respondents in this study commented, '*Hong Kong spas in hotel are very expensive*'; '*Spa in Hong Kong is much more expensive than mainland or Thailand.*' Therefore, pricing is one of the key determinants for price-sensitive millennials in deciding whether to purchase spa services, in addition to promotions such as 'discounts,' 'value-added or upgrades,' or 'loyalty programs.' Hotel spas could follow the hotel brand Moxy to empower millennial guests to be their own marketing force. For example, hotel spas can provide incentives such as coupons to motivate guests to promote and share experiences with their peers via social networking channels (Bowen & Chen McCain, 2015).

Given that the spa industry is human-oriented, in which staff performance directly affects customers' evaluation of service quality, millennials pay extra attention to personnel. Therefore, millennials ranked 'therapists' product and service knowledge' as one of the highest sub-items within the category of therapists. Therapists should use communication and interaction to convey knowledge about treatments to customers. Doing so would not only fulfill millennials' need for novelty, but also satisfy their concerns regarding therapists' knowledge. It is important that therapists educate new spa-goers in terms of products, services, or standard procedures. At the same time, it is also vital for therapists to demonstrate courtesy, such as using a polite tone when helping guests. To further demonstrate their professionalism, spa staff should be attentive to each guest and provide service spontaneously. Spa managers should thus pay attention to the staff-to-customer ratio to ensure attentive and customer-centered service. On a practical level, employing part-time workers on weekends might be helpful in managing a higher influx of customers.

This study's results indicate that product, promotion, location, and price are the factors that lead to millennials' booking intention. Thus, hotel spas might need to constantly change their offerings to cater to the needs of millennials. A unique experience could be created by co-creating products with young spa-goers. One example of co-creation is American Express Travel, which gained a competitive edge by offering exciting travel opportunities to millennials (Adamson & Dev, 2016). For example, they now offer trips where the destination remains unknown until the journey has begun; tourists can download the itinerary each day through their smartphones. This 'mystery' trip is customized according to millennial travelers' personalities. Hotel spas could use a similar co-creation process to provide hospitality services that millennials crave. Launching a 'mystery' package could be one way to attract millennial spa-goers who constantly demand unique experiences. The treatment can remain undisclosed until the end of the experience.

Reisenwitz and Iyer (2009) have suggested that millennials are the least loyal segment ever seen. One reason is that they prefer special and personalized service over benefits from loyalty programs. Therefore, they might be less attracted to traditional tiered loyalty programs, which require them to consume services multiple times before they receive benefits; instead, they may switch to businesses that cater to their needs. Given that traditional loyalty programs are less effective in retaining millennials, providing exclusive rewards might be a better alternative. Hotel spas could consider offering immediate rewards, such as one hour of complimentary access to the swimming pool, to encourage further purchases. In relation to younger millennials, who have not yet entered the workforce, offering student discounts might be a feasible strategy for motivating their spa purchases. For instance, Cathay Pacific implemented the 'pop-up and go' scheme, which offers students a discount on their tourism products (Cathay Pacific, 2017). Thus hotels spas could use student discounts to attract younger millennials.

The effect of technology

The Internet is the 'second brain' of millennials around the world, who are frequently immersed in online activities, including booking hotel services (Bilgihan, 2016; Bowen & Chen McCain, 2015). This study has found that spa attributes are more likely to generate spa booking for frequent mobile device users. For example, our results show that if millennials are highly confident in using smart phones, the importance of spa attributes will result in booking intention. The ease of using technology and electronic devices motivates people to obtain information, while the intrinsic enjoyment of viewing pictures or videos of products and services further lures millennials to stay online (Bilgihan, 2016). Because millennials are price-sensitive, they tend to compare prices online before purchase; as mentioned earlier, women are particularly prone to price-shop. Thus, if people believe that they can find the best value through the Internet, their intention to purchase will increase due to the high self-efficacy attained from the online searching process (Chen, Phelan, & Jai, 2016).

Even though millennials may not fully utilize online booking systems, spa websites remain important for reaching potential spa-goers. Therefore, brochures or promotional messages should be available on spa websites. As discussed earlier, males look for vigorous activities at spas, whereas females are keener on quieter activities. As a result, advertisements should be targeted to gender differences. Similarly, Johanson (2004) also indicated that males' intention to visit spas may decrease if spa brochures mainly feature female models. Thus, photos of a gentleman with an energy drink in the gym or a lady having her nails done could be seen as appropriate promotional messages, and hopefully even if millennials choose not to book online, they will book services by other means such as phone calls. A mobile-friendly website would further facilitate promotion, as millennial respondents are confident mobile users.

Other attributes

Even though hotel spas may possess all the attributes desired by millennials, it is crucial to present ideas and settings to them. Servicescape is critical in influencing customers' cognitive, emotional, and physiological responses and consequently their purchase decisions (Lin, 2004). In this study, components such as lighting and color, sense of tranquility, and privacy are all examples of servicescape, and directly affect millennials' decision-making process (Bitner, 1992; Lin, 2009). The reason is that customers take their first impression from atmospheric cues when evaluating a service provider, before any contact with the concierge (Namasivayam & Lin, 2005).

In hotel spas, pleasant lighting sends implicit cues to customers that the facility is spacious and high-quality, while soft background music creates a relaxing setting for guests to enjoy the tranquility. Olfactory cues are also effective; for example, a pleasant aroma in a bakery can dramatically boost sales by 300% (Lin, 2009), Likewise, a soothing and refreshing scent at a spa can positively alter one's mood and emotions. In addition, young spa-goers pay particular attention to decorations and themes. Therefore, the components of servicescapes should be well designed to increase customers' pleasure levels and reinforce their intention to purchase.

Previous research has shown that spa-goers who visit a spa five times or more per year pay less attention to privacy compared to first-time visitors (Kucukusta & Guillet, 2014). Such a difference in response explains the high rating for 'sense of privacy' as a criterion in this study, as the majority of respondents were unfamiliar with the spa concept. This result indicates that people treat a spa as a private activity in their own individual space, especially when they first experience it. This study agrees with Little (2013) that if hotel spas can effectively address privacy issues, spa-goers will have a stronger desire to visit and the time spent there will be longer. Therefore, managers should ensure privacy in treatment rooms and public areas. Special attention should be paid to common areas such as relaxation lounges or changing rooms, because interactions between spa guests might have an impact on individuals' experience.

Limitations and future research

Caution must be exercised when interpreting the results of this study, as it has some limitations. First, a convenience sampling method was adopted and only a small sample size was obtained; therefore, the results might not reflect the entire market. Second, the younger group (aged 18 to 27) constituted more than half of the research population, and there was also a higher percentage of students compared to other occupations, which may further affect the representativeness of the overall result. Lastly, every culture shapes millennials in different ways, and thus the results of this study might only be applicable to the Hong Kong context. That said, hotel spas around the world can use it as a starting point. For a more comprehensive picture of millennials' intention to visit local hotel spas, further studies using qualitative techniques and specifically focused group interviews could be conducted to validate the findings.

Future research can investigate other characteristics of millennials such as age, income, gender, etc. For example, males are willing to engage in more vigorous spa activities and participate in activities that address physical wellbeing. Sports massage, fitness facilities, and nutrition-related activities are spa services that men generally favor. In contrast, women tend to devote themselves to less demanding activities such as yoga or Pilates (Sherman et al., 2007). Millennials highly value others' comments, as they wish to feel close to their peers; thus, their sense of belonging might decrease if people within the same social circle choose alternative services. This phenomenon has also been noted by Bowen and Chen McCain (2015), who found that almost 40% of millennials had purchased goods and services recommended by friends in the past week. Therefore, future research should consider the potential influence of peers.

Disclosure statement

No potential conflict of interest was reported by the authors.

Funding

This work was supported by the School of Hotel and Tourism Management, The Hong Kong Polytechnic University [G-UAE9].

ORCID

Yixing (Lisa) Gao 🆔 http://orcid.org/0000-0001-6919-434X

References

Adamson, A, & Dev, C. S. (2016). Hospitality branding in the age of the millennial. *Boston Hospitality Review*, 4(3), 1-9.

Bakewell, C., Mitchell, V. W., & Rothwell, M. (2006). UK Generation Y male fashion consciousness. *Journal of Fashion Marketing and Management: an International Journal*, 10 (2), 169–180.

Balda, J. B., & Mora, F. (2011). Adapting leadership theory and practice for the networked, millennial generation. *Journal of Leadership Studies*, 5(3), 13–24.

Bannon, S., Ford, K., & Meltzer, L. (2011). Understanding millennials in the workplace. *CPA Journal*, 81(11), 61–65.

Beekman, T. (2011). Fill in the generation gap. *Strategic Finance*, 93(3), 15–17.

Benckendorff, P., Moscardo, G., & Pendergast, D. (2010). *Tourism and Generation Y*. Wallingford, UK: CABI.

Bilgihan, A. (2016). Gen Y customer loyalty in online shopping: An integrated model of trust, user experience and branding. *Computers in Human Behavior*, 61, 103–113.

Biswas, A. (1992). The moderating role of brand familiarity in reference price perceptions. *Journal of Business Research*, 25(3), 251–262.

Bitner, M. J. (1992). Servicescapes: The impact of physical surroundings on customers and employees. *The Journal of Marketing*, 56(2), 57–71.

Bowen, J. T., & Chen McCain, S.-L. (2015). Transitioning loyalty programs: A commentary on "the relationship between customer loyalty and customer satisfaction". *International Journal of Contemporary Hospitality Management*, 27(3), 415–430.

Cathay Pacific. (2017). Register now for the student discount. *Cathay Pacific*. Retrieved from https://www.cathaypacific.com/cx/zh_HK/registered-account/student-2017.html

Cekada, T. L. (2012). Training a multigenerational workforce. *Professional Safety*, 57(3), 40–44.

Chen, H., Phelan, K. V., & Jai, T. M. (2016). Gender differences in deal hunting: What motivates consumers to search and book hotel deals? *Journal of Hospitality Marketing & Management*, 25(5), 613–639.

Cheung, C., & Law, R. (2009). Have the perceptions of the successful factors for travel web sites changed over time? The case of consumers in Hong Kong. *Journal of Hospitality & Tourism Research*, 33(3), 438–446.

Chu, R. (2001). What online Hong Kong travelers look for on airline/travel websites? *International Journal of Hospitality Management, 20*(1), 95–100.

Cui, Y., Trent, E. S., Sullivan, P. M., & Matiru, G. N. (2003). Cause-related marketing: How generation Y responds. *International Journal of Retail & Distribution Management, 31*(6), 310–320.

Eastman, J., Iyer, R., & Thomas, S. P. (2013). The impact of status consumption on shopping styles: An exploratory look at the millennial generation. *Marketing Management Journal, 23* (1), 57–73.

Eastman, J. K., & Liu, J. (2012). The impact of generational cohorts on status consumption: An exploratory look at generational cohort and demographics on status consumption. *Journal of Consumer Marketing, 29*(2), 93–102.

Ellis, S. (2008). Trends in the global spa industry. In M. Cohen & G. Bodeker (Eds.), *Understanding the global spa industry: Spa management* (pp. 66–84). Oxford: Butterworth-Heinemann.

Ely, J. (2009). Where does the customer Spa experience begin and end? *Spa Management, 19*(8), 28–30.

Farris, R., Chong, F., & Dunning, D. (2002). Generation Y: Purchasing power and implications for marketing. *Academy of Marketing Studies Journal, 6*(1–2), 89–101.

Frost, G. J. (2004). The spa as a model of an optimal healing environment. *Journal of Alternative & Complementary Medicine, 10*(Supplement 1), S85–S92.

Furrer, W. (2010). Top 20 spa trends in 20 years. *Pulse Magazine, 20*, 74–78.

Global Spa and Wellness Summit. (2008). *Global Spa Economy Report 2007*. Retrieved from http://www.globalspaandwellnesssummit.org/images/stories/pdf/gss.spa.economy.report.2008.pdf

Gonzalez, M. E. A., & Brea, J. A. F. (2005). An investigation of the relationship among service quality, customer satisfaction and behavioural intentions in Spanish health spas. *Journal of Hospitality & Leisure Marketing, 12*(2), 67–90.

Guillet, B. D., & Kucukusta, D. (2016). Spa market segmentation according to customer preference. *International Journal of Contemporary Hospitality Management, 28*(2), 418–434.

Guillet, B. D., & Kucukusta, D. (2019). Analyzing attributes of the spa service experience: Perceptions of spa-goers traveling to Hong Kong. *Journal of China Tourism Research, 15*(1), 66–83.

Hayes, A. F., & Montoya, A. K. (2017). A tutorial on testing, visualizing, and probing an interaction involving a multicategorical variable in linear regression analysis. *Communication Methods and Measures, 11*(1), 1–30.

Herbig, P., & Milewicz, J. (1995). The relationship of reputation and credibility to brand success. *Journal of Consumer Marketing, 12*(4), 5–10.

Hong Kong Tourism Board. (2010). *Hong Kong visitor profile report 2010*. Retrieved from http://partnernet.hktourismboard.com

International Spa Association. (2017). *Definition of spa*. Retrieved from https://experienceispa.com/resources/spa-goers

Ip, C., Leung, R., & Law, R. (2011). Progress and development of information and communication technologies in hospitality. *International Journal of Contemporary Hospitality Management, 23*(4), 533–551.

Johanson, M. M. (2004). Health, wellness focus within resort hotels. *FIU Hospitality Review, 22* (1), 24–29.

Joppe, M. (2010). One country's transformation to spa destination: The case of Canada. *Journal of Hospitality and Tourism Management, 17*(1), 117–126.

Kardes, F. R., Cronley, M. L., & Cline, T. W. (2015). *Consumer behaviour*. Stanford: Cengage Learning.

Keri, K., Ottenbacher, M., & Harrington, R. (2007). The North American spa industry: An examination of emergent trends. *FIU Hospitality Review, 25*(1), 50–60.

Kucukusta, D., & Guillet, B. D. (2014). Measuring spa-goers' preferences: A conjoint analysis approach. *International Journal of Hospitality Management, 41*, 115–124.

Kucukusta, D., Law, R., Besbes, A., & Legohérel, P. (2015). Re-examining perceived usefulness and ease of use in online booking: The case of Hong Kong online users. *International Journal of Contemporary Hospitality Management, 27*(2), 185–198.

Kucukusta, D., Pang, L., & Chui, S. (2013). Inbound travelers' selection criteria for hotel spas in Hong Kong. *Journal of Travel & Tourism Marketing, 30*(6), 557–576.

Langvinienė, N. (2011). Specificity of day and resort wellness SPA services in Lithuania. *Social Research, 2*, 45–58.

Lassere, A. (2012). The marketing corner: The purchasing power of Millennials. *Economy & Trade: Epoch Times.* Retrieved from www.theepochtimes.com

Lazarevic, V. (2012). Encouraging brand loyalty in fickle generation Y consumers. *Young Consumers, 13*(1), 45–61.

Lee, M. J. (2015). An investigation of spa-goers' intention to visit a luxury hotel spa: An extension of theory of planned behavior. *Pan-Pacific Journal of Business Research, 6*(2), 15–31.

Lewis, R. A. (2015). Generation Y at work: Insight from experiences in the hotel sector. *International Journal of Business and Management, 3*(1), 1–17.

Lin, I. Y. (2004). Evaluating a servicescape: The effect of cognition and emotion. *International Journal of Hospitality Management, 23*(2), 163–178.

Lin, I. Y. (2009). The combined effect of color and music on customer satisfaction in hotel bars. *Journal of Hospitality Marketing & Management, 19*(1), 22–37.

Lissitsa, S., & Kol, O. (2016). Generation X vs. Generation Y - A decade of online shopping. *Journal of Retailing and Consumer Services, 31*, 304–312.

Little, J. (2013). Pampering, well-being and women's bodies in the therapeutic spaces of the spa. *Social & Cultural Geography, 14*(1), 41–58.

Lo, A., Qu, H., & Wetprasit, P. (2013). Realms of tourism spa experience: The case of mainland Chinese tourists. *Journal of China Tourism Research, 9*(4), 429–451.

Lo, A., Wu, C., & Tsai, H. (2015). The impact of service quality on positive consumption emotions in resort and hotel spa experiences. *Journal of Hospitality Marketing & Management, 24*(2), 155–179.

Lo, A. S., & Wu, C. (2014). Effect of consumption emotion on hotel and resort spa experience. *Journal of Travel & Tourism Marketing, 31*(8), 958–984.

Mak, A. H., Wong, K. K., & Chang, R. C. (2009). Health or self-indulgence? The motivations and characteristics of spa-goers. *International Journal of Tourism Research, 11*(2), 185–199.

Martin, C. A. (2005). From high maintenance to high productivity: What managers need to know about Generation Y. *Industrial and Commercial Training, 37*(1), 39–44.

McNeil, K. R., & Ragins, E. J. (2005). Staying in the spa marketing game: Trends, challenges, strategies and techniques. *Journal of Vacation Marketing, 11*(1), 31–39.

MedSci Communications & Consulting Co. (2006). *2005 Canadian spa goers survey.* Canada: Leading Spas of Canada & Elmcrest College.

Moriarty, R. (2004). Marketers target savvy "Y" spenders: Hip imagery, sophisticated sales pitches, web sites are designed to appeal to youth. *The Post Standard, 8*(2).

Namasivayam, K., & Lin, I. (2005). Accounting for temporality in servicescape effects on consumers' service evaluations. *Journal of Foodservice Business Research, 7*(1), 5–22.

Ng, E. S., Schweitzer, L., & Lyons, S. T. (2010). New generation, great expectations: A field study of the millennial generation. *Journal of Business and Psychology, 25*(2), 281–292.

Nielsen. (2010, September 14). Hong Kong consumers most likely to shop online for booking travels, books and clothing. *Nielsen Insight.* Retrieved from http://hk.nielsen.com/news/20100914.shtml

Noble, S. M., Haytko, D. L., & Phillips, J. (2009). What drives college-age Generation Y consumers? *Journal of Business Research, 62*(6), 617–628.

O'Cass, A., & Frost, H. (2002). Status brands: Examining the effects of non-product-related brand associations on status and conspicuous consumption. *Journal of Product & Brand Management, 11*(2), 67–88.

Okech, R. N. (2014). Promoting the spa tourism industry: Focus on coastal resorts in Kenya. *Athens Journal of Tourism*, 1(1), 67–77.

Ordun, G. (2015). Millennial (Gen Y) consumer behavior their shopping preferences and perceptual maps associated with brand loyalty. *Canadian Social Science*, 11(4), 40–55.

Ozdipciner, N. S. (2010). Electronic marketing in tourism. *Journal of Internet Applications and Management*, 1, 5–22.

Panchal, J. H. (2012). *The Asian spa: A study of tourist motivations, "flow" and the benefits of spa experiences* (doctoral dissertation). James Cook University.

Park, K. S., & Reisinger, Y. (2009). Cultural differences in shopping for luxury goods: Western, Asian, and Hispanic tourists. *Journal of Travel & Tourism Marketing*, 26(8), 762–777.

Phelps, M. (1999). Introducing the millennium kid. *The International Journal of Advertising and Marketing to Children*, 1(2), 135–139.

Phillips, C. (2007). Millennials: Clued in or clueless. *Advertising Age*, 78(46), 12–13.

Puczkó, L., & Bachvarov, M. (2006). Spa, bath, thermae: What's behind the labels? *Tourism Recreation Research*, 31(1), 83–91.

Reisenwitz, T. H., & Iyer, R. (2009). Differences in generation X and generation Y: Implications for the organization and marketers. *The Marketing Management Journal*, 19(2), 91–103.

Remedios, P. (2008). Built environment-spa design. In C. Marc & G. Berard (Eds.), *Understanding the global spa industry* (pp. 281–296). Oxford, UK: Butterworth-Heinemann.

Roesler, P. (2015, May 29). How social media influences consumer buying decisions. *The Business Journals*.

Rohampton, J. (2017). How does social media influence millennials' shopping decisions? *Forbes*. Retrieved from https://www.forbes.com/sites/jimmyrohampton/2017/05/03/does-social-media -influence-millennials-shopping-decisions/#1927ff504cf3

Ruiz-Mafé, C., Sanz-Blas, S., & Aldás-Manzano, J. (2009). Drivers and barriers to online airline ticket purchasing. *Journal of Air Transport Management*, 15(6), 294–298.

Sherman, L., Clemenz, C., & Philipp, S. (2007). Gender-based service preferences of spa-goers. *Advances in Hospitality and Leisure*, 3, 217–229.

Tabacchi, M. H. (2010). Current research and events in the spa industry. *Cornell Hospitality Quarterly*, 51(1), 102–117.

Tang, L. F. I. (2014). *Assessment framework for hotel day spa service and facility provision in Hong Kong* (doctoral dissertation). School of Hotel and Tourism Management, The Hong Kong Polytechnic University, Hong Kong.

Terry, M. (2007). *Spa industry weaknesses—Redefining your focus*. Bountiful, UT: Creative Spa Concepts. Retrieved from www.creativespaconcepts.com/pdf/monaco.pdf

Trihas, N., & Konstantarou, A. (2016). Spa-goers' characteristics, motivations, preferences and perceptions: Evidence from Elounda, Crete. *Almatourism, Journal of Tourism, Culture and Territorial Development*, 7(14), 106–127.

Tsai, H., Suh, E., & Fong, C. (2012). Understanding male hotel spa-goers in Hong Kong. *Journal of Hospitality Marketing & Management*, 21(3), 247–269.

Valentine, D. B., & Powers, T. L. (2013). Generation Y values and lifestyle segments. *Journal of Consumer Marketing*, 30(7), 597–606.

Wakefield, K. L., & Blodgett, J. G. (1994). The importance of servicescapes in leisure service settings. *Journal of Services Marketing*, 8(3), 66–76.

Wolburg, J. M., & Pokrywczunski, J. (2001). A psychographic analysis of generation Y college students. *Journal of Advertising Research*, 41, 33–52.

Wuttke, M., & Cohen, M. (2008). Spa retail. In M. Cohen & G. Bodeker (Eds.), *Understanding the global spa industry: Spa management* (pp. 208–220). Oxford: Butterworth-Heinemann.

Yung, M. (2010, March 22). Spa development in Hong Kong. *Global Trade Net*. Retrieved from http://www.globaltrade.net/f/market-research/text/Hong-Kong-SAR/Fitness-Spa-Cosmetic-Surgery-Spa-Spa-Development-in-Hong-Kong.html

Zhang, T., Abound Omran, B., & Cobanoglu, C. (2017). Generation Y's positive and negative eWOM: Use of social media and mobile technology. *International Journal of Contemporary Hospitality Management*, 29(2), 732–761.

Leisure Mobility of Chinese Millennials

Jieyu (Jade) Shi, Alei Fan and Liping A. Cai

ABSTRACT

This study focuses on Chinese millennials as a unique travel group and investigates how the usage of mobile technology impacts their leisure travel experience and continuous engagement with mobile technology. The study results demonstrate that, among the three major mobile technology functions, the utilitarian and social functions have significant positive impacts on Chinese millennials' leisure travel experience, whereas the hedonic function does not extend any significant influences. In addition, leisure travel experience partially mediates the relationship between the utilitarian function of mobile technology and Chinese millennials' future mobile technology engagement. The findings provide insights for tourism practitioners regarding how to efficiently develop mobile applications through emphasizing utilitarian and social functions to better meet Chinese millennials' needs. The function-improved mobile apps can enhance their leisure travel experience and further contribute to the continuous mobile technology engagement. A virtuous circle will be generated between the mobile technology engagement and leisure travel experience.

移动科技对中国千禧一代休闲旅游体验的影响

摘要

本文着眼于中国千禧一代这个独特的群体，研究了移动科技对他们休闲旅游体验以及未来移动科技参与度的影响。研究结果表明，在移动科技的三大功能中，实用功能和社交功能对中国千禧一代的休闲旅行体验有着显著的积极影响，而娱乐功能则没有任何显著影响。此外，本研究还发现中国千禧一代的休闲旅游体验在移动技术的实用功能和未来移动科技参与度之间具有部分中介影响。本文就旅游从业者应如何有效利用移动科技的实用功能和社交功能开发移动手机应用程序以更好地满足中国千禧一代在休闲旅游过程中的需求提供了见解。经过功能改进的移动手机应用程序不仅可以增强中国千禧一代的休闲旅行体验，而且可以提高他们的移动科技参与度，从而达到移动科技参与度和休闲旅行体验的良性循环。

Introduction

Mobility highlights the movements of people in a free and easy way, and it becomes increasingly important in contemporary society (Scheiner, 2006). People's life is hardly bounded by fixed locations. Instead, traveling to other places has become a core compo-nent of today's lifestyle (Molz, 2006). Leisure mobility refers to the non-work related trips away from the everyday environment, involving both inter-destination and intra-destination movements (Kaspar, 1996). Also, thanks to the new technologies, mobile technology in particular, people assisted by all kinds of mobile appliances can travel more freely and easier than ever in history. The emerging mobile technology and its increasing usage have been greatly changing people's lifestyle, including how people travel (Cohen, Duncan, & Thulemark, 2015). Mobile technology facilitates tourism activities throughout all the three stages of travel: pre-trip, during-trip, and post-trip (Amaro & Duarte, 2017; MacKay & Vogt, 2012; Xiang, Gretzel, & Fesenmaier, 2009). People use various mobile appliances such as smartphones and pads to search for travel information, make pur-chases, communicate with service providers, and kill time during the trip (Hudson & Thal, 2013; Tussyadiah & Zach, 2012). Furthermore, mobile technology helps travelers to create and maintain their social ties in the virtual space when they travel (de Oliveira Nunes & Mayer, 2014; Molz, 2006). They can connect with others including family members, friends, and other travelers, share travel experience, and post reviews.

Meanwhile, tourism destinations take advantage of advanced technologies to provide services for travelers to meet their various needs during different stages of travel (Tussyadiah, 2017). Previous literature has examined how mobile technology is applied to travel (Gretzel, 2010; Hannam, Butler, & Paris, 2014) and how travelers accept various mobile technology appliances (Neuhofer, Buhalis, & Ladkin, 2014; Wang, Xiang, & Fesenmaier, 2016). However, limited research investigates the impact of different functions of mobile technology on tourism experience (Buhalis & Law, 2008). On the other hand, although previous research has examined that different functions of mobile technology influence people's technology engagement in general (Kim, Chan, & Chan, 2007; Kim, Kim, & Wachter, 2013), little attention is paid to the specific tourism context yet. To bridge the research gap, the current study aims to investigate how different functions of mobile technology affect travelers' experience, and whether such experience may lead to their future engagement with mobile technology. Specifically, the study looks into one unique customer group, Chinese millennials, who are recognized as one of the major contributors to the tourism industry today as well as in the future (Dychtwald, 2018).

Millennials or Generation Y, who were born between the early 1980s and the begin-ning of 2000s, have grown up in the information age. They are tagged as the Net Generation and digital natives. Their access to the Internet is ubiquitous. The mobile technology has penetrated almost every aspect of their life, constantly connecting their daily life with the Internet. The younger the age group, the higher percentage of using the Internet for school, work, and leisure (Oblinger, 2003). Unlike the older generation, millennials are more willing to spend time on online interactions and more comfortable to build relationships with others via new technologies (Howard, Rainie, & Jones, 2001; Thayer & Ray, 2006). Chinese millennials refer to those who were born in the 80s and 90s, currently aged between 18 and 37 (Jing & Hu, 2017). They have grown up during the decades when China opened up for its economic reform and have enjoyed the fruits of China's recent prosperity (Russell, 2016). Most of them are the only child in their families due to China's one-child policy that started in 1979 and lasted for almost 40 years in China (Kuo, 2017). As a result, most Chinese millennials are the foci of their parents and grandparents from both sides, and they are often called as 'little emperors' and 'little empresses' of their families (Wang, 2017). On the other hand, Chinese millennials are considered as the loneliest generation group without any siblings. The lack of siblings and the feeling of loneliness increase their desire to connect with the world outside families, to communicate with other people beyond family members, and to share their joys and sorrows with those of similar ages and interests (Yi, Ribbens, & Morgan, 2010). Compared with the Western counterparts, Chinese millennials are more active with the mobile technology since the Internet and mobile technology provide them with the means to satisfy their desire to connect with others and the world without any geographic restrictions (Molz, 2006).

Travel, especially leisure travel, is another popular way for Chinese millennials to connect with the world and get to know others. According to the World Youth Student and Educational Travel Confederation (WYSETC) and the United Nations World Tourism Organization (UNWTO), by 2020, millennials will take about 300 million leisure trips globally. Particularly, Chinese millennials will contribute almost 70% of these leisure travels (Genç, 2013; WYSETC, 2015). Growth from Knowledge (GFK) (2016) reported that 93% of the Post-80s and Post-90s Chinese believe that leisure travel is an indispensable component of their life. Along with Chinese millennials' intensive leisure travel, their usage of mobile technology in travel also shows a constant increase. In 2016, the number of people who booked air tickets, hotel rooms, train tickets, and holiday travels via mobile technology reached to 262 million in China, and 73.7% of them are millennials (CNNIC, 2017).

Leisure mobility underlines both travel and mobile technology usage on the go for today's travelers, especially to Chinese millennials who are one of the major consumption powers for the tourism industry. Therefore, to connect the missing link in previous research and to help tourism service providers have a better understanding of their target customer group, this study aims to answer the following research questions:

- If and to what extent do the utilitarian, hedonic, and social functions of mobile technology influence Chinese millennials' leisure travel experience?
- If and to what extent do the three functions lead Chinese millennials to continue their engagement with mobile technology through the enhanced leisure travel experience facilitated by mobile technology?

The rest of this article is organized as follows. First, the study reviews relevant literature and proposes hypotheses. Next, the methodology is presented and the results are reported. Finally, implications, limitations, and directions for future research are discussed.

Theoretical backgrounds and hypotheses

Mobile technology and leisure travel

Mobile technology refers to the technology that offers people the access to ubiquitous information and services on the move through wireless networks and various mobile appliances such as smartphones and pads (Ito, Okabe, & Matsuda, 2005; Liang, Huang, Yeh, & Lin, 2007). The most significant features of mobile technology are mobility and portability (Liang et al., 2007; Tussyadiah, 2017). Mobile technology and its carriers have penetrated almost every aspect of people's lives, including travel (Lenker, Harris, Taugher, & Smith, 2013). The development of mobile technology has changed the way people search for information and communicate with others (Kim et al., 2013). By adopting mobile technology, the tourism industry can better serve its customers throughout all three stages of travel: pre-trip, during-trip, and post-trip (Gretzel, 2010; Liu & Law, 2013). Prior to a trip, mobile technology helps travelers efficiently make plans and purchases. During a trip, mobile technology facilitates travelers to easily find the destination or service information on-site, to communicate with tourism service providers, to connect with others such as family members and friends, and to share travel experience simultaneously. After a trip, mobile technology provides an easy and convenient way for travelers to post their travel stories with text, pictures, and videos taken and saved in their mobile appliances; and travelers can answer questions and share traveling advice with others anywhere and anytime (Fotis, Buhalis, & Rossides, 2012; Parra-López, Gutiérrez-Taño, Diaz-Armas, & Bulchand-Gidumal, 2012).

Among all three stages throughout traveling, the mobile technology is used most during trips due to mobile appliances' advantages of mobility and portability (Dickinson, Hibbert, & Filimonau, 2016; Wang, Park, & Fesenmaier, 2012). For leisure travel, people intensively use mobile technology during trips for information and services on-site as well as connection with others regardless of time constraints and space limitation (Chung & Buhalis, 2008). For example, travelers utilize mobile apps to check the crowdedness of particular tourist spots at the destination (Brown, Kappes, & Marks, 2013; Ricci, 2010). Recently, mobile technology is increasingly used by travelers for instant communication with others and simultaneous travel experience sharing on social media (White & White, 2007).

Extant literature suggests three major functions of mobile technology: utilitarian, hedonic, and social functions (Kim et al., 2013). Utilitarian function is defined as the acquisition of specific products or services in an effective manner (Venkatesh & Brown, 2001). Mobile technology was originally developed and provided for utilitarian purposes, such as e-mails, calendars, and weather information applications (Hsiao, Chang, & Tang, 2016). The utilitarian function emphasizes the efficiency as users' tasks are fulfilled (Babin, Darden, & Griffin, 1994). With fast technology development and users' ever-growing demands, the other two major functions of mobile technology, namely hedonic function and social function, come under the spotlight. Hedonic function satisfies people's intrinsic needs for fun, excitement, and enjoyment while they are using mobile technology (Kim et al., 2013). Many entertainment-oriented mobile applications are available nowadays to serve hedonic purposes by facilitating users to experience pleasure and obtain enjoyment (Childers, Carr, Peck, & Carson, 2001). Social function reflects the connection and interaction among people in the social network through mobile technology (Rice & Aydin, 1991). This function contributes to maintaining users' social ties and co-creating and sharing personal experiences with other mobile technology users (Edvardsson, Tronvoll, & Gruber, 2011).

In the travel context, mobile technology becomes increasingly important and powerful to facilitate people's leisure travel. With mobile technology, travelers have access to abundant and instant information relevant to destinations, tourism products, and services (Diekmann & McCabe, 2011; Wang et al., 2012). In particular, travelers can solve problems they encounter on the way and complete the travel-related tasks in a more convenient and effective way (Lyons & Urry, 2005). The efficiency brought by mobile technology's utilitarian function helps decrease travelers' perceived risk and uncertainty (Dal Fiore, Mokhtarian, Salomon, & Singer, 2014; Lyons & Urry, 2005), which enhances their leisure travel experience. Chinese millennials have grown up with all kinds of emerging technologies and tend to use mobile technology for information search and online consumption as part of their daily lifestyle (Molz, 2006). Therefore, the positive impact of mobile technology on Chinese millennials' leisure travel may be further improved, as the handy utilitarian function allows them to stay in the comfort zone even when they actually travel away from their familiar environment and daily lifestyle.

Previous literature suggests that mobile technology can add fun to leisure travel and improve the enjoyment and excitement of traveling (Gretzel & Yoo, 2008). Leisure travelers utilize mobile apps to meet their hedonic needs, such as listening to music, watching videos, playing games, and having a fun time by interacting with other users (Chung & Buhalis, 2008), which in turn leads to the pleased leisure travel experience. As for millennials, having fun with various mobile apps has become a part of their daily life (Howard et al., 2001). Entertainments fulfilled by mobile technology are important resources for Chinese millennials to satisfy their hedonic demands during leisure trips (Eastman, Iyer, Liao-Troth, Williams, & Griffin, 2014; Li, Dong, & Chen, 2012). Hence, the hedonic function of mobile technology may further improve Chinese millennials' entire leisure travel experience.

Mobile technology also enables travelers to instantly communicate with family, friends, and other mobile users (Gotardi, Senn, Cholakova, Liebrich, & Wozniak, 2015). The interaction not only makes the leisure travel less perilous and less lonely (Jain & Lyons, 2008; Lyons & Urry, 2005), but also meets travelers' social needs during trips (Mascheroni, 2007; White & White, 2007). This is especially true for Chinese millennial travelers. Chinese millennials' parents usually keep in close contact with their children to make sure that their only child is safe during traveling and able to get immediate help on the move (Nasar, Hecht, & Wener, 2007). Meanwhile, Chinese millennials themselves heavily rely on mobile technology to maintain their social connections and to eliminate their feeling of loneliness (Yang, 1997; Yi et al., 2010). During their leisure travel, Chinese millennials tend to directly communicate with other people, post their travel photos and videos, and get updated about others' status through various social media (Dewan & Benckendorff, 2013; Ling & Yttri, 2002). Furthermore, some mobile apps provide Chinese millennials the channel to expand their social networks during trips. For instance, Mafengwo app, as one of the most popular mobile apps among Chinese young people, aims at both travel and social purposes (Jia, Li, & He, 2016). It helps travelers to meet and communicate with strangers who share the same interests by following, posting, commenting, and messaging. Such social function well meets one of the goals for Chinese millennial travelers: to make new friends on the trip. Thus, the mobile technology's social function fulfills Chinese millennials' social needs during their leisure travel and in turn is likely to improve their leisure travel experience.

Travel experience is seen as a psychological outcome resulting from their participation in tourism-related activities (Chen & Chen, 2010). It is a multi-dimensional concept and investigated by scholars from different aspects. A number of studies captured travel experience by evaluating travelers' perceived satisfaction based on the comparison between expectations and actual performance (Chen & Chen, 2010; Kim et al., 2013). If the comparison brings out travelers' feelings of gratification, then travelers are likely to obtain the enhanced leisure travel experience (Reisinger & Turner, 2003). Other researchers identify travel experience with such realms as entertainment and enjoyment (e.g. He, Wu, & Li, 2018; Oh, Fiore, & Jeoung, 2007). In particular, they argue that taking leisure trips makes travelers feel excited, helps them relax, and receive happiness.

Mobile technology has become travel companions for the majority of people, young travelers in particular, resulting in the connection between their travel experience and the development of mobile technology (Tussyadiah, 2013). A study conducted by Lalicic and Weismayer (2016) indicated that mobile technology usage involves psychological processes, which in turn influences traveler's overall experience. Following previous literature (Chen & Chen, 2010), the current study considers leisure travel experience as a holistic concept to evaluate the quality of Chinese millennials' travel experience according to their emotional responses toward the usage of mobile technology for utilitarian, hedonic, and social needs. Once their specific demands are achieved through using mobile technology at the during-trip stage, Chinese millennials will further obtain the enhanced overall leisure travel experience.

Put together, this study proposes the following hypotheses:

H1: The mobile technology functions positively impact on Chinese millennials' leisure travel experience at the during-trip stage, specifically

H1a: The utilitarian function of mobile technology has a positive impact on leisure travel experience.

H1b: The hedonic function of mobile technology has a positive impact on leisure travel experience.

H1c: The social function of mobile technology has a positive impact on leisure travel experience.

Mobile technology engagement in the tourism context

Engagement is defined as a status that people are involved, occupied, retained, and intrinsically interested in something (Pagani & Mirabello, 2011). It is not a temporary state, but a more persistent and pervasive cognitive-affective state (Schaufeli, Salanova, González-Romá, & Bakker, 2002). Mobile technology engagement highlights people's involvement and continuous use of various mobile devices and applications (Kowatsch & Maass, 2010). Extant studies have identified three major factors that influence mobile users' engagement: utilitarian, hedonic, and social functions (Kim et al., 2007; Venkatesh, Thong, & Xu, 2012). According to the technology acceptance model (TAM), the technology users tend to continue using a certain technology if they perceive its usefulness in task completion or performance improvement (Hsiao et al., 2016). In other words, technology's utilitarian advantages positively influence users' engagement with it, so does mobile technology. Similarly, the hedonic function is another key predictor of users' engagement with mobile technology (Brown & Venkatesh, 2005; Lee & Jun, 2005). Particularly, Ayeh, Au, and Law (2013) find the positive relationship between mobile technology's hedonic benefits and people's intention to continue using it for

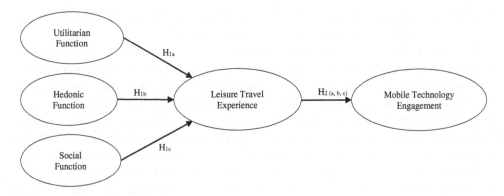

Figure 1. The conceptual model.
*Note: *p < .05, **p < .01, ***p < .001.*

travel planning. The third major factor impacting users' engagement with mobile technology is the social function (Karaiskos, Drossos, Tsiaousis, Giaglis, & Fouskas, 2012). To maintain their social networks, people frequently use various instant communication mobile apps (Ellison, Steinfield, & Lampe, 2007; Salehan & Negahban, 2013). As a result, how well mobile technology's social function meets people's social needs during their travel may strongly affect users' continuous engagement with technology. Travelers' experience of using mobile technology during trips may affect their decision on whether to continue using it in their future leisure travels (Gretzel, 2011). Hereby, it is hypothesized:

H2: The mobile technology functions positively affect Chinese millennials' future mobile technology engagement through the enhanced leisure travel experience, specifically

H2a: The utilitarian function positively affects Chinese millennials' future mobile technology engagement through the enhanced leisure travel experience.

H2b: The hedonic function positively affects Chinese millennials' future mobile technology engagement through the enhanced leisure travel experience.

H2c: The social function positively affects Chinese millennials' future mobile technology engagement through the enhanced leisure travel experience.

Figure 1 shows the proposed conceptual model and hypotheses.

Methodology

Procedures

The study developed and employed a self-administered web-based questionnaire to test the hypotheses. The survey was first designed in English and then translated into Mandarin. Before the questionnaire was sent out, two bilingual Chinese-English faculty members who were familiar with the study conducted the back-to-back translation to confirm the correctness and accuracy of the questionnaire.

Respondents were recruited through snowball sampling approach. Chinese consumers tend to be suspicious of surveys, in particular if they come from unfamiliar sources (Fan, Mattila, & Zhao, 2015). Thus, to ensure the quality of data, this study employed this technique to recruit participants through WeChat, which is considered as the most popular social media platform and mobile application among Chinese young people. Participants must be Chinese millennials who are native mainland Chinese and aged between 18 and 37. The data was collected on Qualtrics, a professional web-based survey collection platform. Total 576 responses were collected, and 315 of them were valid and used in the final analysis after excluding 147 incomplete responses, 52 with zero travel experience in the past 12 months, 37 answering the attention check questions incorrectly, and 25 indicating no use of mobile technology during trips.

Measurements

The proposed conceptual model includes utilitarian, hedonic, and social mobile technology functions, leisure travel experience, and mobile technology engagement. All the items were measured with a 7-point Likert scale (i.e. from 1 = totally disagree, 7 = totally agree). The measures for three mobile technology functions were adopted from the study conducted by Kim et al. (2013). The scale items are available inAppendix A Tables A1–A3. Leisure travel experience was assessed by nine items that were adapted from previous literature (Chen & Chen, 2010). Appendix A Table A4 demonstrates the detailed scale items. Mobile technology engagement was measured by a scale adapted from Kim et al.'s (2013) study (Appendix A Table A5).

The study conducted confirmatory factor analysis (CFA) to test the overall fit of the measurement model. The model fits were estimated by comparative fit index (CFI), the normed fit index (NFI), and the root mean square error of approximation (RMSEA) (Chen, Petrick, & Shahvali, 2016). If CFI exceeds .93; NFI is greater than .9.0; RMSEA is less than .80, a model is considered as acceptable (Byrne, 1998). According to the results of CFA, $\chi 2$ value was significant at 1% level ($\chi 2 = 485.1$, p < .000, df = 199). Furthermore, CFI was .94; NFI equaled to .90; RMSEA was .068. Overall, the goodness of fit indicators suggested that the measurement model fit the data well.

Convergent validity was assessed by the following methods. Firstly, it is commonly suggested that .70 or higher standardized factor loadings indicate that items converge on a common point (Hair, Anderson, Tatham, & Black, 1998). Shown in Table 1, the results of standardized factor loadings implied that the measurement had convergent validity. In addition, composite reliability (CR) and average variance extracted (AVE) were calculated. The results showed that all CR values ranged from .92 to .97 were over the suggested cutoff value .70 (Hair et al., 1998). The AVEs for all constructs, ranged from .79 to .91, exceeded the minimum threshold of .50, indicating that the convergent validity of the scales was high, and a large portion of the variance was explained by the constructs (Fornell & Larcker, 1981; Netemeyer, Bearden, & Sharma, 2003). Also, this study employed Cronbach's alpha to check the internal consistency of each scale. All alpha values ranged from .70 to .88, which met the .70 minimum requirement suggested by Nunnally (1989). To sum up, convergent validity for each construct was satisfied.

Table 1. Results of confirmatory factor analysis.

Constructs	Standardized Factor Loadings	Error Variances	Cronbach's α	Composite Reliabilities	Average Variance Extracted (AVE)
Utilitarian function			.79	.94	.84
UF-1	.71	.10			
UF-2	.77	.10			
UF-3	.76	.11			
Hedonic function			.81	.94	.85
HF-1	.78	.11			
HF-2	.73	.13			
HF-3	.80	.10			
Social function			.70	.92	.79
SF-1	.80	.09			
SF-2	.71	.10			
SF-3	.73	.10			
Leisure travel experience			.94	.99	.89
LTE-1	.79	.06			
LTE-2	.77	.09			
LTE-3	.80	.08			
LTE-4	.81	.07			
LTE-5	.86	.06			
LTE-6	.75	.09			
LTE-7	.80	.08			
LTE-8	.72	.08			
LTE-9	.84	.06			
Mobile technology engagement			.88	.97	.90
MTE-1	.76	.08			
MTE-2	.85	.05			
MTE-3	.88	.06			
MTE-4	.73	.09			

Table 2. Results of discriminant validity.

	UF	HF	SF	LTE	MTE
UF	(.84)				
HF	.461	(.85)			
SF	.619	.549	(.79)		
LTE	.228	.192	.241	(.89)	
MTE	.175	.130	.151	.366	(.90)

Note: The diagonal numbers in parentheses represent AVE. The remaining numbers show squared correlations.

Discriminant validity was assessed by comparing the average variance extracted (AVE) with the squared correlation between constructs (Fornell & Larcker, 1981). As shown in Table 2, AVEs for all five constructs were greater than the squared correlations. The discriminant validity was high. The results of CFA suggested that the measurement model demonstrated the soundness of its measurement properties.

Results

Descriptive statistics

Table 3 shows the respondents' demographic information. In general, the survey sample had more respondents in age groups 21–25 and 26–30, accounting for 50% and 31% respectively. Among the 315 valid responses, the gender split was 63% female and 37%

Table 3. Demographic and personal information.

Respondent characteristics	Frequency	Percentage
Age		
≤20	31	10%
21–25	158	50%
26–30	96	31%
31–35	19	6%
36–40	7	2%
41–45	0	0%
≥46	4	1%
Gender		
Female	197	63%
Male	118	37%
Marital status		
Single	256	81%
Married	56	18%
Others	3	1%
The only child		
Yes	213	68%
No	102	32%
Occupation		
Student	138	43%
Businessperson	5	2%
Company employee	124	40%
Self-employed	11	3%
Unemployed	7	2%
Industrial/Agricultural worker	2	1%
Government employee	10	3%
Others	18	6%
Education level		
Middle school or below	1	0%
High school or equivalent	8	3%
Some college, but no degree	27	8%
Bachelor's degree	167	53%
Graduate degrees	112	36%

male. The majority of the participants (81%) were unmarried. More than half of them (68%) were the only child of their families. Over one third of participants (43%) were still at school, followed by company employees which accounted for 40%. Almost 90% of the respondents had bachelors or graduate degrees (53% for the former and 36% for the latter).

Multiple regression analyses

To test the proposed hypotheses, multiple regressions were conducted. The results in Table 4 revealed that utilitarian and social functions had significantly positive impacts on Chinese millennials' leisure travel experience at the during-trip stage: the utilitarian function ($\beta_{utilitarian}$ = .21, p-value = .010; H_{1a} supported) and the social function (β_{social} = .24, p-value = .007; H_{1c} supported). However, the relationship between hedonic function and Chinese millennials' leisure travel experience was insignificant ($\beta_{hedonic}$ = .12, p-value = .11; H_{1b} rejected). Therefore, H_1 was partially supported: when Chinese millennials use mobile technology at the during-trip stage, among all three mobile technology functions, utilitarian and social functions positively affect their leisure travel experience, but the hedonic function does not have positive impacts on their leisure travel experience. In particular, between utilitarian and social functions, Chinese millennials' leisure travel experience is influenced more by the social function than the utilitarian function (β_{social} = .24 > $\beta_{utilitarian}$ = .21).

Table 4. Results of multiple regression analyses.

Variables	Leisure travel experience
Intercept	2.4*** (.26)
Utilitarian function	.21* (.07)
Hedonic function	.12 (.06)
Social function	.24** (.08)

Note: *$p < .05$, **$p < .01$, ***$p < .0001$. The numbers in parentheses represent SE.

Mediation test analyses

To investigate the mediation effect of leisure travel experience between the three mobile technology functions and mobile technology engagement and test H_2 (a, b, c), the following four conditions must be satisfied (Baron & Kenny, 1986): a significant relationship between the independent variable and the dependent variable; a significant relationship between the independent variable and the mediator; when both the independent variable and the mediator are predictors of the dependent variable, a significant relationship between the mediator and the dependent variable must exist; when the mediator is added, the relationship between the independent variable and the dependent variable must be either insignificant or significantly reduced (Prayag, Hosany, & Odeh, 2013).

According to the results of the multiple regression analyses in Table 4, utilitarian ($\beta_{utilitarian} = .21$, p-value $= .010$) and social functions ($\beta_{social} = .24$, p-value $= .007$) were significantly related to leisure travel experience, but hedonic function was not ($\beta_{hedonic} = .12$, p-value $= .11$). In addition, only utilitarian function positively influenced Chinese millennials' future mobile technology engagement ($\beta_{utilitarian} = .27$, p-value $= .002$; $\beta_{hedonic} = .10$, p-value $= .20$; $\beta_{social} = 0.10$, p-value $= .27$). Leisure travel experience also positively affected Chinese millennials' future mobile technology engagement ($\beta_{leisure\ travel\ experience} = 0.61$, p-value $< .001$). Thus, the mediation effect of leisure travel experience can only be conducted between utilitarian function and mobile technology engagement. Based on the statistical results, the beta coefficient of utilitarian function was significantly reduced from .27 in the direct path to .17 when the mediator was added in Figure 2. Therefore, leisure travel experience was a partial mediator between utilitarian function and mobile technology engagement. H_{2a} was partially supported, and H_{2b} and H_{2c} were not supported.

General discussion

Conclusion

This study focuses on Chinese millennials and investigates how mobile technology usage influences their leisure travel experience and future engagement with it. The results demonstrate that utilitarian and social functions of mobile technology positively affect Chinese millennials' leisure travel experience with social function contributing more during their leisure trips, whereas hedonic function does not. The findings indicate that when Chinese millennials take leisure trips, they use mobile technology mostly for information search and social networking. Unlike utilitarian and social functions, Chinese millennial travelers seem to have less interest in the hedonic function of mobile technology on the move. Traveling and relevant activities are more attractive and

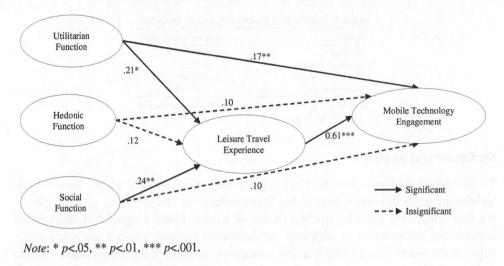

Note: * p<.05, ** p<.01, *** p<.001.

Figure 2. The conceptual model with results.

enjoyable than entertainments facilitated by mobile technology. Furthermore, the findings identify that leisure travel experience partially mediates the positive relationship between utilitarian function and Chinese millennials' mobile technology engagement, implying that the enhanced leisure travel experience facilitated by the utilitarian function of mobile technology also prompts Chinese millennials' future engagement with it during travel.

Theoretical implications

The current study contributes to both mobile technology research and millennial studies in the tourism context. Previous technology research mainly focuses on travelers' acceptance and attitudes toward emerging technology and innovations (Molz & Paris, 2015; Wang et al., 2016). For instance, Kim, Park, and Morrison (2008) identify that two external variables of technology experience and trip experience and two influential determinants, which are perceived usefulness and perceived ease of use, jointly affect users' willingness to use mobile technology during their travel. The current study is one of the few to further investigate what specific attributes of mobile technology improve the travel experience. The findings show that among all three functions of mobile technology, only utilitarian and social functions positively influence Chinese millennials' leisure travel experience. It is noteworthy that Chinese millennials care less about the hedonic function of mobile technology, which means their happiness and enjoyment are more likely to be tied with leisure travel itself rather than the fun features offered by mobile technology applications. It is timely to systemically examine how to leverage mobile technology, especially its utilitarian and social functions, to improve young travelers' experience, as they can hardly live in a technology-free zone, no matter on the way or at the destination.

Young and Hinesly (2012) suggest that mobile technology penetrates almost every aspect of millennials' lives and significantly influences their behaviors, including travel.

Gretzel (2010) finds that travelers' experience of using mobile technology has impacts on their intention to continuously use it. Consistent with previous studies, the current study also shows that enhanced leisure travel experience facilitated by mobile technology significantly influences Chinese millennials' engagement with it in their future travel.

Additionally, this study selects one unique market segment, Chinese millennials, to examine the relationship between mobile technology usage and leisure travel experience. Millennials are seen as one of the super consumer groups due to their strong spending power (Eastman et al., 2014; Nowak, Thach, & Olsen, 2006). As grown up with constant technology breakthroughs, this generation's travel style is heavily influenced by the emerging mobile technology (Wilska, 2003). Among the entire millennial population, Chinese millennials stand out as the most important and strongest consumption power for tourism and related industries (Dychtwald, 2018; Wang, 2017). Therefore, the findings lay a foundation for future research in Chinese millennials' travel behaviors and consumption patterns.

Managerial implications

This research benefits the tourism industry, especially those companies considering Chinese millennials as their target market segmentation. Amaro, Duarte, and Henriques (2016) pointed out the need and significance of knowing the target market in adapting online marketing strategies. Millennials have become the major workforce in China and one of the most important consumption powers for both domestic and international travels (Gursoy, Maier, & Chi, 2008). A better understanding of this unique consumer group and their travel consumption preferences can help the tourism industry better serve them and in turn, to enhance their travel experience (Smith & Diekmann, 2017; Van Boven & Gilovich, 2003).

The current study also provides insights and guidelines for tourism practitioners and destination marketers about developing mobile apps in order to better meet travelers' needs, especially the unique utilitarian and social needs of the major consumption group of Chinese millennials. Consistent with the extant literature (Mascheroni, 2007; White & White, 2007), this research confirms Chinese millennials' desire to constantly stay connected with different groups of people, such as friends, parents, travel service providers, and other mobile users, through the mobile technology on the move. As a result, service providers and mobile apps developers may consider including more social services in designing the apps that can facilitate tourism services to Chinese millennials. To maximize the outcome, as suggested by Tussyadiah and Zach (2013), knowledgeable and experienced Chinese millennial travelers can be invited to participate in the new products and services creation and development.

According to Tussyadiah (2017), as technology has become an integral component in the tourism context, the design of tourism technologies focuses more on generating influence on travelers' experience at the during-trip stage. As the study results show, the better the mobile technology functioning in utilitarian and social terms, the better Chinese millennials' travel experience. And the improved travel experience further prompts Chinese millennials' future engagement with mobile technology. Therefore, tourism practitioners may take advantage of such a reciprocal relationship between leisure travel and mobile technology to better serve travelers. Particularly, they can provide easy Wi-Fi access for travelers to use mobile technology both on the go and at the destination. Besides, when developing travel mobile apps, instead of focusing on the hedonic function of mobile technology, the practitioners may consider features that are able to meet young travelers' utilitarian needs. More importantly, they may think about how to integrate the social function to make mobile apps more social networking friendly. The function-improved mobile apps can improve travelers' experience, and in turn, the enhanced experience tends to keep them using the apps and becoming loyal customers. Thus, a virtuous circle will be generated between the mobile technology engagement and travel experience.

Limitations and future research

The study has several limitations. Given that mobile technology is most frequently used during traveling (Dickinson et al., 2016; Wang et al., 2012), this research only focuses on the during-trip stage. However, mobile technology usage is also involved in the pre-trip and post-trip stages (Gretzel, Fesenmaier, Formica, & O'Leary, 2006). Future research is needed to examine how various mobile technology functions influence travelers' experience at those two stages. Furthermore, different purposes of travel may lead to different weights on each mobile technology function (Amaro et al., 2016). For example, the utilitarian function may have more impacts on business travelers, while the social function may be more important for leisure travelers. Researchers can look into these unsolved issues.

The current research targets at one unique market segment – Chinese millennials. This group of people may have a unique preference and dependence on specific platforms of mobile technology when they travel. It would be meaningful to investigate what are the specific platforms and how they influence Chinese millennials' leisure travel experience. Furthermore, future studies may be conducted among different generations to explore whether there are any age differences between young generations who live a technology lifestyle and senior generations who are not very much technology-oriented. Also, as national culture differences play an important role in travelers' behavior and experience in terms of the use of mobile technology to fulfill their needs (Amaro & Duarte, 2017), future research can expand to millennials in other countries for a cross-cultural study to examine the cultural differences.

Disclosure statement

No potential conflict of interest was reported by the authors.

References

Amaro, S., & Duarte, P. (2017). Social media use for travel purposes: A cross cultural comparison between Portugal and the UK. *Information Technology & Tourism, 17*(2), 161–181.

Amaro, S., Duarte, P., & Henriques, C. (2016). Travelers' use of social media: A clustering approach. *Annals of Tourism Research, 59*, 1–15.

Ayeh, J. K., Au, N., & Law, R. (2013). "Do we believe in TripAdvisor?" Examining credibility perceptions and online travelers' attitude toward using user-generated content. *Journal of Travel Research, 52*(4), 437–452.

Babin, B. J., Darden, W. R., & Griffin, M. (1994). Darden WR 9 Griffin M. Work and/or fun: Measuring hedonic and utilitarian shopping value. *Journal of Consumer Research, 20*(4), 644–656.

Baron, R. M., & Kenny, D. A. (1986). The moderator-mediator variable distinction in social psychological research: Conceptual, strategic, and statistical considerations. *Journal of Personality and Social Psychology, 51*(6), 1173–1182.

Brown, A., Kappes, J., & Marks, J. (2013). Mitigating theme park crowding with incentives and information on mobile devices. *Journal of Travel Research, 52*(4), 426–436.

Brown, S. A., & Venkatesh, V. (2005). Model of adoption of technology in households: A baseline model test and extension incorporating household life cycle. *MIS Quarterly, 29* (3), 399–426.

Buhalis, D., & Law, R. (2008). Progress in information technology and tourism management: 20 years on and 10 years after the Internet—The state of eTourism research. *Tourism Management, 29*(4), 609–623.

Byrne, B. M. (1998). *Structural equation modeling with LISREL, PRELIS, and SIMPLIS*. London: Lawrence Erlbaum.

Chen, C. C., Petrick, J. F., & Shahvali, M. (2016). Tourism experiences as a stress reliever: Examining the effects of tourism recovery experiences on life satisfaction. *Journal of Travel Research, 55*(2), 150–160.

Chen, C. F., & Chen, F. S. (2010). Experience quality, perceived value, satisfaction and behavioral intentions for heritage tourists. *Tourism Management, 31*(1), 29–35.

Childers, T. L., Carr, C. L., Peck, J., & Carson, S. (2001). Hedonic and utilitarian motivations for online retail shopping behavior. *Journal of Retailing, 77*(4), 511–535.

China Internet Network Information Center (CNNIC). (2017). *Statistical report on internet development in China* (January 2017). Retrieved from https://cnnic.com.cn/IDR/ReportDownloads/201706/P020170608523740585924.pdf

Chung, J. Y., & Buhalis, D. (2008). Information needs in online social networks. *Information Technology & Tourism, 10*(4), 267–281.

Cohen, S. A., Duncan, T., & Thulemark, M. (2015). Lifestyle mobilities: The crossroads of travel, leisure and migration. *Mobilities, 10*(1), 155–172.

Dal Fiore, F., Mokhtarian, P. L., Salomon, I., & Singer, M. E. (2014). "Nomads at last"? A set of perspectives on how mobile technology may affect travel. *Journal of Transport Geography, 41*, 97–106.

de Oliveira Nunes, M., & Mayer, V. F. (2014). Mobile technology, games and nature areas: The tourist perspective. *Tourism & Management Studies, 10*(1), 53–58.

Dewan, I., & Benckendorff, P. (2013). Impact of tech savviness and impulsiveness on the mobile information search behaviour of young travellers. *e-Review of Tourism Research, ENTER 2013, 4*, 1–5.

Dickinson, J. E., Hibbert, J. F., & Filimonau, V. (2016). Mobile technology and the tourist experience: (Dis) connection at the campsite. *Tourism Management, 57*, 193–201.

Diekmann, A., & McCabe, S. (2011). Systems of social tourism in the European Union: A critical review. *Current Issues in Tourism, 14*(5), 417–430.

Dychtwald, Z. (2018). *Young China: How the restless generation will change their country and the world*. New York: St. Martin's Press.

Eastman, J. K., Iyer, R., Liao-Troth, S., Williams, D. F., & Griffin, M. (2014). The role of involvement on millennials' mobile technology behaviors: The moderating impact of status consumption, innovation, and opinion leadership. *Journal of Marketing Theory and Practice, 22* (4), 455–470.

Edvardsson, B., Tronvoll, B., & Gruber, T. (2011). Expanding understanding of service exchange and value co-creation: A social construction approach. *Journal of the Academy of Marketing Science, 39*(2), 327–339.

Ellison, N. B., Steinfield, C., & Lampe, C. (2007). The benefits of Facebook "friends:" Social capital and college students' use of online social network sites. *Journal of Computer-Mediated Communication, 12*(4), 1143–1168.

Fan, A., Mattila, A. S., & Zhao, X. (2015). How does social distance impact customers' complaint intentions? A cross-cultural examination. *International Journal of Hospitality Management, 47*, 35–42.

Fornell, C., & Larcker, D. F. (1981). Evaluating structural equation models with unobservable variables and measurement error. *Journal of Marketing Research, 18*(1), 39–50.

Fotis, J., Buhalis, D., & Rossides, N. (2012). Social media use and impact during the holiday travel planning process. In M. Fuchs, F. Ricci, & L. Cantoni (Eds.), *Information and communication Technologies in Tourism 2012* (pp. 13–24). New York: Springer-Verlag.

Genç, M. (2013). Migration and tourism flows to New Zealand. In Á. Matias, P. Nijkamp, & M. Sarmento (Eds.), *Quantitative methods in tourism economics* (pp. 113–126). Berlin: Springer-Verlag.

Gotardi, L., Senn, Y., Cholakova, E., Liebrich, A., & Wozniak, T. (2015). How do millennial travellers use their mobile devices in a city destination? – Empirical evidence from Switzerland. *e-Review of Tourism Research, ENTER 2015, 6*, 1–5.

Gretzel, U. (2010). Travel in the network: Redirected gazes, ubiquitous connections and new frontiers. In M. Levina & G. Kien (Eds.), *Post-global network and everyday life* (pp. 41–58). New York: Peter Lang.

Gretzel, U. (2011). Intelligent systems in tourism: A social science perspective. *Annals of Tourism Research, 38*(3), 757–779.

Gretzel, U., Fesenmaier, D. R., Formica, S., & O'Leary, J. T. (2006). Searching for the future: Challenges faced by destination marketing organizations. *Journal of Travel Research, 45*(2), 116–126.

Gretzel, U., & Yoo, K. H. (2008). Use and impact of online travel reviews. In P. O'Connor, W. Höpken, & U. Gretzel (Eds.), *Information and communication technologies in tourism 2008* (pp. 35–46). New York: Springer.

Growth from Knowledge. (2016). *Chinese tourists spend 229 million USD in 2015*. Retrieved from https://www.gfk.com/insights/press-release/chinese-tourists-spend-229-billion-usd-in-2015/

Gursoy, D., Maier, T. A., & Chi, C. G. (2008). Generational differences: An examination of work values and generational gaps in the hospitality workforce. *International Journal of Hospitality Management, 27*(3), 448–458.

Hair, J. F., Anderson, R. E., Tatham, R. L., & Black, W. C. (1998). *Multivariate data analysis*. Englewood Cliffs, NJ: Prentice Hall.

Hannam, K., Butler, G., & Paris, C. M. (2014). Developments and key issues in tourism mobilities. *Annals of Tourism Research, 44*, 171–185.

He, Z., Wu, L., & Li, X. R. (2018). When art meets tech: The role of augmented reality in enhancing museum experiences and purchase intentions. *Tourism Management, 68*, 127–139.

Howard, P. E., Rainie, L., & Jones, S. (2001). Days and nights on the Internet: The impact of a diffusing technology. *American Behavioral Scientist, 45*(3), 383–404.

Hsiao, C. H., Chang, J. J., & Tang, K. Y. (2016). Exploring the influential factors in continuance usage of mobile social Apps: Satisfaction, habit, and customer value perspectives. *Telematics and Informatics, 33*(2), 342–355.

Hudson, S., & Thal, K. (2013). The impact of social media on the consumer decision process: Implications for tourism marketing. *Journal of Travel & Tourism Marketing, 30*(1–2), 156–160.

Ito, M. E., Okabe, D. E., & Matsuda, M. E. (2005). *Personal, portable, pedestrian: Mobile phones in Japanese life.* Cambridge, MA: The MIT Press.

Jain, J., & Lyons, G. (2008). The gift of travel time. *Journal of Transport Geography, 16*(2), 81–89.

Jia, Z., Li, D., & He, F. (2016). Analysis and reviews on tourism and travel mobile apps of China. In C. Liu, G. R. Chang, & Z. Luo (Eds.), *Proceedings of international conference on electronics, mechanics, culture and medicine* (pp. 62–66). Paris: Atlantis Press.

Jing, S., & Hu, Y. (2017). Millennials drive a retail revival. *China Daily.* Retrieved from http://africa.chinadaily.com.cn/weekly/2017-03/03/content_28418327.htm

Karaiskos, D. C., Drossos, D. A., Tsiaousis, A. S., Giaglis, G. M., & Fouskas, K. G. (2012). Affective and social determinants of mobile data services adoption. *Behaviour & Information Technology, 31*(3), 209–219.

Kaspar, C. (1996). *The tourism theory in the plan.* Bern: Haupt.

Kim, D. Y., Park, J., & Morrison, A. M. (2008). A model of traveller acceptance of mobile technology. *International Journal of Tourism Research, 10*(5), 393–407.

Kim, H. W., Chan, H. C., & Chan, Y. P. (2007). A balanced thinking–Feelings model of information systems continuance. *International Journal of Human-Computer Studies, 65*(6), 511–525.

Kim, Y. H., Kim, D. J., & Wachter, K. (2013). A study of mobile user engagement (MoEN): Engagement motivations, perceived value, satisfaction, and continued engagement intention. *Decision Support Systems, 56,* 361–370.

Kowatsch, T., & Maass, W. (2010). In-store consumer behavior: How mobile recommendation agents influence usage intentions, product purchases, and store preferences. *Computers in Human Behavior, 26*(4), 697–704.

Kuo, M. A. (2017). *China's millennials: Consumer superpower.* Retrieved from https://thediplomat.com/2017/05/chinas-millennials-consumer-superpower/

Lalicic, L., & Weismayer, C. (2016). The passionate use of mobiles phones among tourists. *Information Technology & Tourism, 16*(2), 153–173.

Lee, T., & Jun, J. (2005). Contextual perceived usefulness? Toward an understanding of mobile commerce acceptance. In *Proceedings of the international conference on mobile business* (pp. 255–261). Washington, DC: IEEE Computer Society.

Lenker, J. A., Harris, F., Taugher, M., & Smith, R. O. (2013). Consumer perspectives on assistive technology outcomes. *Disability and Rehabilitation: Assistive Technology, 8*(5), 373–380.

Li, M., Dong, Z. Y., & Chen, X. (2012). Factors influencing consumption experience of mobile commerce: A study from experiential view. *Internet Research, 22*(2), 120–141.

Liang, T. P., Huang, C. W., Yeh, Y. H., & Lin, B. (2007). Adoption of mobile technology in business: A fit-viability model. *Industrial Management & Data Systems, 107*(8), 1154–1169.

Ling, R., & Yttri, B. (2002). Hyper-coordination via mobile phones in Norway. In J. E. Katz & M. Aakhus (Eds.), *Perpetual contact: Mobile communication, private space, public performance* (pp. 139–169). Cambridge, UK: Cambridge University Press.

Liu, Y., & Law, R. (2013). The adoption of smartphone applications by airlines. In L. Cantoni & Z. Xiang (Eds.), *Information and communication technologies in tourism 2013* (pp. 47–57). Berlin-Heidelberg, Germany: Springer.

Lyons, G., & Urry, J. (2005). Travel time use in the information age. *Transportation Research Part A: Policy and Practice, 39*(2–3), 257–276.

MacKay, K., & Vogt, C. (2012). Information technology in everyday and vacation contexts. *Annals of Tourism Research, 39*(3), 1380–1401.

Mascheroni, G. (2007). Global nomads' network and mobile sociality: Exploring new media uses on the move. *Information, Communication & Society, 10*(4), 527–546.

Molz, J. G. (2006). 'Watch us wander': Mobile surveillance and the surveillance of mobility. *Environment and Planning A, 38*(2), 377–393.

Molz, J. G., & Paris, C. M. (2015). The social affordances of flashpacking: Exploring the mobility nexus of travel and communication. *Mobilities, 10*(2), 173–192.

Nasar, J., Hecht, P., & Wener, R. (2007). 'Call if you have trouble': Mobile phones and safety among college students. *International Journal of Urban and Regional Research*, *31*(4), 863–873.

Netemeyer, R. G., Bearden, W. O., & Sharma, S. (2003). *Scaling procedures: Issues and applications*. Thousand Oaks, CA: Sage.

Neuhofer, B., Buhalis, D., & Ladkin, A. (2014). A typology of technology-enhanced tourism experiences. *International Journal of Tourism Research*, *16*(4), 340–350.

Nowak, L., Thach, L., & Olsen, J. E. (2006). Wowing the millennials: Creating brand equity in the wine industry. *Journal of Product & Brand Management*, *15*(5), 316–323.

Nunnally, J. C. (1989). *Psychometric theory*. New York: McGraw- Hill.

Oblinger, D. (2003). Boomers gen-xers millennials. *EDUCAUSE Review*, *500*(4), 37–47.

Oh, H., Fiore, A. M., & Jeoung, M. (2007). Measuring experience economy concepts: Tourism applications. *Journal of Travel Research*, *46*(2), 119–132.

Pagani, M., & Mirabello, A. (2011). The influence of personal and social-interactive engagement in social TV web sites. *International Journal of Electronic Commerce*, *16*(2), 41–68.

Parra-López, E., Gutiérrez-Taño, D., Diaz-Armas, R. J., & Bulchand-Gidumal, J. (2012). Travellers 2.0: Motivation, opportunity and ability to use social media. In M. Sigala, E. Christou, & U. Gretzel (Eds.), *Social media in travel, tourism and hospitality: Theory, practice and cases* (pp. 171–189). Surrey, UK: Ashgate.

Prayag, G., Hosany, S., & Odeh, K. (2013). The role of tourists' emotional experiences and satisfaction in understanding behavioral intentions. *Journal of Destination Marketing & Management*, *2*(2), 118–127.

Reisinger, Y., & Turner, L. W. (2003). *Cross-cultural behavior in tourism: Concept and analysis*. New York: Routledge.

Ricci, F. (2010). Mobile recommender systems. *Information Technology & Tourism*, *12*(3), 205–231.

Rice, R. E., & Aydin, C. (1991). Attitudes toward new organizational technology: Network proximity as a mechanism for social information processing. *Administrative Science Quarterly*, *36*(2), 219–244.

Russell, C. (2016). *New youth: Understanding China's millennials*. Retrieved from http://knowl edge.ckgsb.edu.cn/2016/02/03/demographics/new-youth-understanding-chinas-millennials/

Salehan, M., & Negahban, A. (2013). Social networking on smartphones: When mobile phones become addictive. *Computers in Human Behavior*, *29*(6), 2632–2639.

Schaufeli, W. B., Salanova, M., González-Romá, V., & Bakker, A. B. (2002). The measurement of engagement and burnout: A two sample confirmatory factor analytic approach. *Journal of Happiness Studies*, *3*(1), 71–92.

Scheiner, J. (2006). Housing mobility and travel behaviour: A process-oriented approach to spatial mobility: Evidence from a new research field in Germany. *Journal of Transport Geography*, *14* (4), 287–298.

Smith, M. K., & Diekmann, A. (2017). Tourism and wellbeing. *Annals of Tourism Research*, *66*, 1–13.

Thayer, S. E., & Ray, S. (2006). Online communication preferences across age, gender, and duration of Internet use. *Cyber Psychology & Behavior*, *9*(4), 432–440.

Tussyadiah, I., & Zach, F. (2013). Social media strategy and capacity for consumer co-creation among destination marketing organizations. In L. Cantoni & Z. Xiang (Eds.), *Information and communication technologies in tourism 2013* (pp. 242–253). Berlin-Heidelberg, Germany: Springer.

Tussyadiah, I. P. (2013). Expectation of travel experiences with wearable computing devices. In Z. Xiang & I. Tussyadiah (Eds.), *Information and communication technologies in tourism 2014* (pp. 539–552). Cham, Switzerland: Springer.

Tussyadiah, I. P. (2017). Technology and behavioral design in tourism. In D. R. Fesenmaier & Z. Xiang (Eds.), *Design science in tourism: Foundations of destination management* (pp. 173–191). Cham, Switzerland: Springer.

Tussyadiah, I. P., & Zach, F. J. (2012). The role of geo-based technology in place experiences. *Annals of Tourism Research*, *39*(2), 780–800.

Van Boven, L., & Gilovich, T. (2003). To do or to have? That is the question. *Journal of Personality and Social Psychology*, *85*(6), 1193–1202.

Venkatesh, V., & Brown, S. A. (2001). A longitudinal investigation of personal computers in homes: Adoption determinants and emerging challenges. *MIS Quarterly, 25*(1), 71–102.

Venkatesh, V., Thong, J. Y. L., & Xu, X. (2012). Consumer acceptance and use of information technology: Extending the unified theory of acceptance and use of technology. *MIS Quarterly, 36*(1), 157–178.

Wang, D., Park, S., & Fesenmaier, D. R. (2012). The role of smartphones in mediating the touristic experience. *Journal of Travel Research, 51*(4), 371–387.

Wang, D., Xiang, Z., & Fesenmaier, D. R. (2016). Smartphone use in everyday life and travel. *Journal of Travel Research, 55*(1), 52–63.

Wang, H. H. (2017). *The real reason Chinese millennials are super consumers.* Retrieved from https://www.forbes.com/sites/helenwang/2017/03/27/the-real-reason-chinese-millennials-are-super-consumers/#2c141ed84053

White, N. R., & White, P. B. (2007). Home and away: Tourists in a connected world. *Annals of Tourism Research, 34*(1), 88–104.

Wilska, T. A. (2003). Mobile phone use as part of young people's consumption styles. *Journal of Consumer Policy, 26*(4), 441–463.

WYSE Travel Confederation (WYSETC). (2015). *Youth and student travellers age 15 to 29 represent 23% of international tourist arrivals.* Retrieved from http://knowledge.ckgsb.edu.cn/2016/02/03/demographics/new-youth-understanding-chinas-millennials/

Xiang, Z., Gretzel, U., & Fesenmaier, D. R. (2009). Semantic representation of tourism on the Internet. *Journal of Travel Research, 47*(4), 440–453.

Yang, D. P. (1997). Generational conflicts and the one child generation. *Youth Studies, 12*, 6–9.

Yi, X., Ribbens, B., & Morgan, C. N. (2010). Generational differences in China: Career implications. *Career Development International, 15*(6), 601–620.

Young, A. M., & Hinesly, M. D. (2012). Identifying millennials' key influencers from early childhood: Insights into current consumer preferences. *Journal of Consumer Marketing, 29*(2), 146–155.

Appendix A. Measurement scales

Please indicate how much you agree with the following statements using the scale of 1 = *'totally disagree'* to 7 = *'totally agree'*.

Table A1. Utilitarian function of the mobile technology at during-trip stage.

Items	Adapted from
Helps me find out travel-related information.	Kim et al., 2013
Keeps me informed and updated about others.	
Helps me with daily activities (e.g. checking e-mails).	

Table A2. Hedonic function of the mobile technology at during-trip stage.

Items	Adapted from
Helps me get rest and relaxation.	Kim et al., 2013
Helps me enjoy the variety of contents (e.g. voice, text, and commenting will bring different interactive experience to you).	
Makes me feel happy.	

Table A3. Social function of the mobile technology at during-trip stage.

Items	Adapted from
Helps me keep in touch/share events with others.	Kim et al., 2013
Helps me make friends with people who share common interests with me.	
Offers me with the opportunity to share my travel experience with others.	

Table A4. Leisure travel experience.

Items	Adapted from
I think leisure travel itself is very entertaining.	Chen & Chen, 2010
I think leisure travel is attractive and catching.	
I think leisure travel entertains me.	
I am thrilled about having such leisure travel experience.	
I really enjoy this leisure travel experience.	
This leisure travel experience is exciting.	
I am indulged in this leisure travel and related activities.	
Overall, I am satisfied with this leisure trip.	
As a whole, I am happy with this leisure trip.	

Table A5. Mobile technology engagement.

Items	Adapted from
In the future, I will continue to engage in using mobile technology in my daily life.	Kim et al., 2013
In the future, I will continue to engage in using mobile technology during my leisure travel.	
In the future, I will continue to interact with others by using mobile technology during my leisure travel.	
In the future, I will recommend my engagement in mobile technology to others.	

Corporate Social Responsibility Communications on Social Media and Consumers' Brand Engagement: A Case Study of Hotels in Hong Kong

Cheukhei Danny Chung, Yixing (Lisa) Gao (iD) and Daniel Leung(iD)

ABSTRACT

This paper aims to investigate how the communication of the three major types of corporate social responsibility (CSR) initiatives (i.e. environmental, societal and stakeholders' CSR) on Facebook affect consumers' brand engagement. A preliminary content analysis on 100 hotels' Facebook was conducted to identify the current usage of Facebook for CSR communication among hotel firms in Hong Kong. Then, a consumer survey was conducted with 314 Facebook users in order to collect data for testing the conceptual framework. The empirical findings unveil that disclosure of societal CSR on Facebook has a strong explanatory power of consumer brand engagement, whereas that of environmental CSR was close to reasonable. This study provides insights into hotel firms' usage of Facebook as a platform for CSR communication. The findings might ease industry practitioners' apprehension of disclosure of CSR initiatives on Facebook.

社交媒体上的企业社会责任传播与消费者品牌参与：以香港酒店为例

摘要

本文旨在研究Facebook上三种主要类型的企业社会责任倡议的传播（即"环境"、"社会"和"利益相关者"的企业社会责任）如何影响消费者的品牌参与。首先，本文对100家酒店的Facebook进行了内容分析，以确定目前香港酒店企业使用Facebook进行企业社会责任沟通的情况。然后，本文对314名Facebook用户进行了一项消费者调查，以测试本文提出的概念框架。结果表明，Facebook上有关"社会"的企业社会责任的披露对消费者品牌参与具有较强的解释力，而有关"环境"的企业社会责任的披露则接近合理。本研究为酒店企业利用Facebook作为企业社会责任沟通平台提供了视角。这些发现会缓解业内人士对Facebook披露企业社会责任举措的担忧。

Introduction

As the business rewards brought by incorporating socially responsible behavior into the organizational strategy are increasingly recognized (Du, Bhattacharya, & Sen, 2010;

Holcomb, Upchurch, & Okumus, 2007; Sen, Bhattacharya, & Korschun, 2006), many tourism and hospitality businesses now voluntarily engage in corporate social responsibility (CSR) activities and communicate their CSR initiatives to the general public. Bonilla-Priego, Font, and Pacheco (2014) research and report that eleven international cruise companies demonstrated their sustainability accountability and reported their CSR practices in the forms of written reports in the year 2011. Another recent study by Guix, Bonilla-Priego, and Font (2018) also reports that over one-third of the largest hotel groups in the world compile CSR reports that contain social, environmental and economic issues associated with their operations.

Although CSR communications in the hotel context have already been extensively researched (e.g. De Grosbois, 2012; Holcomb et al., 2007; Kennedy Nyahunzvi, 2013), it is surprising that online CSR communications and particularly those available in social media were rarely investigated (Ettinger, Grabner-Kraeuter, & Terlutter, 2018). As over 40% of the world population now actively engage with social media (We are social, 2018), social media and particularly Facebook do enrich hospitality companies' capability in reaching their stakeholders for CSR communication. Facebook has been recognized as a dominant communication platform for hospitality companies (Hsu, 2012; Kang, Tang, & Fiore, 2014; McCarthy, Stock, & Verma, 2010). Facebook overtook other platforms such as Google with number of unique visitors per week and its referral conversion rates far exceed those from other online travel sites (McCarthy et al., 2010). Features of Facebook such as profiles, fan page, event, advertisement allow hotels to find, connect, and communicate to their target markets (Hsu, 2012). While this notion was coined for several years and many hotels have already embraced Facebook to communicate hospitality companies' CSR practices (Kwok & Yu, 2016), to the best of the authors' knowledge, the question of 'what CSR messages were communicated by hotels on Facebook' has never been investigated.

In addition to the dearth of research exploring CSR communications by hotels on Facebook, the examination of whether and how CSR communication influences consumers' engagement or engagement with the communicated hotel brands is another area which is largely overlooked by previous researchers (Serra-Cantallops, Peña-Miranda, Ramón-Cardona, & Martorell-Cunill, 2018). According to Simmons and Becker-Olsen (2006), brands can differentiate themselves and reinforce their positioning via communicating themselves as a 'socially responsible' brand. Several literatures from the general management field also assert that complementing business operations with CSR practices can often result into better business performance (e.g. Basu & Palazzo, 2008; Yuan, Bao, & Verbeke, 2011). While some recent studies conducting in the hotel setting have empirically proven that the implementation of CSR practices can effectively enhance hotels' financial performance (Gao & Mattila, 2014; Kang, Stein, Heo, & Lee, 2012), the question of 'whether (and which type of) CSR messages communicated by hotels can affect receivers' post-reading perceptions towards the communicated hotel brands?' remains unknown at the moment of this writing.

In light of the existence of the aforementioned research gaps, using hotels in Hong Kong as the case study, this exploratory study is designed to achieve the following two objectives: (1) To identify the types of CSR message hotels in Hong Kong communicate to customers on Facebook; (2) To examine the relationship between each type of CSR message the hotels communicate on Facebook and customers' level of brand engagement. Unlike prior studies which mostly focus on one aspect, the current study makes an initial attempt to investigate how hotels communicate their CSR initiatives in three different domains – (1) *societal CSR* referring to all corporate activities that contribute to the society's well-being (Turker, 2009); (2) *stakeholders' CSR* referring to all corporate activities that are related to owners, customers, employees and the community (Torres, Bijmolt, Tribo, & Verhoef, 2012); and (3) *environmental CSR* referring to all corporate activities that emphasize the protection of global environment (Liu, Wong, Shi, Chu, & Brock, 2014).

Literature review

CSR research in tourism and hospitality

Being one of most extensively researched areas in hospitality and tourism, Font and Lynes (2018) latest work shows that over 360 CSR-related articles have been published in refereed journals and conference proceedings between 2004 and 2017. The definition of CSR varies across different studies. Business in the Community (2018) defines CSR as managing a company's positive impacts on the society and environment through its operations and interaction with stakeholders such as investors, suppliers, employees and customers. Carroll (1979) states that the social responsibility of businesses encompasses the economic, legal, ethical, and discretionary expectations that society has of organizations. Although CSR is generally defined based on the premise that companies are accountable for ensuring all aspects of their businesses have a positive impact on the society, several studies show that stakeholders often consider CSR as secondary to the business. For instance, Chang and Yeh's (2016) study shows that stakeholders of a Taiwanese airport prioritize service quality and corporate governance over employee management and work environment management. Leung and Snell (2017) also investigate and report that operators of Macao's gaming industry only emphasize the symbolic contribution of the gaming industry to the city's economy while other social issues like gambling addiction were largely overlooked.

One of the two major streams of research about CSR in tourism and hospitality is to investigate the benefit of incorporating CSR into a business's strategy. As part of a firm's internationalization strategy, Jung, Kim, Kang, and Kim (2018) theorize that CSR activities have the opportunity to contribute to image formation and adaptation to local markets. Another report published by Business for Social Responsibility (2006) shows that 67% of the executives strongly agreed that implementing CSR initiatives can improve customers' perceived corporate reputation, and this will further lead to a positive impact on brand preference (Alamro & Rowley, 2011; Porter & Kramer, 2006). In the hotel and tourism industries, previous researchers note that the major benefits derived by CSR activities profoundly lie on a pronounced and favorable organizational image, higher market shares, higher market values and profitability, the ability to charge premium prices and easier access to financing (Martínez, Pérez, & Del Bosque, 2014; O'Neill & Mattila, 2006; Wildes, 2008). Although customers' interpretations of CSR initiative vary considerably (Caruana, Glozer, Crane, & McCabe, 2014), the effective communication of CSR initiatives can positively affect perceptions of corporate reputation and customer satisfaction. This in return will raise the likelihood to repeat business (Jarvis, Stoeckl, & Liu, 2016), increase customer loyalty (Pérez & Rodriguez Del Bosque, 2015) and increase customer resistance to negative information (Xie, Bagozzi, & Grønhaug, 2015). In view of these instrumental benefits, it is understandable to witness why many hotel managers now spend time and resources in the hotel's CSR initiatives.

Another major stream of research about CSR in tourism and hospitality is to explore the variation in the forms of CSR activities embraced by hotel and tourism businesses. According to a study conducted by Holcomb et al. (2007), 80 percent of the top ten hotel companies reported that the socially responsible acts performed by them are mostly related to charitable donations. Sixty percent were with diversity policy and fifty percent supported an employee volunteer program. Tzschentke, Kirk, and Lynch (2008) conduct a similar study with independently owned lodging establishments in Scotland. Their empirical findings show that most of the CSR practices adopted by hotels in Scotland are related to the environment such as towel recycling schemes and the usage of eco-friendly products. Given that guests often value guest experience-related green practices more than those focusing on minimizing adverse ecological impacts, some hotels in China stipulated that sufficient sunlight, fresh air, clean drinking water, and green plants must be available in their property (Heung, Fei, & Hu, 2006). Apart from those environment-related practices, promotion of local culture, employment of local people and purchase of fair-trade products are other typical examples of CSR practices which are prevalent among hotels in less-developed regions (Kasim, 2004).

Major types of CSR initiatives

Societal CSR

Referring to all activities that contribute to the society's wellbeing (Turker, 2009), societal CSR emerges at the time when companies faced increasing pressure both to maintain profitability and behave in socially responsible ways (Mohr, Webb, & Harris, 2001). The measurements of a firm's societal CSR include assessing the extent to which that firm (1) supports non-governmental organizations working in problematic areas, (2) contributes to campaigns and projects that promote the well-being of the society, (3) makes investment for creating a better life for future generations, and (4) targets sustainable growth for the sake of future generations (Liu et al., 2014).

The positive impact brought by societal CSR has been verified in various studies. Murray and Vogel (1997) assert that societal CSR activities could predispose people to a more positive impression towards the company. Thanks to the input by 293 undergraduate students, Ricks (2005) experiments and empirically verifies there is a positive relationship between corporate philanthropy activities and corporate brand association. Singh, Sanchez, and Del Bosque (2008) also demonstrate that CSR behaviors focusing on social interests are positively associated with the brand image. Using examples of many firms' active engagement in various activities to restore local communities after the 2004 Indian Ocean tsunami in Phuket, Henderson's (2007) study demonstrates that firms' sincere and generous outreach activities to the community in need can significantly enhance their brand image and consumers' evaluation.

Stakeholders' CSR

Defined as the management of a corporation's relationships with its stakeholders including government, customers, employees, suppliers and shareholders (Torres et al., 2012; Turker, 2009), stakeholders' CSR comprises all CSR activities that are in relation to various stakeholders of the organization, such as owners, customers, employees and the community. The measurements of a firm's stakeholders' CSR include assessing the extent to which that firm (1) respects consumer rights beyond the legal requirements, (2) prohibits pornography, gambling, and drug abuse, (3) discloses full and accurate information about its products/services to customers, as well as (4) provides a healthy and safe working environment for employees (Liu et al., 2014).

The benefits of stakeholders' CSR are acquired through strengthening or creating a positive relationship between firms and stakeholders (Peloza & Shang, 2011). Creyer and Ross (1997) found that stakeholder-related socially responsible acts are favored by customers. These acts will later be recalled and taken into consideration when customers make a purchase decision. Maignan and Ferrell (2004) noted that communication of CSR concerns and activities related to stakeholders could not only entice customers' awareness for CSR and enhance customers' brand image, but also create a bond between the company and its stakeholders. Using panel data consisting of 57 global brands from ten countries, Torres et al. (2012) recently found that stakeholders' CSR can make a positive impact on global brand equity, stating that global brands respecting local communities' value would yield stronger brand equity.

Environmental CSR

In spite of its late emergence, environmental CSR has been coming to attention because of its visibility and feasibility (Pedersen, 2010; Williamson, Lynch-Wood, & Ramsay, 2006). In short, environmental CSR includes practices such as pollution prevention, efficient use of energy and green production/service (Kalisch, 2002). The measurements of a firm's environmental CSR include assessing the extent to which that firm (1) promotes environmental protection and green consumption concepts, (2) embeds environmental-friendly design to protect natural landscapes and heritage, (3) implements consumption reduction program, and (4) implements programs that improve public security, fire control and food safety and reduce pollution (Liu et al., 2014).

Since environmental CSR is easy to understand and is highly recognized by consumers and media (Rahbar & Wahid, 2011), a plethora of research demonstrates that corporates can enhance their reputation (Marin & Ruiz, 2007) or/and increase consumer satisfaction (Chen, 2010) by communicating their environmentally friendly brand image. Laroche, Bergeron, and Barbaro-Forleo (2001) find and report that consumers with a more ecologically friendly lifestyle have a strong purchase intention toward products by companies associated with ecologically friendly practices. Besides service-providers, Cheung, Welford, and Hills (2009) also note that manufacturers can also enjoy the increased consumers' purchase intentions and company evaluation resulted from environmental CSR.

Impact of CSR communications on consumers' brand engagement

In recent decades, a research stream highlighting the dynamics related to specific consumer/brand relationships has emerged (Aaker, Fournier, & Brasel, 2004; Fournier, 1998). Within this growing body of work, significant attention has been given to consumer brand engagement, which reflects a consumer's level of interest, confidence, integrity, pride, and passion in a certain brand in the brand (Bowden, 2009; Coulter, Price, & Feick, 2003;

Hollebeek, Glynn, & Brodie, 2014; Kumar et al., 2010). Recently published studies are shifting to concepts which explain this dynamic more explicitly (Bolton & Saxena-Iyer, 2009; Malthouse & Hofacker, 2010) because of the increasing recognition of consumers' active roles in brand-based processes (Pagani, Hofacker, & Goldsmith, 2011; Singh & Sonnenburg, 2012). The newly developed concept is being seen to be representing an important new metric for measuring brand performance. Recent research has emphasized the possible benefits of the construct, such as bringing organizations superior performance outcomes such as sales growth, brand referrals, cost reductions, enhanced consumer contributions to product development processes, co-creative experiences, loyalty and profitability (Bowden, 2009; Sawhney, Verona, & Prandelli, 2005). Brand engagement can be a process for both new customers and repeat customers, and can be experienced both online and offline (Bolton, 2011; Bowden, 2009).

Being a strategic tool through which organizations/brands can engage with their customers, Ahluwalia, Burnkrant, and Unnava (2000) found that customers' positive experience with a CSR initiative can result in positive attitudinal and behavioral change towards the brand. The impact of CSR on customers' engagement was also affirmed in the works by Bhattacharya and Sen (2003) as well as Du et al. (2010). Du et al. (2010) emphasized that effective communication of CSR can positively impact a brand's awareness, identification, and lead to consumer purchase, loyalty, and positive word-of-mouth. Although some studies (e.g. Torelli, Monga, & Kaikati, 2011) counter-argued that CSR communications may induce a negative impact on the brand evaluation if the brand is associated with self-enhancement concept, a majority of previous literature generally agree that CSR communication can positively affect consumers' brand evaluations (e.g. Du et al., 2010; He & Li, 2011). With reference to the previous research findings, this study postulates that:

H1: Societal CSR message on a hotel's Facebook page will have a positive impact on consumers' brand engagement with the hotel.

H2: Stakeholder's CSR message on a hotel's Facebook page will have a positive impact on consumers' brand engagement with the hotel.

H3: Environmental CSR message on a hotel's Facebook page will have a positive impact on consumers' brand engagement with the hotel.

Figure 1 summarizes the research hypotheses in a graphical form.

Methodology

Study 1: Preliminary content analysis

To achieve the first objective (i.e. to identify the types of CSR message hotels in Hong Kong communicate to customers on Facebook), an analysis on the content of posts available on Hong Kong hotels' Facebook pages was conducted. Although we acknowledge that hotels in Hong Kong have been embracing multiple types of social media (e.g. Twitter, Instagram, Pinterest) for marketing and external communication, Facebook was the one and only platform which was used by all hotels in Hong Kong (Chan & Guillet, 2011).

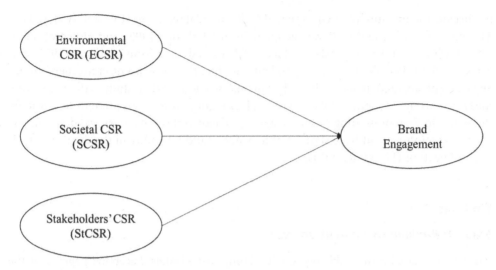

Figure 1. Conceptual framework.

In February 2018, the authors manually reviewed all posts published on 100 Hong Kong hotels' Facebook pages over the past two years (from 2015 to 2017). If any CSR-related post was identified, it was recorded in an Excel spreadsheet. After extracting all CSR-related Facebook posts, the authors individually analyzed the content and then codified each post following Liu et al.'s (2014) definitions of societal, environmental and stakeholders' CSR.

Study 2: Consumer survey

Samples and procedures

To achieve the second objective (i.e. to examine the relationship between each type of CSR message the hotels communicate on Facebook and customers' level of brand engagement), a web-based survey was conducted with 314 Facebook users. The online questionnaire was designed using Qualtrics, and it includes three sections. The questions in the first and second section embed the selected measurement scales with the wordings modified to fit the context of hotels' CSR communication on Facebook. The last section asked for the respondents' demographic information. The questionnaire was set in English in the first place, and it was translated into Chinese by the first author as well as another bilingual speaker harnessing the back-translation method.

Prior to the main data collection, a pilot study was conducted with 30 Facebook users. Having received the feedbacks from the respondents, some minor amendments on wordings and formatting were made. The convenience sampling approach was adopted to identify target respondents.

Measures of CSR communications and brand *engagement*

The current research employed and adapted the well-established scales to measure the three CSR communications and consumers' brand engagement (e.g. Kotler, 2008; Liu et al., 2014; Matten & Crane, 2005; Mohr et al., 2001; Pedersen, 2010; Turker, 2009). To be specific, the measure of environmental CSR was adapted from Holcomb et al. (2007). The measure of societal CSR was adapted from Clarkson (1995) and Holcomb et al. (2007), while the measure of stakeholders' CSR was adapted from Clarkson (1995) and Turker (2009). Pertinent to the dependent variable, the measure of consumers' brand engagement adapted from Hollebeek, Glynn, Brodie's (2014) study. All items were measured using a 7-point Likert-type scale ranging from 1 (representing 'strongly disagree') to 7 (representing 'strongly agree'). These scales have been validated in the previous literatures and have shown strong validity and reliability in the context of CSR communication (Liu et al., 2014).

Findings

Study 1: Preliminary content analysis

After analyzing all posts published on 100 Hong Kong hotels' Facebook pages over the past two years (from 2015 to 2017), this study found that the usage of Facebook as a platform to communicate CSR initiatives is prevalent among hotels in Hong Kong. Over eight percent (83%) of the analyzed 100 hotels in Hong Kong has published at least one CSR-related post in the previous two years. Though communicating CSR initiatives via Facebook is found to be a common practice, the frequency of CSR posting on Facebook is generally low. Among those hotels that communicated CSR initiatives on Facebook, around 34.94% have posted less than 10 CSR messages in the past two years (0.25 post per month). Over ninety percent (96.39%) have posted less than 60 messages (1 post per month), and only 3.61% have posted more than 60 messages in the past two years.

Table 1 shows the frequency of each type of CSR posts found on the hotels' Facebook page. Generally speaking, societal CSR (SCSR) messages and stakeholders' CSR (StCSR) messages have been posted most frequently in the past two years. Among these, 59 posts were found to include more than one type of CSR initiatives, exemplified by a post about the employees spending quality time together at a company's campaign of cleaning the beach, which includes both environmental and stakeholders' initiatives (i.e. the hotel participates in environmental protection activities and it provides a healthy working environment for the employees). Among those environmental CSR (ESCR) messages, communicating the hotel's 'promotion on environmental protection and participation in related activities' were the most prevalent type of ECSR messages published on Facebook (21.77%), followed by 'implementation of special programs or usage of relevant facilities' (5.54%) and 'special design of the hotel that protects the surrounding natural landscape and places of historical interest' (0.05%). For those SCSR messages, messages regarding the hotels' 'supports for nongovernmental organizations working in problematic areas' account for the most (23.09%) while those on the hotel's 'contribution to campaigns and projects promoting the well-being of the society' comes second (12.7%). Regarding StCSR communications, messages about the hotels' 'provision of a healthy and safe working environment for employees' have the highest number (22.67%), followed by those for 'highly valuing customer satisfaction' (12.70%) and 'respect for consumer rights beyond legal requirements' (1.48%).

Most of the identified CSR messages are posts combining photos/videos with texts. Examples of the texts of each type of messages are presented as follow (specific Facebook posts information will be available upon request).

Table 1. Frequency of hotels' CSR posting on facebook.

Type	CSR Messages	Freq. (Percent)
Environmental CSR (ECSR)	• Promoting environmental protection and green consumption concepts to customers and participates in related activities. (e.g. Hyatt's earth hour campaign)	413 (21.77%)
	• Having environmentally-friendly design to protect natural landscapes, places of cultural and historical interest". (e.g. ibis's beach cleaning campaign)	1 (0.05%)
	• Implementing special programs to reduce consumption, improve public security, fire control and food safety, save and use energy efficiently, and utilizes renewable energy. (e.g. Silka Far East's Charter on External Lighting program)	105 (5.54%)
Societal CSR (SCSR)	• Supporting nongovernmental organizations working in problematic areas. (e.g. Crown Plaza's collaboration with Red Cross on blood donation)	438 (23.09%)
	• Contributing to campaigns and projects that promote the well-being of the society. (e.g. W hotel's Run to Give charity run)	241 (12.70%)
	• Making investment to create a better life for future generations.	0 (0%)
	• Targeting sustainable growth which considers future generations.	0 (0%)
Stakeholders' CSR (StCSR)	• Respecting consumer rights beyond legal requirements. (e.g. Marco Polo's Mandatory Provident Fund schemes award)	28 (1.48%)
	• Providing full and accurate information about its products/services to customers.	0 (0%)
	• Customers' satisfaction is highly important for this hotel. (e.g. Four Season's best bridal award)	241 (12.70%)
	• Providing a healthy and safe working environment for employees. (e.g. Lanson Place Hotel's employee fun day event)	430 (22.67%)
	Total	**1,897 (100%)**

ECSR messages: 'Join the global event Earth Hour and show your care for the planet. The lights in our restaurants and part of public areas in the hotel will remain dimmed from 8:30pm to 9:30pm this Saturday.'

SCSR messages: 'Can you imagine how many meals can we create with the 13 tones food donation in 2015 to Food link Foundation? The answer is approximately 20,800 meals. However, our ultimate goal is not to donate more, but to reduce the leftovers. Next time when you come to our restaurants, don't be shy and ask for a take away box if you cannot consume all ordered foods, our staffs are more than happy to help with taking away the leftovers.'

StCSR messages: 'Kiddie's Christmas Party. The three Hyatt hotels in Hong Kong have organized the annual Hyatt Kiddie's Party on last Sunday Hyatt Regency Sha Tin for our staff and their families to celebrate Christmas together. We have arranged numerous activities including booth games, magic shows, a selection of delicious snacks and drinks. Santa Claus has also distributed Christmas gifts to children.'

Study 2: Consumer survey

Respondent profiles

Table 2 presents the demographic profile of the respondents. Considering the gender of the respondents, 63.7% of the sample was female. In terms of age, 32.8% are 18 to 24 years old; 30.8% are 25 to 23 years old. Regarding the place of origin, 97.5% of the respondents were from Hong Kong, 1.6% were from Mainland China and 1% were from other countries such as South Korea. Regarding the respondents' education level, 72.9% had a bachelor degree, 4.1% earned a diploma and 13.4% completed a master degree or above. Pertinent to the respondents' personal monthly income, 43.3% had a monthly income of less than HK$20,000 (US$1 = HK$7.85). Finally, 40.8% had stayed in a hotel for more than twice in the past month.

Measurement model

Although all measurement items used in this study were adapted from previous literature (i.e. Hollebeek et al., 2014; Liu et al., 2014), an exploratory factor analysis was conducted using SPSS to specify the relationships between the observed measures and their posited underlying factors (Hair, Black, Babin, & Anderson, 2010). Specifically, principal components analysis with varimax rotation was used to extract the maximum variance with each component so that the simplest possible solution with sufficient explanatory power can be found (Tabachnick & Fidell, 2007). Four factors (with 24 items) were extracted based on the exploratory factor analysis results. One item of stakeholders' CSR (i.e. Pornography, drug abuse, and gambling are prohibited in this hotel) is removed because its communalities figure is lower than 0.5. Other than that, the content of each factor largely corroborates the original conceptualization. A confirmatory factor analysis was conducted to determine the adequacy of fit of the four-factor model and it is considered a good fit to the data (χ^2/df = 1.87; GFI = 0.902; CFI = 0.960; TLI = 0.951; RMSEA = 0.053). In addition, Cronbach's α values of the constructs are higher than 0.7, indicating an acceptable level of reliability for each construct (See Table 3).

Table 2. Respondents' demographic profile.

	Freq.	Percent
Gender		
Male	113	36.0
Female	200	63.7
Others	1	0.3
Age		
Under 18	8	2.5
18–24	103	32.8
25–34	97	30.9
35–44	64	20.4
45–54	35	11.1
55 or above	4	1.3
Missing	3	1.0
Place of origin		
China	5	1.6
Hong Kong	306	97.5
Others	3	1.0
Education level		
High school or below	30	9.6
Diploma	13	4.1
Bachelor degree	229	72.9
Master degree or above	42	13.4
Personal monthly income (in HK$)		
Below $20,000	136	43.3
$20,000 – $39,999	113	36.0
$40,000 – $59,999	45	14.3
$60,000 – $79,999	16	5.1
$80,000 – $99,999	2	.6
Above $100,000	2	.6
Number of hotel stay in the past month		
None	186	59.2
1 time	79	25.2
2 times	29	9.2
3 times	16	5.1
4 times	1	.3
5 times or above	3	1.0

Hypotheses testing

The structural model constructed based on the three hypotheses was tested using AMOS 25. The results show that societal CSR message has a significant influence on consumers' brand engagement ($\beta = 0.259$, $p < 0.05$). Therefore, H1 was supported. However, the influence of environmental CSR ($\beta = 0.016$, $p > 0.05$) and stakeholders' CSR ($\beta = 0.147$, $p > 0.05$) failed to reach at the significant level. Thus, H2 and H3 were not supported (Figure 2).

Discussion

Theoretical implications

This study examined how the communication of the three major domains of CSR initiatives on Facebook affects consumers' brand engagement in the context of hotels in Hong Kong. The results suggest that hotels can increase the level of their guests' brand engagement through communicating their CSR initiatives related to the society on social media. Recent research suggests that interacting types of CSR messages (as

Table 3. Results of factor analysis.

	Mean	SD	alpha
Environmental CSR			0.891
This hotel promotes environmental protection and green consumption concepts to customers and participates in related activities	4.95	1.249	
This hotel has environmentally-friendly design to protect natural landscapes, places of cultural and historical interest	4.96	1.290	
This hotel implements programs to reduce consumption, e.g. decrease usage of disposable goods	5.20	1.303	
This hotel implements programs and uses relevant facilities to improve public security, fire control and food safety	5.43	1.358	
This hotel implements programs and uses relevant facilities to save and use energy efficiently, and utilizes renewable energy	5.07	1.347	
This hotel implements programs and uses relevant facilities to reduce polluted water, noise and rubbish emissions	5.28	1.313	
Social CSR			0.890
This hotel supports nongovernmental organizations working in problematic areas	4.50	1.413	
This hotel contributes to campaigns and projects that promote the well-being of the society	4.64	1.350	
This hotel makes investment to create a better life for future generations	4.85	1.266	
This hotel targets sustainable growth which considers future generations	5.11	1.222	
Stakeholders' CSR			0.824
This hotel respects consumer rights beyond legal requirements	5.01	1.276	
This hotel provides full and accurate information about its products/services to customers	5.65	1.188	
Customers' satisfaction is highly important for this hotel	5.84	1.111	
This hotel provides a healthy and safe working environment for employees	5.59	1.236	
Brand Engagement			0.931
This hotel is important to me	5.16	1.304	
This hotel is interesting to me	4.36	1.239	
This hotel is relevant to me	4.45	1.294	
This hotel is exciting to me	4.32	1.266	
This hotel is meaningful to me	4.68	1.233	
This hotel is appealing to me	4.65	1.212	
This hotel is fascinating to me	4.26	1.147	
This hotel is valuable to me	5.09	1.262	
This hotel is involving to me	4.70	1.311	
This hotel is needed to me	5.10	1.283	

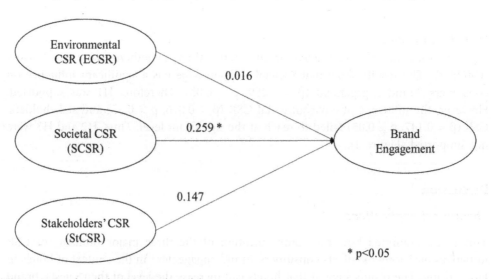

Figure 2. Results of the structural model.

opposed to informing types) on Facebook bring companies benefits of public engagement and relationship building (Cho, Furey, & Mohr, 2017). As the types of CSR
messages embody strategies such as 'announcing corporate partnership with community leaders and nonprofit organizations' and 'highlighting corporate engagement with
local communities' are related to societal CSR, these messages communicated on social
media were found to have a significant influence on consumers' brand engagement.

The findings of this current study do not complement the notion that CSR initiatives
related to the stakeholders and environment have the strongest impact on Chinese
customers' brand preference among the three CSR domains (Kucukusta, Mak, & Chan,
2013; Liu et al., 2014). One of the possible explanations could be because social media
allow messages to turn viral through interactions (Kesavan, Bernacchi, & Mascarenhas,
2013). Hence, the general public might consider corporate social media marketing as
invasive (Cohen, 2012); and this negativity couples with publics' tendency to be highly
skeptical towards certain types of CSR messages (Cho et al., 2017).

The current study contributes to the growing body of CSR research in multiple ways.
First, social media's role as a platform for CSR communication is lacking in the
literature. Our findings contribute to the CSR communication literature by specifying
which type of CSR message is more effective on social media. Second, a key gap in the
literature lies in our understanding of where an organization should focus its CSR
efforts on (O'Brien, Jarvis, & Soutar, 2015). While the literature has suggested that the
fit between an organization and a cause can positively affect the effectiveness of a CSR
campaign (File & Prince, 1998; Gupta & Pirsch, 2006), there is insufficient empirical
evidence to affirm the kind of fit that provokes more positive customer responses. This
research marks one of the first efforts to demonstrate that compared to stakeholder's
and environmental CSR messages, societal CSR messages are more effective in creating
brand engagement for hotel companies. Third, despite the shift in the literature to
establishing concepts that explain or predict the dynamics related to specific consumer/
brand relationships explicitly (Bolton & Saxena-Iyer, 2009; Malthouse & Hofacker,
2010) because of the increasing recognition of consumers' active roles in brand-based
processes (Pagani et al., 2011; Singh & Sonnenburg, 2012), studies in the hospitality
context mostly focuses on the end results CSR can lead to, e.g. brand preference (Liu
et al., 2014) without taking into account the underlying construct that affects these end
results and its antecedent, i.e. brand engagement (Hollebeek et al., 2014). This study
bridges this gap by identifying which type of CSR communication is more effective in
influencing consumers' brand engagement.

Managerial implications

The empirical results of this study provide hotel managers insights into how they can
incorporate social media in the communication of CSR initiatives to obtain the instrumental benefits of the properties' investments in CSR. First, this study contributes to
hotel managers' strategies by presenting a status quo of the social media usage for CSR
communication among hotels in Hong Kong, i.e. most of the hotels do post messages
related to their CSR initiatives on Facebook; the CSR domains most messages pertain to
are societal CSR, stakeholders' CSR and environmental CSR respectively; and most of
the hotels communicate the messages on the platform at a low frequency, which

complements the notion that most companies are underutilizing the branding benefits possibly brought by CSR communication through social media, as well as the call for identifying CSR communication strategies that engage the external publics (Cho et al., 2017). Hotel managers might adjust the mix of the types of CSR messages on social media in relation to the market according to the reference this study has provided.

Second, the results of the consumer survey suggest that hotels in Hong Kong should keep adopting social media as a platform for CSR communication especially for disclosing societal CSR initiatives because it can increase the level of customers' brand engagement, which is found to be an antecedent of the engagement concept (O'Brien et al., 2015). Hotel managers' apprehension of intensely using social media for CSR communication is attributed to the possible public skepticism. The positive relationship between disclosing societal CSR initiatives on social media and consumers' brand engagement found by this study affirms hotel managers that they could utilize social media for the communication more frequently than they do now, especially when social media are found to 'work better' than traditional corporate websites in CSR communication because they can reach the 'critical mass' much more easily through 'sharing', 'liking' and 'commenting' and fulfill consumers' preferences of information with a short response time in today's world (Kesavan et al., 2013).

Third, since local consumers and local communities are stakeholders of local hotels (Muller, 2006; Werther & Chandler, 2010). Effective CSR communication can increase stakeholders' engagement with the hotel brands, and benefit the hotel's brand reputation and satisfaction. Last but not least, to minimize possible cynicism towards the hotels' motives when their CSR initiatives are disclosed on social media, hotel managers, when choosing what types of messages to communicate, can focus on the hotels' participations in local social issues that are related to their core business because these are interactive messages that customers would prefer (Cho et al., 2017; O'Brien et al., 2015; Simmons & Becker-Olsen, 2006).

Conclusion and limitations

This current study was conducted out of the growing scholarly attention towards the dynamics pertaining to the explicit interactions between companies and customers, as well as the prevalent usage of social media in hotels' external communication nowadays. Specifically, this study investigated how the three major domains of CSR messages as identified in the literatures will affect hotel guests' brand engagement as an antecedent of consumer brand engagement that activates guests' behavior intentions in the context of hotels' social media.

The study was started with a content analysis on the Facebook pages of 100 hotels in Hong Kong to identify the current situation of the social media's usage for CSR communication in the industry in the region. The results showed that most of the hotels were disclosing their CSR initiatives on Facebook at a low frequency, which suggest that hotel companies should enhance their CSR communication on social media (Cha, Yi, & Bagozzi, 2016; Kleinrichert, Ergul, Johnson, & Uydaci, 2012). Further, through a quantitative approach, a consumer survey with 314 respondents was conducted and it found that CSR related to the society has a significant predictive power towards the increase in consumers' brand engagement, whereas that of environmental CSR has a certain trend towards significance.

However, the results of this study may not be generalizable to other industries without further study. Besides, the sample size was relatively small and that most of the respondents are young and with a relatively low income, which may not represent the customers of Hong Kong hotels accurately. Thus, the results of this study may bear limited significance to Hong Kong hotels who seek to increase their brand engagement using Facebook to communicate their CSR initiatives. In addition, the convenience sampling method may suffer biases. Therefore, future research should take these hotel guests into account and use random sampling methods. Some interesting topics remain unexplored regarding hotels' CSR communication on social media. Future studies may investigate, with a bigger sample size and designated proportions of respondents, how consumers' brand engagement level differs with certain demographic characteristics or personal traits. Besides, as there is a variety of social media nowadays, future studies may also look into how the impacts of hotels' CSR communication on different social media on customers' brand engagement differ from each other. In light of the growing scholarly emphasis on studying the underlying construct from the customers' perspectives through which the instrumental benefits of CSR are resulted, future studies may, taking the results of this study into account, explore how the types of CSR messages on different communication platforms of hotel companies would affect brand engagement as well as the directionality between the components of the concepts.

Disclosure statement

No potential conflict of interest was reported by the authors.

ORCID

Yixing (Lisa) Gao ⓘ http://orcid.org/0000-0001-6919-434X
Daniel Leung ⓘ http://orcid.org/0000-0002-2621-853X

References

Aaker, J., Fournier, S., & Brasel, A. S. (2004). When good brands do bad. *Journal of Consumer Research, 31*(1), 1–16.

Ahluwalia, R., Burnkrant, R., & Unnava, H. (2000). Consumer response to negative publicity: The moderating role of commitment. *Journal of Marketing Research, 37*(2), 203–214.

Alamro, A., & Rowley, J. (2011). Antecedents of brand preference for mobile telecommunications services. *Journal of Product & Brand Management, 20*(6), 475–486.

Basu, K., & Palazzo, G. (2008). Corporate social responsibility: A process model of sense making. *Academy of Management Review, 33*(1), 122–136.

Bhattacharya, C., & Sen, S. (2003). Consumer-company identification: A framework for understanding consumers' relationships with companies. *Journal of Marketing, 67*(2), 76–88.

Bolton, R. N. (2011). Comment: Customer engagement: Opportunities and challenges for organizations. *Journal of Service Research, 14*(3), 272–274.

Bolton, R. N., & Saxena-Iyer, S. (2009). Interactive services: A framework, synthesis and research directions. *Journal of Interactive Marketing, 23*(1), 91–104.

Bonilla-Priego, M. J., Font, X., & Pacheco, R. (2014). Corporate sustainability reporting index and baseline data for the cruise industry. *Tourism Management, 44*, 149–160.

Bowden, J. L. H. (2009). The process of customer engagement: A conceptual framework. *Journal of Marketing Theory and Practice, 17*(1), 63–74.

Business for Social Responsibility. (2006). *Taking the temperature of CSR leaders.* Retrieved from www.bsr.org/Meta/BSRleaders_survey.pdf

Business in the Community. (2018, November 22). *What is corporate social responsibility?* Retrieved from https://www.bitc.ie/about-us/what-is-csr/

Carroll, A. (1979). A three-dimensional conceptual model of corporate performance. *Academy of Management Review, 4*(4), 497–505.

Caruana, R., Glozer, S., Crane, A., & McCabe, S. (2014). Tourists' accounts of responsible tourism. *Annals of Tourism Research, 46*, 115–129.

Cha, M. K., Yi, Y., & Bagozzi, R. P. (2016). Effects of customer participation in corporate social responsibility (CSR) programs on the CSR-brand fit and brand loyalty. *Cornell Hospitality Quarterly, 57*(3), 235–249.

Chan, N. L., & Guillet, B. D. (2011). Investigation of social media marketing: How does the hotel industry in Hong Kong perform in marketing on social media websites?. *Journal of Travel & Tourism Marketing, 28*(4), 345–368.

Chang, Y. H., & Yeh, C. H. (2016). Managing corporate social responsibility strategies of airports: The case of Taiwan's Taoyuan international airport corporation. *Transportation Research Part A: Policy and Practice, 92*, 338–348.

Chen, Y. (2010). The drivers of green brand equity: Green brand image, green satisfaction, and green trust. *Journal of Business Ethics, 93*(2), 307–319.

Cheung, D., Welford, R., & Hills, P. (2009). CSR & the environment: Business-supply chain partnerships in Hong Kong & the PRDR of China. *Corporate Social Responsibility and Environmental Management, 16*(5), 250–263.

Cho, M., Furey, L. D., & Mohr, T. (2017). Communicating corporate social responsibility on social media: Strategies, stakeholders, and public engagement on corporate Facebook. *Business and Professional Communication Quarterly, 80*(1), 52–69.

Clarkson, M. B. E. (1995). A stakeholder framework for analyzing and evaluating corporate social performance. *Academy of Management Review, 20*(1), 92–117.

Cohen, D. (2012). Brands, maintain a Facebook page, but don't bother me. *Social Times.* Retrieved from http://www.adweek.com/socialtimes/facebook-page-consum-ers/382017

Coulter, R., Price, L., & Feick, L. (2003). Rethinking the origins of involvement and brand commitment: Insights from postsocialist Europe. *Journal of Consumer Research, 30*(2), 151–169.

Creyer, E., & Ross, W. (1997). The influence of firm behavior on purchase intention: Do consumers really care about business ethics?. *Journal of Consumer Marketing, 14*(6), 421–432.

De Grosbois, D. (2012). Corporate social responsibility reporting by the global hotel industry: Commitment, initiatives and performance. *International Journal of Hospitality Management*, *31*(3), 896–905.

Du, S., Bhattacharya, C., & Sen, S. (2010). Maximizing business returns to corporate social responsibility (CSR): The role of CSR communication. *International Journal of Management Reviews*, *12*(1), 8–19.

Ettinger, A., Grabner-Kraeuter, S., & Terlutter, R. (2018). Online CSR communication in the hotel industry: Evidence from small hotels. *International Journal of Hospitality Management*, *68*, 94–104.

File, K. M., & Prince, R. A. (1998). Cause related marketing and corporate philanthropy in the privately held enterprise. *Journal of Business Ethics*, *17*(14), 1529–1539.

Font, X., & Lynes, J. (2018). Corporate social responsibility in tourism and hospitality. *Journal of Sustainable Tourism*, *26*(7), 1027–1042.

Fournier, S. M. (1998). Consumers and their brands: Developing relationship theory in consumer research. *Journal of Consumer Research*, *24*(4), 343–353.

Gao, Y. L., & Mattila, A. S. (2014). Improving consumer satisfaction in green hotels: The roles of perceived warmth, perceived competence, and CSR motive. *International Journal of Hospitality Management*, *42*, 20–31.

Guix, M., Bonilla-Priego, M. J., & Font, X. (2018). The process of sustainability reporting in international hotel groups: An analysis of stakeholder inclusiveness, materiality and responsiveness. *Journal of Sustainable Tourism*, *26*(7), 1063–1084.

Gupta, S., & Pirsch, J. (2006). The company-cause-customer fit decision in cause-related marketing. *Journal of Consumer Marketing*, *23*(6), 314–326.

Hair, J. F., Black, W. C., Babin, B. J., & Anderson, R. E. (2010). *Multivariate data analysis* (7th ed.). Upper Saddle River, NJ: Prentice Hall.

He, H., & Li, Y. (2011). CSR and service brand: The mediating effect of brand identification and moderating effect of service quality. *Journal of Business Ethics*, *100*(4), 673–688.

Henderson, J. (2007). Corporate social responsibility and tourism: Hotel companies in Phuket, Thailand, after the Indian Ocean tsunami. *International Journal of Hospitality Management*, *26*(1), 228–239.

Heung, V. C., Fei, C., & Hu, C. (2006). Customer and employee perception of a green hotel-the case of five-star hotels in China. *China Tourism Research*, *2*(3), 246–297.

Holcomb, J. L., Upchurch, R. S., & Okumus, F. (2007). Corporate social responsibility: What are top hotel companies reporting? *International Journal of Contemporary Hospitality Management*, *19*(6), 461–475.

Hollebeek, L. D., Glynn, M. S., & Brodie, R. J. (2014). Consumer brand engagement in social media: Conceptualization, scale development and validation. *Journal of Interactive Marketing*, *28*, 149–165.

Hsu, Y. L. (2012). Facebook as international eMarketing strategy of Taiwan hotels. *International Journal of Hospitality Management*, *31*(3), 972–980.

Jarvis, D., Stoeckl, N., & Liu, H. (2016). The impact of economic, social and environmental factors on trip satisfaction and the likelihood of visitors returning. *Tourism Management*, *52*, 1–18.

Jung, S., Kim, J. H., Kang, K. H., & Kim, B. (2018). Internationalization and corporate social responsibility in the restaurant industry: Risk perspective. *Journal of Sustainable Tourism*, *26*(7), 1105–1123.

Kalisch, A. (2002). *Corporate futures: Social responsibility in the tourism industry*. London: Tourism Concern.

Kang, J., Tang, L., & Fiore, A. M. (2014). Enhancing consumer-brand relationships on restaurant Facebook fan pages: Maximizing consumer benefits and increasing active participation. *International Journal of Hospitality Management*, *36*, 145–155.

Kang, K. H., Stein, L., Heo, C. Y., & Lee, S. (2012). Consumers' willingness to pay for green initiatives of the hotel industry. *International Journal of Hospitality Management*, *31*, 2564–2572.

Kasim, A. (2004). BESR in the hotel sector: A look at tourists' propensity towards environmentally and socially friendly hotel attributes in Pulau Pinang, Malaysia. *International Journal of Hospitality & Tourism Administration, 5*(2), 61–83.

Kennedy Nyahunzvi, D. (2013). CSR reporting among Zimbabwe's hotel groups: A content analysis. *International Journal of Contemporary Hospitality Management, 25*(4), 595–613.

Kesavan, R., Bernacchi, M., & Mascarenhas, O. (2013). Word of mouse: CSR communication and the social media. *International Management Review, 9*(1), 58–66.

Kleinrichert, D., Ergul, M., Johnson, C., & Uydaci, M. (2012). Boutique hotels: Technology, social media and green practices. *Journal of Hospitality and Tourism Technology, 3*(3), 211–225.

Kotler, P. (2008). *Marketing management.* Upper Saddle River, NJ: Prentice-Hall.

Kucukusta, D., Mak, A., & Chan, X. (2013). Corporate social responsibility practices in four and five-star hotels: Perspectives from Hong Kong visitors. *International Journal of Hospitality Management, 34*, 19–30.

Kumar, V., Aksoy, L., Donkers, B., Venkatesan, R., Wiesel, T., & Tillmanns, S. (2010). Undervalued or overvalued customers: Capturing total customer engagement value. *Journal of Service Research, 13*(3), 297–310.

Kwok, L., & Yu, B. (2016). Taxonomy of Facebook messages in business-to-consumer communications: What really works?. *Tourism and Hospitality Research, 16*(4), 311–328.

Laroche, M., Bergeron, J., & Barbaro-Forleo, G. (2001). Targeting consumers who are willing to pay more for environmentally friendly products. *Journal of Consumer Marketing, 18*(6), 503–520.

Leung, T. C. H., & Snell, R. S. (2017). Attraction or distraction? Corporate social responsibility in Macao's gambling industry. *Journal of Business Ethics, 145*, 637–658.

Liu, M. T. C., Wong, I. A., Shi, G. C., Chu, R., & Brock, J. L. (2014). The impact of corporate social responsibility (CSR) performance and perceived brand quality on customer-based brand preference. *Journal of Services Marketing, 28*(3), 181–194.

Maignan, I., & Ferrell, O. C. (2004). Corporate social responsibility and marketing: An integrative framework. *Journal of the Academy of Marketing Science, 32*(1), 3–19.

Malthouse, E., & Hofacker, C. (2010). Looking back and looking forward with interactive marketing. *Journal of Interactive Marketing, 24*(3), 181–184.

Marin, L., & Ruiz, S. (2007). I need you too! Corporate identity attractiveness for consumers and the role of social responsibility. *Journal of Business Ethics, 71*(3), 245–260.

Martínez, P., Pérez, A., & Del Bosque, I. R. (2014). Exploring the role of CSR in the organizational identity of hospitality companies: A case from the Spanish tourism industry. *Journal of Business Ethics, 124*(1), 47–66.

Matten, D., & Crane, A. (2005). Corporate citizenship: Toward an extended theoretical conceptualization. *Academy of Management Review, 30*(1), 166–179.

McCarthy, L., Stock, D., & Verma, R. (2010). How travelers use online and social media channels to make hotel-choice decisions. *Cornell Hospitality Report, 10*(18), 6–18.

Mohr, L., Webb, D., & Harris, K. (2001). Do consumers expect companies to be socially responsible? The impact of corporate social responsibility on buying behavior. *Journal of Consumer Affairs, 35*(1), 45–72.

Muller, A. (2006). Global versus local CSR strategies. *European Management Journal, 24*(2–3), 189–198.

Murray, K. B., & Vogel, C. M. (1997). Using a hierarchy-of-effects approach to gauge the effectiveness of corporate social responsibility to generate goodwill toward the firm: Financial versus nonfinancial impacts. *Journal of Business Research, 38*(2), 141–159.

O'Brien, I. M., Jarvis, W., & Soutar, G. N. (2015). Integrating social issues and customer engagement to drive loyalty in a service organisation. *Journal of Services Marketing, 29*(6/7), 547–559.

O'Neill, J. W., & Mattila, A. S. (2006). Strategic hotel development and positioning: The effect of revenue drivers on profitability. *The Cornell Hotel and Restaurant Administration Quarterly, 47*(2), 146–154.

Pagani, M., Hofacker, C. F., & Goldsmith, R. E. (2011). The influence of personality on active and passive use of social networking sites. *Psychology & Marketing, 28*(5), 441–456.

Pedersen, E. R. (2010). Modeling CSR: How managers understand the responsibilities of business towards society. *Journal of Business Ethics, 91*(2), 155–166.

Peloza, J., & Shang, J. (2011). How can corporate social responsibility activities create value for stakeholders? A systematic review. *Journal of the Academy Marketing Science, 39*(1), 117–135.

Pérez, A., & Rodriguez Del Bosque, I. (2015). Corporate social responsibility and customer loyalty: Exploring the role of identification, satisfaction and type of company. *Journal of Services Marketing, 29*(1), 15–25.

Porter, M., & Kramer, M. (2006). Strategy and society: The link between competitive advantage and corporate social responsibility. *Harvard Business Review, 84*(12), 78–89.

Rahbar, E., & Wahid, N. (2011). Investigation of green marketing tools' effect on consumers' purchase behavior. *Business Strategy Series, 12*(2), 73–83.

Ricks, J. M. (2005). An assessment of strategic corporate philanthropy on perceptions of brand equity variables. *Journal of Consumer Marketing, 22*(3), 121–134.

Sawhney, M., Verona, G., & Prandelli, E. (2005). Collaborating to create: The Internet as a platform for customer engagement in product innovation. *Journal of Interactive Marketing, 19*(4), 4–17.

Sen, S., Bhattacharya, C., & Korschun, D. (2006). The role of corporate social responsibility in strengthening multiple stakeholder relationships: A field experiment. *Journal of the Academy of Marketing Science, 34*(2), 158–166.

Serra-Cantallops, A., Peña-Miranda, D. D., Ramón-Cardona, J., & Martorell-Cunill, O. (2018). Progress in research on CSR and the hotel industry (2006-2015). *Cornell Hospitality Quarterly, 59*(1), 15–38.

Simmons, C., & Becker-Olsen, K. (2006). Achieving marketing objectives through social sponsorships. *Journal of Marketing, 70*(4), 154–169.

Singh, J., Sanchez, M., & Del Bosque, I. (2008). Understanding corporate social responsibility and product perceptions in consumer market: A cross-culture evolution. *Journal of Business Ethics, 80*(3), 597–611.

Singh, S., & Sonnenburg, S. (2012). Brand performances in social media. *Journal of Interactive Marketing, 26*(4), 189–197.

Tabachnick, B. G., & Fidell, L. S. (2007). *Using multivariate statistics* (5th ed.). Boston, MA: Allyn & Bacon.

Torelli, C. J., Monga, A. B., & Kaikati, A. M. (2011). Doing poorly by doing good: Corporate social responsibility and brand concepts. *Journal of Consumer Research, 38*(5), 948–963.

Torres, A., Bijmolt, T., Tribo, J., & Verhoef, P. (2012). Generating global brand equity through corporate social responsibility to key stakeholders. *International Journal of Research in Marketing, 29*(1), 13–24.

Turker, D. (2009). Measuring corporate social responsibility: A scale development study. *Journal of Business Ethics, 85*(4), 411–427.

Tzschentke, N., Kirk, D., & Lynch, P. (2008). Ahead of their time? Barriers to action in green tourism firms. *Service Industries Journal, 28*(2), 167–178.

We are social. (2018, November 22). *Digital in 2018: World's Internet users pass the 4 billion mark.* Retrieved from https://digitalreport.wearesocial.com/

Werther, W. B., Jr., & Chandler, D. (2010). *Strategic corporate social responsibility: Stakeholders in a global environment.* Los Angeles: Sage.

Wildes, V. J. (2008). How can organizational leaders really lead and serve at the same time?. *International Journal of Contemporary Hospitality Management, 20*(1), 67–78.

Williamson, D., Lynch-Wood, G., & Ramsay, J. (2006). Drivers of environmental behaviour in manufacturing SMEs and the implications for CSR. *Journal of Business Ethics, 67*(3), 317–330.

Xie, C., Bagozzi, R., & Grønhaug, K. (2015). The role of moral emotions and individual differences in consumer responses to corporate green and non-green actions. *Journal of the Academy of Marketing Science, 43*(3), 333–356.

Yuan, W., Bao, Y., & Verbeke, A. (2011). Integrating CSR initiatives in business: An organizing framework. *Journal of Business Ethics, 101*(1), 75–92.

Channeling Life Satisfaction to Tourist Satisfaction: New Conceptualization and Evidence

Yong Chen

ABSTRACT

This study developed a model that predicts tourist satisfaction with a destination based on their life satisfaction in their home country. The model was grounded on an assumption that tourist consumption does not necessarily entail consuming commodities, on which the expectancy-disconfirmation framework is built. The model was tested with 1,048 inbound tourists in Switzerland from eight countries. We found that among all the structural relationships, those between life satisfaction, positive affect, destination image, and tourist satisfaction were the most significant and robust across all nine models. This suggests that life satisfaction at home boosts tourist satisfaction at the destination through the mediations of positive affect and destination image. By contrast, all structural relationships related to negative affect were either nonsignificant or extremely weak. We conclude that life satisfaction at home can be channeled to the destination through experience-based affect and destination image, which eventually affects tourist satisfaction.

生活满意度对旅游满意度的溢出效应：理论新解与证据

摘要

本研究旨在探讨旅游者在其惯常环境中的生活满意度对其在目的地的旅游满意度影响的成因和机制。与其他消费活动相比，旅游体验可以但无需完全建立在消费具体的商品和服务的基础上，因此旅游者在旅游过程中未必会产生基于具体商品和服务的购买前的期望与购买后的评判，而这二者的差异则是经典消费者满意度建立的基础。基于这一假设，本研究认为旅游满意度可以部分来自于旅游者在其惯常环境中生活满意度的溢出，即较高的生活满意度可以产生较高的旅游满意度。通过收集1048名来自八个国家的游客在瑞士的旅游数据以检测模型的有效性，本研究发现，所有基于生活满意度、积极情绪、目的地形象以及旅游满意度之间关系的假设都被证实，而所有与消极情绪相关的假设都不显著或者非常微弱。这一发现表明，旅游者在其惯常环境中所获得的生活满意度会影响其在目的地的旅游满意度，而生活满意度对旅游满意度的影响是通过旅游者在旅游过程中所产生的积极情绪和对目的地形象的正面感知而形成的。

1. Introduction

Tourist satisfaction is a vital indicator of service performance in various tourism and hospitality sectors as well as the competitiveness of a destination (Song, van der Veen, Li, & Chen, 2012). Previous research on tourist satisfaction was grounded on the expectancy-disconfirmation framework (Oliver, 1980), in which tourist satisfaction is nothing more than customer satisfaction derived from the discrepancy between consumers' expectation for, and perceived performance of, a product (Chan et al., 2003; Song et al., 2012). In this conceptualization, tourist consumption is relegated to the consumption of merely fragmented products and services at the destination. Yet tourist consumption is more complex as it is intertwined with enormous hedonic and transcendent experiences that may have little to do with specific products and services, nor with service performance of the industry (Gillet, Schmitz, & Mitas, 2016; Kler & Tribe, 2012; Tsaur, Yen, & Hsiao, 2013). The assumption that customer satisfaction entails an expectation as a prerequisite is problematic in the tourism context, since the expectation itself cannot be anticipated when a vacation is improvised, an activity is haphazard, or even the destination itself is rather obscure. These issues cast doubt on the validity of the expectancy-disconfirmation framework in explaining tourist satisfaction despite its wide application in consumer behavior research.

Empirical evidence has shown that tourist satisfaction is culturally biased, with Western tourists stubbornly more satisfied than their Eastern counterparts (Song & Chon, 2015). This cultural difference might be owing to the disparities of the *ex-ante* life satisfaction that varies across cultures and nationalities. In other words, tourist satisfaction with a destination might be determined prior to a vacation or travel activities at the destination. Studies suggested that tourist satisfaction with a particular destination (Hong Kong) tends to increase over time (Chen, Schuckert, Song, & Chon, 2016; Song & Chon, 2015), which might be mirrored in tourists' growing life satisfaction at home. While life satisfaction at home and tourist satisfaction with a destination are divided, the fact that vacation becomes instrumental in shaping people's daily life lends support to the causal relationship between the two. On the one hand, vacation can boost positive affect and life satisfaction (Chen & Li, 2018; Neal, Sirgy, & Uysal, 1999, 2004; Neal, Uysal, & Sirgy, 2007) and, on the other, research has shown that happy people tend to project an optimistic view on the products they bought, the people they interacted as well as the decisions they made (Adaval, 2003; Forgas, 1990; Forgas & Ciarrochi, 2001; Wright & Bower, 1992). These studies suggest that tourist satisfaction with a destination is, at least in part, internalized in life satisfaction at home.

Vacation boosts happiness and life satisfaction because people's satisfaction with vacation as a specific life domain can spill over upward to their general life domain (Neal et al., 1999, 2004, 2007). We argue that life satisfaction can spill over downward to affect people's satisfaction in their specific life domains, including their evaluation of a trip or a leisure activity, and therefore determines tourist satisfaction at the destination. We aim to examine whether and how people's life satisfaction at home can predict their satisfaction with the destination, namely tourist satisfaction. Since tourist consumption at the destination is filled with experiences that can evoke either positive affect (such as excitement and joyfulness associated with transcendent experiences) or negative affect (such as anxiety and stress associated with fatigue and burnout) (Fritz & Sonnentag, 2006; Gilbert & Abdullah, 2004; Steyn, Saayman, & Nienaber, 2004), we look further into whether and how positive and negative affect can mediate the relationship between people's life satisfaction at home and their satisfaction with the destination.

2. Literature review

2.1. Life satisfaction, happiness, and consumer evaluation

Life satisfaction and happiness have been used interchangeably in the literature to refer to subjective well-being as opposed to material well-being, or gross domestic product (GDP) (Deaton, 2013; Stiglitz, Sen, & Fitoussi, 2009). As an objective measure and statistic of both a nation's wealth and living standard for almost a century up to date, GDP has, since the last decade or two, been discredited as being insufficient to measure the genuine quality of life and well-being (Stiglitz et al., 2009). Economists have been considering alternative measures that include subjective well-being in order to more accurately assess a nation's economic prosperity and social progress (Deaton, 2013; Stiglitz et al., 2009). Empirical research on happiness, though, was originated in positive psychology but has gone on to penetrate a wide range of social sciences, from economics, sociology, to political sciences (Easterlin, 2001, 2004, 2013; Johns & Ormerod, 2007). When it comes to tourism, research has confirmed the positive effect of vacation and leisure on life satisfaction and happiness, which is robust across different travel or leisure activities (Neal et al., 1999, 2004, 2007).

Studies, on the other hand, have shown that happiness affects individuals' personal development, decision making, as well as judgement (Lyubomirsky, King, & Diener, 2005a; Mogilner, Aaker, & Kamvar, 2012). Lyubomirsky et al. (2005a) found that happiness is not only associated with, but can also predict, personal success. A wealth of research also showed that having a positive mood – a component of happiness – can affect people's choice through influencing their cognitive processing of information in decision making (Mogilner et al., 2012; Schwarz & Clore, 1983). Lyubomirsky, Sheldon, and Schkade (2005b) found that people feeling happy are more likely to make better choices both in their personal (e.g. drinking less alcohol, smoking less) and professional lives (e.g. behaving in less retaliatory ways to coworkers, searching for and securing more job interviews). Numerous studies have shown that people in a positive mood tend to be optimistic about favorable events occurring as well as to evaluate people and objects in a more favorable way (Adaval, 2003; Forgas, 1990; Forgas & Ciarrochi, 2001; Wright & Bower, 1992), which indicates that happiness leads to satisfaction as well as a tolerance of dissatisfaction.

2.2. Effects of vacation on happiness

The relationship between life satisfaction and vacation is mainly about whether and how vacation can boost life satisfaction and happiness (Gilbert & Abdullah, 2004; Kim & Woo, 2014; Lounsbury & Hoopes, 1986; Nawijn, Marchand, Veenhoven, & Vingerhoets, 2010). This line of research articulated the differences in life satisfaction between vacationers and non-vacationers (Gilbert & Abdullah, 2004; Lounsbury & Hoopes, 1986). Gilbert and Abdullah's (2004) study showed that vacationers experience higher subjective well-being in both pre- and post-travel periods compared to non-vacationers. According to Gilbert and Abdullah (2004), vacation participation can enhance happiness, especially for those who enjoy and value travel. While no significant difference was found between vacationers and non-vacationers in their post-trip happiness, Nawijn et al.'s (2010) study found that the former have higher pre-trip happiness. Although travel can lead to burnout and fatigue (Steyn et al., 2004), Gilbert and Abdullah (2004) concluded that vacation would, after all, not make people physically worse off.

While a number of sociodemographic variables, such as income, marital status and employment, can affect happiness either positively or negatively, vacation can somewhat mediate the relationships between these sociodemographic variables and happiness (Lounsbury & Hoopes, 1986; McCabe & Johnson, 2013; McCabe, Joldersma, & Li, 2010). Even after controlling for the effects of these sociodemographic variables on life satisfaction, vacation can still have a significantly positive effect on life satisfaction (Lounsbury & Hoopes, 1986). While low life satisfaction is normally associated with low income (Cone & Gilovich, 2010), people who are economically disadvantaged also see their happiness increase through vacation participation. This argument was evidenced in a community of the United Kingdom, where low-income households reported an increase in their life satisfaction after taking a sponsored vacation (McCabe & Johnson, 2013; McCabe et al., 2010).

2.3. Tourist experiences and happiness

Tourist consumption is more associated with mood and happiness than generic consumption (Nawijn, 2010b; Strauss-Blasche, Ekmekcioglu, & Marktl, 2000). Nawijn (2010b) found that mood is generated and can fade at different phases of travel, and mood climaxes around the completion of 70% of a holiday. Nawijn et al. (2010) found no difference in post-trip happiness between vacationers and non-vacationers, but vacationers report higher pre-trip happiness. This is perhaps because vacationers' anticipation of their holiday brings them positive affect concluded by Nawijn et al. (2010). Strauss-Blasche et al. (2000) found that compared to the pre-vacation period, tourists reported improved mood in the post-vacation period. The fact that mood and emotion are volatile has led some researchers to conclude that the effects of vacation on happiness are transitory, meaning that its effect on life satisfaction is inconclusive (Nawijn, 2010a; Nawijn et al., 2010). Nawijn (2010a) argued that vacation only has a marginal effect on the hedonic level of happiness, implying that vacation affects some dimensions of happiness, such as emotions, mood, and affect. This is perhaps because vacationing is positively reminisced, and is thus more associated with positive affect (Nawijn, 2010a).

Travel experience is also associated with health complaints and burnout, which in turn affect tourist satisfaction, yet the effects of travel experience, along with negative affect at the destination, have not been addressed in conventional customer satisfaction frameworks. Fritz and Sonnentag (2006) found that vacationers' health complaints and burnout first decline approximately one week before vacation and plummet when the vacation is about to conclude, and then increase in the post-vacation period. This indicates that the negative effect of vacation fades during the whole trip. It was found that recuperation is negatively associated with the number of stressful days at home after vacation while positively associated with the length of vacation and the number of non-stressful days (Strauss-Blasche et al., 2000).

Different tourist activities are associated with different facets of happiness (Kler & Tribe, 2012; Tsaur et al., 2013; Voigt, Howat, & Brown, 2010). Based on the classification of travel experience on a spectrum from hedonism to eudaimonia, Voigt et al. (2010) found that spa visitation is on the hedonic end, spiritual retreat experiences are on the eudaimonic end, and lifestyle resort experiences are somewhere in between. The facets of eudaimonia were found to be associated with highly-engaging travel activities, such as scuba diving, which can provide participants with meaning and fulfillment through learning and personal growth (Kler & Tribe, 2012; Matteucci & Filep, 2017). Matteucci and Filep (2017) argued that tourists' experience of flamenco music and dance in Spain is eudaimonic as the pursuit of flamenco involves hardship, sacrifice as well as an enthusiastic craving for self-discovery, all of which are obscured in commonplace travel activities. Tsaur et al. (2013) surveyed mountain climbers and found that mountain climbing is filled with transcendent experience, which boosts hedonic enjoyment and happiness, especially for professional climbers. Hosany (2012) argued that appraisals of pleasantness, goal congruence, and internal self-compatibility are the main drivers of positive emotions.

2.4. Spillover effects: From tourist happiness to life satisfaction

The mechanism by which tourist satisfaction or happiness can increase life satisfaction is based on the spillover theory (Neal, 2000; Neal et al., 1999, 2004, 2007). This theory regards life satisfaction as a hierarchy that builds on people's satisfaction with a wide range of specific life domains, including leisure and vacation (Neal, 2000; Neal et al., 1999, 2004, 2007). Since the leisure domain is placed at the bottom of the hierarchy, satisfaction with leisure and vacation spills over upward to superordinate domains, and eventually affects life satisfaction (Neal et al., 1999, 2007). With a comprehensive literature review on the linkages between leisure and happiness, Newman, Tay, and Diener (2014) proposed five core psychological domains that can explain why leisure can boost happiness, which are detachment-recovery, autonomy, mastery, meaning, and affiliation (DRAMMA). These five psychological domains are the most relevant and applicable to life satisfaction with leisure and, to a larger extent, with tourism. The DRAMMA model was based on a re-conceptualization of leisure on two dimension. One is the structural dimension, which distinguishes between leisure and obligated work, and the other dimension is subjective, indicating people's perceived engagement in leisure activities (Newman et al., 2014)

2.5. From life satisfaction, customer satisfaction to tourist satisfaction

Customer satisfaction theories are built upon the expectancy-disconfirmation framework, which consists of four interconnected constructs: expectation, perceived performance, disconfirmation, and satisfaction (Fornell, 1992; Oliver, 1980). This framework has been widely applied in customer satisfaction research in various contexts, including tourism and hospitality where tourism and even a destination are seen as a product (Chan et al., 2003; De Ruyter, Bloemer, & Peeters, 1997a; Song et al., 2012). Underlying this framework is a conjecture that consumers develop expectations of a product prior to purchase, and then compare its actual performance with their expectations. As such, customer satisfaction is essentially consumers' evaluation of the perceived discrepancy between their expectation of a product before consumption and perceived performance of the product after consumption (Churchill & Surprenant, 1982; Halstead, Hartman, & Schmidt, 1994). This framework, along with a wealth of research that builds on it, suggests that customer satisfaction depends on the assessed value of the product which, in turn, is measured by the price paid by consumers versus the quality delivered (De Ruyter, Wetzels, Lemmink, & Mattson, 1997b; Rust & Oliver, 1994).

Despite the widespread application of the expectancy-disconfirmation framework, some assumptions that make the framework function in a generic consumption context may not apply to tourist consumption. First, tourists are not obliged to purchase a product to fulfil their travel goals; if anything, they actually purchase a combination of products and services from a wide range of suppliers to generate a holistic travel experience. Thus, customer satisfaction that builds on a single product or service may not work well in the tourism context. Second, product- or service-based customer satisfaction may obscure the discriminability between satisfaction and service quality, leading some studies to interchangeably use service quality and customer satisfaction (Mattsson, 1992; Spreng & Singh, 1993). Third, tourist consumption is nothing but experience creation despite the fact that products and services help build such experience (Andersson, 2007). In some travel activities such as backpacking, pilgrim, and dark tourism, the creation of tourist experience entails no presence of specific, commercialized products or services. In Cohen's (1972) tourist typology, drifters simply avoid commercial tourism establishments during their travel in order to obtain an authentic travel experience. Finally, since tourist consumption occurs in different travel phases, expectation becomes elusive as tourists pass through one phase to another during the whole trip. Therefore, the boundary between expectation and perception is blurred, so is the disparity between them, which affects customer satisfaction.

Studies aiming at unraveling the effects of vacation on happiness concluded that vacation can bring happiness and positive emotions (Chen & Li, 2018; Neal et al., 1999, 2004, 2007). Nevertheless, little is known about how life satisfaction would affect tourist consumption and, in particular, tourist satisfaction at the destination. Tourist satisfaction, especially with a destination, has more to do with tourist experience than separate tourism products and services. Whether tourists value travel and see travel as a means of self-fulfillment also matters to their satisfaction with the destination, which in turn can be predicted by their life satisfaction before a vacation actually takes place. Yet these issues, which pertain specifically to tourist consumption, have not fully been accounted for by conventional customer satisfaction frameworks, nor has empirical evidence been provided for this matter.

3. Research methods

3.1. Model and hypotheses

We assume that tourist satisfaction at a destination is rooted in people's life satisfaction at home. Given that tourist experience is created by various travel activities at the destination, we examine how both positive and negative affect would influence tourist satisfaction. Tourism research has shown that destination image affects tourist evaluation of the destination, such as tourist satisfaction and loyalty (Bigné, Sánchez, & Sánchez, 2001; del bosque & martín, 2008) and can therefore affect their destination choice (Bigné et al., 2001; Telisman-Kosuta, 1989). In particular, Bigné et al. (2001) confirmed that destination image has direct effects on tourist satisfaction and behavioral intentions. Chen and Li's (2018) study found that not only does destination image affect tourist satisfaction, but it also affects life satisfaction and emotions. As argued by Del Bosque and Martín (2008), destination image is one of the key drivers of tourists' commitment to the destination. We therefore hypothesize that destination image is influenced by tourists' affect at the destination as well as their life satisfaction at home. Figure 1 shows the conceptual model that consists of nine hypotheses:

$H_{1\text{-}1}$:   Life satisfaction has a positive effect on positive affect at the destination.

$H_{1\text{-}2}$:   Life satisfaction has a negative effect on negative affect at the destination.

$H_{1\text{-}3}$:   Life satisfaction has a positive effect on destination image.

$H_{1\text{-}4}$:   Life satisfaction has a positive effect on tourist satisfaction with the destination.

$H_{2\text{-}1}$:   Positive affect has a positive effect on destination image.

$H_{2\text{-}2}$:   Positive affect has a positive effect on tourist satisfaction with the destination.

$H_{3\text{-}1}$:   Negative affect has a negative effect on destination image.

$H_{3\text{-}2}$:   Negative affect has a negative effect on tourist satisfaction with the destination.

H_4 Destination image has a positive effect on tourist satisfaction with the destination.

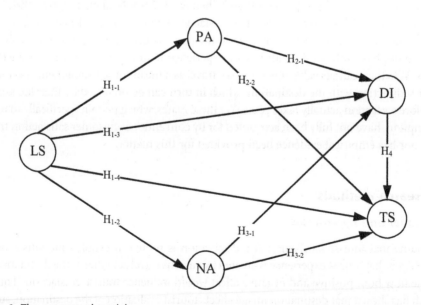

Figure 1. The conceptual model.

3.2. Research design

In order to test the effect of tourists' life satisfaction on tourist happiness, we need to ensure that life satisfaction cannot be affected by tourist experience at the destination, in other words, life satisfaction is exogenous in the model. We adopted a two-phase research design to dictate the sequence of the questions regarding life satisfaction (pre-travel phase) and tourist satisfaction (post-travel phase) being asked. In the first phase, respondents were required to provide information about their life satisfaction at home and how they viewed their life prior to their most recent trip to the destination (Switzerland). In this phase, respondents were unaware of both the questions regarding their travel experience at the destination and the relationship between the two sets of questions. This was to ensure that information collected for life satisfaction was not affected by their most recent travel experience. In the second phase, respondents were required to provide information about their travel experience, ranging from their travel activities, emotions, happiness, to their satisfaction with the destination. It was plausible under this research design, as we hypothesized, that respondents' experience at the destination would not affect their life satisfaction at home.

In order to account for the differences of respondents' life satisfaction that varies with their nationalities, we adopted a quota sampling approach for surveying tourists from eight countries (Germany, the United Kingdom, France, Italy, the United States, Canada, China, and Japan), which were the eight largest source markets of Switzerland measured by hotel room nights at the time of this study (Federal Statistical Office (FSO), 2014). We excluded one-day visitors and transit travelers in our survey as they did not experience the destination thoroughly, and therefore could not accumulate sufficient travel experiences that served the purpose of this study.

3.3. Data and measurement

Life satisfaction was measured with the *Satisfaction with Life Scale* developed by Diener et al. (1985), and extended by Pavot and Diener (2008). This scale consists of five statements: (1) 'In most ways my life is close to my ideal,' (2) 'The conditions of my life are excellent,' (3) 'I am satisfied with my life,' (4) 'So far I have gotten the important things I want in life,' and (5) 'If I could live my life over, I would change almost nothing.' Destination image was used to capture tourists' perception of a destination, including environmental quality, political security, social connectivity, and economic affordability (Chen & Li, 2018), which shape tourists' experience and influence their satisfaction and happiness. The items pertaining to destination image were drawn from Del Bosque and Martín (2008) and Jenkins (1999). Tourist satisfaction was measured by three indicators: overall satisfaction, comparison with expectations, and comparison with the ideal (Chan et al., 2003; Fornell, 1992; Song et al., 2012). Positive affect included relaxation, contentedness, joy, and excitement, while negative affect included anxiety, stress, depression, and sadness, both of which were drawn from the measurement of subjective well-being suggested by the Organization for Economic Co-operation and Development (OECD, 2013). All these indicators were measured on an 11-point Likert scale, with 0 indicating tourists' complete disagreement with a statement and 10, complete agreement.

We employed a cross-sectional study to collect information on tourists' most recent trip in Switzerland. Data were collected from tourists from the eight countries aforementioned, who traveled to and stayed overnight in Switzerland between January and December 2015. A questionnaire incorporating the questions about tourists' life satisfaction before their trip and their satisfaction with Switzerland after the trip was administered to respondents in January 2016 by a professional market research firm. Data collection began with the link of the questionnaire sent to the respondents in a panel database of the firm. Based on the speeding check results, of the 4,607 respondents who started the survey, 1,450 completed it, including 1,048 international tourists from the eight countries, and were used for analysis.

3.4. Data analysis

A structural equation modeling (SEM) approach was used to test the hypotheses of the study, and a partial least squares SEM (PLS-SEM) was used to analyze the model (Hair, Hult, Ringle, & Sarstedt, 2017). We adopted the variance-based SEM to analyze the data as we focused on the explanatory power of the model in explaining tourist satisfaction instead of confirming an existing theory. We expected that the predictors, particularly life satisfaction at home, have considerable power in predicting tourist satisfaction at the destination. Data analysis consisted of testing and verifying a model that ran on the aggregate sample of all respondents and eight models on eight national samples respectively. This two-stage process allowed us, on the one hand, to check whether the whole model was valid or not and, on the other, to examine whether the structural relationships between life satisfaction and tourist satisfaction were stable and robust across the eight national samples.

4. Results and discussion

4.1. Respondent profiles

Table 1 presents the sociodemographic profiles of the respondents. Of the 1,048 respondents surveyed, more than 55% were males. Married tourists accounted for nearly two-thirds of the respondents. The respondents were relatively young, with a combined 65.5% of the respondents between 25 and 44 years old, and a combined 21% or so between 45 and 64 years old. The respondents were well educated, with nearly 60% having obtained a college/university education and more than 25% having obtained a postgraduate education or above. As for occupation and employment, a vast majority of the respondents (82.5%) reported that they were employed before or during their most recent trip in Switzerland. Since the respondent samples from different countries were aggregated, which significantly reduced income disparities across these countries, the distribution of household income was relatively even compared to that of other sociodemographic attributes.

Table 1. Sociodemographic of the respondents (*N* = 1,048).

Category	N	%	Category	N	%
Gender			Primary/elementary school	10	1.0
Male	579	55.2	Secondary/high school	150	14.3
Female	469	44.8	College/university	616	58.8
Marital status			Postgraduate	254	24.2
Single	315	30.1	Other	13	1.2
Married	652	62.2	*Occupation*		
Divorced	26	2.5	Employed	865	82.5
Separated	10	1.0	Unemployed	23	2.2
Widowed	15	1.4	Retired	41	3.9
Other	30	2.9	Student	54	5.2
Age			Housewife	40	3.8
15–24	103	9.8	Other	25	2.4
25–34	402	38.4	*Household income[1]*		
35–44	284	27.1	Less than US$20,000	62	5.9
45–54	145	13.8	US$20,000–39,999	188	17.9
55–64	82	7.8	US$40,000–59,999	253	24.1
65 +	32	3.1	US$60,000–79,999	228	21.8
Education			US$80,000–99,999	149	14.2
No formal education	5	.5	US$100,000 or more	163	15.6

Missing values for household income.

4.2. Reliability and validity of the models

Table 2 presents the results of the measurement model tested on the aggregate sample. The factor loadings of all constructs were statistically significant and above the threshold value of .70, suggesting that the indicators exactly measured their corresponding constructs (Bagozzi & Yi, 1988; Hair, Hult, Ringle, & Sarstedt, 2014). The Cronbach's αs of all constructs far exceeded .70, indicating satisfactory internal consistency of the constructs (Nunnally, 1978; Nunnally & Bernstein, 1994). Composite reliability was also used to assess the internal consistency of the constructs as Cronbach's α tends to underestimate the internal consistency (Hair et al., 2014). The results show that the composite reliability of the four constructs exceeded the threshold value of .70 (Hair et al., 2014), indicating high levels of internal consistency. All four dependent constructs, except negative affect, were explained, to a substantial degree, by their predictors in the model. Specifically, 79.4% of the variance in tourist satisfaction was explained by its four predictors, namely life satisfaction, positive affect, negative affect, and destination image; 71.2% of the variance in destination image was explained by the three predictors; and 31.4% of the variance in positive affect was explained by life satisfaction.

Table 3 shows that the AVEs of all constructs far exceeded the cutoff value of .50 (Fornell & Larcker, 1981; Hair et al., 2014), indicating that the constructs had adequate and satisfactory convergent validity. Table 3 also shows that the square roots of all the constructs' AVEs were larger than the corresponding inter-construct correlation coefficients, indicating that the measurement model achieved satisfactory discriminant validity (Fornell & Larcker, 1981; Hair et al., 2014).

4.3. Effects of life satisfaction on tourist satisfaction

Table 4 shows the path coefficients of the nine models, namely one model on the aggregate sample and eight models on the eight national samples. All paths in the aggregate model were statistically significant and had expected signs. We found that

Table 2. Reliability of the measurement model (N = 1,048).

Indictor	Factor loading	rho_A	Composite reliability	Cronbach's a	R^2
Life satisfaction		.944	.948	.931	
Life close to ideal	.906***				
Conditions of life were excellent	.923***				
Satisfied with life	.913***				
Gotten the important things	.884***				
Would change almost nothing	.796***				
Positive affect		.938	.954	.936	.314
Relaxed	.914***				
Content	.935***				
Joyful	.934***				
Excited	.881***				
Negative affect		1.000	.978	.970	.006
Anxious	.926***				
Stressed	.959***				
Depressed	.978***				
Sad	.967***				
Destination image		.943	.954	.943	.712
Environment	.879***				
Landscape	.871***				
Weather	.855***				
Safe and secure	.899***				
People reliable and trustworthy	.910***				
People friendly and hospitable	.874***				
Tourist satisfaction		.915	.942	.908	.794
Overall satisfaction	.935***				
Comparison with expectations	.889***				
Comparison with ideal	.934***				

* p < .05, ** p < .01, *** p < .001.

Table 3. Validity of the measurement model (N = 1,048).

Construct	LS	PA	NA	DI	TS
Life satisfaction (LS)	(.886)				
Positive affect (PA)	.561	(.916)			
Negative affect (NA)	.077	−.128	(.958)		
Destination image (DI)	.558	.830	−.188	(.881)	
Tourist satisfaction (TS)	.559	.848	−.104	.853	(.919)
Average Variance Extracted (AVE)	.785	.840	.917	.777	.845

Values in parentheses are the square roots of the AVEs of the corresponding constructs.

four structural relationships were supported across almost all nine models, which were the associations between life satisfaction and positive affect, between positive affect and destination image, between positive affect and tourist satisfaction, and between destination image and tourist satisfaction. However, there was no compelling evidence to suggest that life satisfaction directly affects tourist satisfaction as this relationship was confirmed in three models only (aggregate, USA, and China). Even though in these three models the direct effects of life satisfaction on tourist satisfaction were statistically significant, the magnitude of these effects were negligible. Therefore, we conclude that there is no direct effect of life satisfaction on tourist satisfaction. The effects of life satisfaction on positive affect were statistically significant and strong, indicating that life satisfaction brings about positive emotions. In other words, happy tourists tend to generate more positive emotions through vacation participation at the destination.

4.4. Effects of affect on tourist satisfaction

The direct effect of life satisfaction on tourist satisfaction was not verified probably because of the mediation effects of positive affect and destination image in the model. We found that life satisfaction had a statistically positive effect on positive affect (Table 4). Among all the significant structural relationships was the positive one between life satisfaction and positive affect, which was pronounced in all nine models, indicating that happy tourists tend to have positive affect at the destination. Also, happy tourists were more likely to project a favorable image of the destination, and the relationship between life satisfaction and positive affect was among the strongest in the results. It is worth noting that there was a positive yet weak relationship between life satisfaction and negative affect, indicating that happy tourists may also encounter negative affect. This finding has been confirmed by a number of studies, suggesting that negative affect helps to strike an emotional balance that ultimately leads to happiness (Liu, Wang, & Lü, 2013; Moriwaki, 1974; Ryff, 1989).

We found that positive affect had strong effects on both destination image and tourist satisfaction with the destination (Table 4), indicating that positive affect helps tourists project a favorable image of the destination as well as makes them more satisfied with the destination. On the other hand, the effects of negative affect were either nonsignificant in some models or negatively associated with destination image (Table 4). Note that negative affect had a positive effect on tourist satisfaction, despite that the effect was negligible. In addition, we found that destination image had a statistically positive effect on tourist satisfaction. While travel activities may end up with negative emotions, which are either physically (such as fatigue), psychologically (sadness), or socially (loneliness) related, we found that these negative emotions, if anything, had negligible effects on tourist satisfaction.

As Figure 2 shows, among all the structural relationships, those between life satisfaction (LS), positive affect (PA), destination image (DI), and tourist satisfaction (TS) (LS → PA → DI → TS) were the most significant and robust across all nine models. This result suggests that life satisfaction at home affects tourist satisfaction at the destination only through the mediations of positive affect and destination image. By contrast, all structural relationships involving negative affect were either nonsignificant or extremely weak. As argued by Chen and Li (2018), tourists are reluctant to link their travel experience to negative affect, despite the fact that vacation can bring about negative emotions.

Table 4. Path estimates.

Path	All (N = 1048)	Germany (N = 105)	France (N = 105)	Italy (N = 105)	UK (N = 105)	USA (N = 157)	Canada (N = 157)	China (N = 157)	Japan (N = 157)
LS → PA	.561***	.533***	.625***	.433***	.346**	.460***	.551***	.731***	.480***
LS → NA	.077*	.016	.083	.253*	.153	.115	.204*	−.041	.065
LS → DI	.158***	.127	.205**	.163	.073	.071	.328***	.126*	.120
LS → TS	.050*	.010	.087	−.082	.046	.093*	.062	.104*	.078
PA → DI	.727***	.670***	.719***	.761***	.616***	.809***	.609***	.814***	.778***
PA → TS	.431***	.363***	.303**	.391**	.431***	.410***	.174	.623***	.656***
NA → DI	−.107***	−.206***	.037	−.111*	−.226**	−.090*	−.185***	−.022	−.039
NA → TS	.037**	.118**	.134**	.077	−.080	.117**	−.014	−.041	.025
DI → TS	.474**	.586***	.550***	.587***	.419***	.463***	.703***	.241*	.238*

LS = Life satisfaction, PA = Positive affect, NA = Negative affect, DI = Destination image, TS = Tourist satisfaction. * $p < .05$, ** $p < .01$, *** $p < .001$.

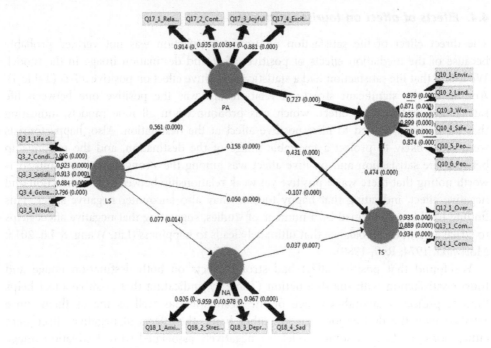

Figure 2. Estimated model (*N* = 1,048).

5. Conclusion

This study has shown that the effects of life satisfaction on tourist satisfaction were almost completely mediated by both positive affect and destination image. The strongest paths in the models were found between life satisfaction, positive affect, destination image, and tourist satisfaction. This result suggests that life satisfaction at home can be channeled to the destination through two mediators (experience-based affect and destination image) that are specific to tourist consumption. It also suggests that life satisfaction eventually affects tourist satisfaction. On the one hand, we found that life satisfaction was strongly associated with tourists' positive affect, and on the other hand, it lends support to the pivotal role of positive affect in determining tourist satisfaction at the destination. Not only does positive affect directly influence tourist satisfaction, but it also influences tourist satisfaction through affecting destination image. The pivotal role of positive affect is largely due to the fact that vacation is hedonic by its nature, and thus is strongly associated with positive affect. The hedonic nature of tourist consumption can also explain why negative affect has no role to play in our model: it does not affect tourist satisfaction even though negative affect is indeed associated with travel activities at the destination.

5.1. Theoretical implications

We have provided an alternative approach to studying customer satisfaction in general and tourist satisfaction in particular. This approach conjectures that tourist satisfaction evoked at the destination is originated from life satisfaction at home, and is augmented by positive affect at the destination. We conclude a series of mediations:

LS (life satisfaction) → PA (positive affect) → DI (destination image) → TS (tourist satisfaction). This framework conceptualizes customer satisfaction in the tourism context, in which intangible experiences triumph over tangible commodities. It implies that tourist satisfaction might be independent of service performance at the destination, a view that differs drastically from conventional customer satisfaction frameworks, which see satisfaction as being built upon the consumption of concrete commodities and a consequence of service quality. Our study has shown that tourist satisfaction can be seen as a spillover of life satisfaction associated with the destination. Since tourist consumption, above anything else, is a process and experience, transferring life satisfaction into tourist satisfaction requires tourists to experience the destination. Since tourist satisfaction is rooted in people's life satisfaction, it can be stationary across destinations but varies across the nationalities of tourists. Tourist satisfaction may also deviate from life satisfaction because tourists' affect and destination image vary from one destination to another.

Given the crucial role of affect in mediating the relationship between life satisfaction and tourist satisfaction, conventional customer satisfaction frameworks that do not encompass emotions may be insufficient to assess the outcome of tourist consumption. Therefore, recent studies in tourism advocate that tourist happiness might be a better measure of tourist fulfillment at the destination (Chen & Li, 2018; Filep, 2008; Filep & Deery, 2010). Since emotions are always associated with different travel experiences at the destination, the product/transaction-based satisfaction scale has little power in explaining tourist satisfaction without emotions at play. Recent research has shown that emotion, affect, and eudaimonia are the defining elements of tourist consumption (Chen & Li, 2018; Fritz & Sonnentag, 2006; Hosany, 2012; Kler & Tribe, 2012; Matteucci & Filep, 2017), which are absent in conventional consumption settings. Also, tourist experience is not necessarily associated with commercial hospitality establishments, which renders conventional customer satisfaction frameworks less applicable in the tourism context. Our study has shown that destination image matters to tourist satisfaction, which entails no transactions between tourists and suppliers at the destination.

5.2. Practical implications

This study suggests that customer satisfaction is not entirely determined by consumers' perception and expectation when they purchase a product or engage in a particular transaction. Customer satisfaction, at least in part, is rooted in people's life satisfaction prior to any consumption or experience, and therefore can be independent of product or service provision. Not only has this point been shed light on by happiness research in relation to the effect of happiness on consumer judgement (Lyubomirsky et al., 2005a; Mogilner et al., 2012), this study also provided evidence in the tourism context. This requires managers to factor life satisfaction in measuring customer satisfaction and tourist satisfaction, and thus assess to what extent tourist satisfaction, in particular, can be attributed to a product or service which managers can control. On the other hand, manages need to better understand life satisfaction of consumers and further segment tourists based not only on visible sociodemographic profiles but also on the levels of life satisfaction. A lot of happiness reports and statistics, such as the *World Happiness*

Report and *Gallup Life Satisfaction Survey*, to name a few, have already provided the information to the industry and firms.

Managers also need to bear in mind that the extent to which life satisfaction affects tourist happiness depends on the product or service that tourists consume or the travel activities that tourists undertake. We tested the model in the tourism context simply because tourist consumption can easily invoke emotion and is strongly associated with tourist happiness (Chen & Li, 2018). Studies also show that tourist experience with different activities can be measured on a continuum from hedonism to eudaimonia (Voigt et al., 2010), consumption or activities closely related to eudaimonia, for instance, would end up with higher levels of tourist satisfaction and happiness. Thus in product development, managers should focus on eliciting the eudaimonia dimension of a product or service offering, especially for consumers with higher life satisfaction in the first place. This helps channel life satisfaction at home to tourist satisfaction at the destination, and eventually augment tourist satisfaction.

5.3. Limitations

This study has a few limitations. First, since we adopted a cross-sectional research design, in which both life satisfaction in the pre-travel phase and tourist satisfaction in the post-travel phase were asked in a single survey after tourists concluded their travel activities, their responses to the questions of life satisfaction might still be affected by their travel experience at the destination. Despite the fact that we tried to avoid the reverse causality between life satisfaction and tourist satisfaction by dictating the sequence of the two types of questions, the reverse causality may still exist. If so, what we examined might be the effects of vacation and tourist satisfaction on life satisfaction, a predominant theme in tourist happiness studies (Chen & Li, 2018; Hoopes & Lounsbury, 1989; Kim & Woo, 2014; Neal et al., 1999, 2004, 2007). Second, while this study aimed to provide an alternative framework for customer satisfaction in the tourism context by referring to life satisfaction, the measure of tourist satisfaction was still grounded on the expectancy-disconfirmation framework. Therefore, the predictors in the model supposed to account for the new conceptualization of tourist satisfaction may not fully explain tourist consumption per se. Third, despite culture being closely related to life satisfaction, nowhere did we carry out a cross-cultural analysis of the relationship between life satisfaction and tourist satisfaction.

From a theoretical point of view, we would like draw the relevance of technology advancement to the study of life satisfaction at home and of tourist satisfaction at the destination. A perplexing issue is that on the one hand, people's high reliance on technology at home might be detrimental to their pursuit of happiness and life satisfaction – the antecedent of our conceptualization of customer/tourist satisfaction; on the other hand, people crave the convenience that technology, such as Wi-Fi connection and mobile payment, brings while traveling. Studies on the one side have indicated the adverse effect of technology that leads to depression and anxiety, thereby decreasing life satisfaction (Roberts & David, 2016), while on the other side have shown that tourists, especially Chinese, see technology as one of the most important elements in determining their satisfaction at the destination (Lee & Mills, 2007; Wang, So, & Sparks, 2017). As a matter fact, mainstream life satisfaction and happiness statistics, such as the *World Happiness Report*, have not yet to include technology as one dimension on which people's happiness at home is based. Future research should look at whether, and why, people view technology at home and at the destination differently in relation to their life satisfaction and tourist satisfaction, and, importantly how their views affect their travel experience at the destination.

Disclosure statement

No potential conflict of interest was reported by the author.

Funding

This work was funded by the University of Applied Sciences and Arts Western Switzerland, HES-SO under Grant N° SAGE-X: 42116.

References

Adaval, R. (2003). How good gets better and bad gets worse: Understanding the impact of affect on evaluations of known brands. *Journal of Consumer Research*, 30(3), 352–367.

Andersson, T. D. (2007). The tourist in the experience economy. *Scandinavian Journal of Hospitality and Tourism*, 7(1), 46–58.

Bagozzi, R. P., & Yi, Y. (1988). On the evaluation of structural equation model. *Journal of Academy of Marketing Science*, 16(1), 74–94.

Bigné, J. E., Sánchez, M. I., & Sánchez, J. (2001). Tourism image, evaluation variables and after purchase behaviour: Inter-relationship. *Tourism Management*, 22(6), 607–616.

Chan, L. K., Hui, Y. V., Lo, H. P., Tse, S. K., Tso, G. K., & Wu, M. L. (2003). Consumer satisfaction index: New practice and findings. *European Journal of Marketing*, 37(5/6), 872–909.

Chen, Y., & Li, R. (2018). Does a happy destination bring you happiness? Evidence from Swiss inbound tourism. *Tourism Management*, 65, 256–266.

Chen, Y., Schuckert, M., Song, H., & Chon, K. (2016). Why can package tours hurt tourists? Evidence from China's tourism demand in Hong Kong. *Journal of Travel Research*, 55(4), 427–439.

Churchill, G. A., & Surprenant, C. (1982). An investigation into the determinants of customer satisfaction. *Journal of Marketing Research*, 19(4), 491–504.

Cohen, E. (1972). Toward a sociology of international tourism. *Social Research*, 39(1), 164–182.

Cone, J., & Gilovich, T. (2010). Understanding money's limits: People's beliefs about the income-happiness correlation. *Journal of Positive Psychology*, 5(4), 294–301.

De Ruyter, K., Bloemer, J., & Peeters, P. (1997a). Merging service quality and service satisfaction: An empirical test of an integrative model. *Journal of Economic Psychology*, 18(4), 387–406.

De Ruyter, K., Wetzels, M., Lemmink, J., & Mattson, J. (1997b). The dynamics of the service delivery process: A value-based approach. *International Journal of Research in Marketing*, 14(3), 231–243.

Deaton, A. (2013). *The great escape: Health, wealth, and the origins of inequality*. Princeton, New Jersey: Princeton University Press.

Del Bosque, I. R., & Martín, H. S. (2008). Tourist satisfaction: A cognitive-affective model. *Annals of Tourism Research, 35*(2), 551–573.

Diener, E., Emmons, R. A., Larsen, R. J., & Griffin, S. (1985). The satisfaction with life scale. *Journal of Personality Assessment, 49*(1), 71–75.

Easterlin, R. A. (2001). Income and happiness: Towards a unified theory. *The Economic Journal, 111*(473), 465–484.

Easterlin, R. A. (2004). The economics of happiness. *Daedalus, 133*(2), 26–33.

Easterlin, R. A. (2013). Happiness, growth, and public policy. *Economic Inquiry, 51*(1), 1–15.

Federal Statistical Office (FSO). (2014). *Swiss Tourism Statistics 2013*. Neuchâtel: Office fédéral de la statistique.

Filep, S. (2008). Measuring happiness: A new look at tourist satisfaction. In S. Richardson, L. Fredline, A. Patiar, & M. Ternel (Eds.), *CAUTHE 2008: Tourism and hospitality research, training and practice: Where the 'bloody hell' are we?* (pp. 13–19). Gold Coast: Griffith University.

Filep, S., & Deery, M. (2010). Towards a picture of tourists' happiness. *Tourism Analysis, 15*(4), 399–410.

Forgas, J. P. (1990). Affective influences on individual and group judgments. *European Journal of Social Psychology, 20*(5), 441–453.

Forgas, J. P., & Ciarrochi, J. (2001). On being happy and possessive: The interactive effects of mood and personality on consumer judgments. *Psychology and Marketing, 18*(3), 239–260.

Fornell, C. (1992). A national customer satisfaction barometer: The Swedish experience. *Journal of Marketing, 56*(1), 6–21.

Fornell, C., & Larcker, D. F. (1981). Evaluating structural equation models with unobservable variables and measurement error. *Journal of Marketing Research, 18*(1), 39–50.

Fritz, C., & Sonnentag, S. (2006). Recovery, well-being, and performance-related outcomes: The role of workload and vacation experiences. *Journal of Applied Psychology, 91*(4), 936–945.

Gilbert, D., & Abdullah, J. (2004). Holidaytaking and the sense of well-being. *Annals of Tourism Research, 31*(1), 103–121.

Gillet, S., Schmitz, P., & Mitas, O. (2016). The snap-happy tourist: The effects of photographing behavior on tourists' happiness. *Journal of Hospitality & Tourism Research, 40*(1), 37–57.

Hair, J. F., Hult, G. T. M., Ringle, C. M., & Sarstedt, M. (2014). *A primer on partial least squares structural equation modeling (PLS-SEM)*. Thousand Oaks, CA: Sage.

Hair, J. F., Hult, G. T. M., Ringle, C. M., & Sarstedt, M. (2017). *A primer on partial least squares structural equation modeling (PLS-SEM)* (2nd ed.). Thousand Oaks, CA: Sage.

Halstead, D., Hartman, D., & Schmidt, S. L. (1994). Multisource effects on the satisfaction formation process. *Journal of the Academy of Marketing Science, 22*(2), 114–129.

Hoopes, L. L., & Lounsbury, J. W. (1989). An investigation of life satisfaction following a vacation: A domain-specific approach. *Journal of Community Psychology, 17*(2), 129–140.

Hosany, S. (2012). Appraisal determinants of tourist emotional responses. *Journal of Travel Research, 51*(3), 303–314.

Jenkins, O. H. (1999). Understanding and measuring tourist destination images. *International Journal of Tourism Research, 1*(1), 1–15.

Johns, H., & Ormerod, P. (2007). *Happiness, economics and public policy* (SSRN Scholarly Paper No. ID 1020246). Rochester, NY: Social Science Research Network. Retrieved from http://papers.ssrn.com/abstract=1020246

Kim, H., & Woo, E. (2014). An examination of missing links between quality of life and tourist motivation. *Tourism Analysis, 19*(5), 629–636.

Kler, B. K., & Tribe, J. (2012). Flourishing through scuba: Understanding the pursuit of dive experiences. *Tourism in Marine Environments, 8*(1–2), 19–32.

Lee, J., & Mills, J. (2007). Exploring tourist satisfaction with mobile technology. *Information and Communication Technologies in Tourism, 2007*, 141–152.

Liu, Y., Wang, Z., & Lü, W. (2013). Resilience and affect balance as mediators between trait emotional intelligence and life satisfaction. *Personality and Individual Differences, 54*(7), 850–855.

Lounsbury, J. W., & Hoopes, L. L. (1986). A vacation from work: Changes in work and nonwork outcomes. *Journal of Applied Psychology, 71*(3), 392–401.

Lyubomirsky, S., King, L., & Diener, E. (2005a). The benefits of frequent positive affect: Does happiness lead to success? *Psychological Bulletin, 131*(6), 803–855.

Lyubomirsky, S., Sheldon, K. M., & Schkade, D. (2005b). Pursuing happiness: The architecture of sustainable change. *Review of General Psychology, 9*(2), 111–131.

Matteucci, X., & Filep, S. (2017). Eudaimonic tourist experiences: The case of flamenco. *Leisure Studies, 36*(1), 39–52.

Mattsson, J. (1992). A service quality model based on an ideal value standard. *International Journal of Service Industry Management, 3*(3), 18–33.

McCabe, S., & Johnson, S. (2013). The happiness factor in tourism: Subjective well-being and social tourism. *Annals of Tourism Research, 41*(1), 42–65.

McCabe, S., Joldersma, T., & Li, C. (2010). Understanding the benefits of social tourism: Linking participation to subjective well-being and quality of life. *International Journal of Tourism Research, 12*(6), 761–773.

Mogilner, C., Aaker, J., & Kamvar, S. D. (2012). How happiness affects choice. *Journal of Consumer Research, 39*(2), 429–443.

Moriwaki, S. Y. (1974). The affect balance scale: A validity study with aged samples. *Journal of Gerontology, 29*(1), 73–78.

Nawijn, J. (2010a). Happiness through vacationing: Just a temporary boost or long-term benefits? *Journal of Happiness Studies, 12*(4), 651–665.

Nawijn, J. (2010b). The holiday happiness curve: A preliminary investigation into mood during a holiday abroad. *International Journal of Tourism Research, 12*(3), 281–290.

Nawijn, J., Marchand, M. A., Veenhoven, R., & Vingerhoets, A. J. (2010). Vacationers happier, but most not happier after a holiday. *Applied Research in Quality of Life, 5*(1), 35–47.

Neal, J. D. (2000). *The effects of different aspects of tourism services on travelers' quality of life: Model validation, refinement, and extension* (Doctoral dissertation). Virginia Tech.

Neal, J. D., Sirgy, M. J., & Uysal, M. (1999). The role of satisfaction with leisure travel/tourism services and experience in satisfaction with leisure life and overall life. *Journal of Business Research, 44*(3), 153–163.

Neal, J. D., Sirgy, M. J., & Uysal, M. (2004). Measuring the effect of tourism services on travelers' quality of life: Further validation. *Social Indicators Research, 69*(3), 243–277.

Neal, J. D., Uysal, M., & Sirgy, M. J. (2007). The effect of tourism services on travelers' quality of life. *Journal of Travel Research, 46*(2), 154–163.

Newman, D. B., Tay, L., & Diener, E. (2014). Leisure and subjective well-being: A model of psychological mechanisms as mediating factors. *Journal of Happiness Studies, 15*(3), 555–578.

Nunnally, J. (1978). *Psychometric theory* (2nd ed.). New York: McGraw-Hill.

Nunnally, J., & Bernstein, I. H. (1994). *Psychometric theory* (3rd ed.). New York: McGraw-Hill.

OECD. (2013). *OECD guidelines on measuring subjective well-being*. Author. doi:10.1787/9789264191655-en

Oliver, R. L. (1980). A cognitive model of the antecedents and consequences of satisfaction decisions. *Journal of Marketing Research, 17*(4), 460–469.

Pavot, W., & Diener, E. (2008). The satisfaction with life scale and the emerging construct of life satisfaction. *Journal of Positive Psychology, 3*(2), 137–152.

Roberts, J. A., & David, M. E. (2016). My life has become a major distraction from my cell phone: Partner phubbing and relationship satisfaction among romantic partners. *Computers in Human Behavior, 54*, 134–141.

Rust, R. T., & Oliver, R. L. (1994). Service quality: Insights and managerial implications from the frontier. In R. T. Rust & R. L. Oliver (Eds.), *Service quality: New directions in theory and practice* (pp. 1–19). Thousand Oaks, CA: Sage Publications.

Ryff, C. D. (1989). Happiness is everything, or is it? Explorations on the meaning of psychological well-being. *Journal of Personality and Social Psychology, 57*(6), 1069–1081.

Schwarz, N., & Clore, G. L. (1983). Mood, misattribution, and judgments of well-being: Informative and directive functions of affective states. *Journal of Personality and Social Psychology, 45*(3), 512–523.

Song, H., & Chon, K. (2015). *The Hong Kong tourist satisfaction index and tourism service quality index 2014*. The Hong Kong Polytechnic University. Retrieved from http://www.touristsatisfaction.org/uploads/1/6/5/1/16512380/tsi_tsqi_2014_report.pdf

Song, H., van der Veen, R., Li, G., & Chen, J. L. (2012). The Hong Kong tourist satisfaction index. *Annals of Tourism Research, 39*(1), 459–479.

Spreng, R. A., & Singh, A. K. (1993). An empirical assessment of the SERVQUAL scale and the relationship between service quality and satisfaction. In D. W. Cravens & P. R. Dickson (Eds.), *Enhancing knowledge development in marketing* (pp. 1–6). Chicago, IL: American Marketing Association.

Steyn, S., Saayman, M., & Nienaber, A. (2004). The impact of tourist and travel activities on facets of psychological well-being. *South African Journal for Research in Sport, Physical Education and Recreation, 26*(1), 97–106.

Stiglitz, J. E., Sen, A., & Fitoussi, J.-P. (2009). *Report by the commission on the measurement of economic performance and social progress*. Retrieved from http://www.voced.edu.au/content/ngv:44133

Strauss-Blasche, G., Ekmekcioglu, C., & Marktl, W. (2000). Does vacation enable recuperation? Changes in well-being associated with time away from work. *Occupational Medicine, 50*(3), 167–172.

Telisman-Kosuta, N. (1989). Tourist destination image. In S. F. Witt & L. Moutinho (Eds.), *Tourism marketing & management handbook* (pp. 557–561). Cambridge, UK: Prentice Hall.

Tsaur, S.-H., Yen, C.-H., & Hsiao, S.-L. (2013). Transcendent experience, flow and happiness for mountain climbers. *International Journal of Tourism Research, 15*(4), 360–374.

Voigt, C., Howat, G., & Brown, G. (2010). Hedonic and eudaimonic experiences among wellness tourists: An exploratory enquiry. *Annals of Leisure Research, 13*(3), 541–562.

Wang, Y., So, K. K. F., & Sparks, B. A. (2017). Technology readiness and customer satisfaction with travel technologies: A cross-country investigation. *Journal of Travel Research, 56*(5), 563–577.

Wright, W. F., & Bower, G. H. (1992). Mood effects on subjective probability assessment. *Organizational Behavior and Human Decision Processes, 52*(2), 276–291.

Relationship between Hotels' Website Quality and Consumers' Booking Intentions with Internet Experience as Moderator

Liang Wang and Rob Law ⓘ

ABSTRACT

This study examines how perceived hotel website attributes influence consumers' booking intentions. From a dynamic view, this study integrates privacy, security and consumers' perceived protection against online purchasing risks into the empirical model obtained from existing literature. Moreover, consumers' Internet experiences, as a dynamic learning process, are considered a moderator in the relationship between website quality and booking intentions. Empirical results support the expected hypotheses concerning the effects of website dimensions on booking intentions wherein website usability and booking intentions are the strongest. Moreover, the power law of practice exists as daily and yearly Internet experience can moderate such causal relationship. Implications for hoteliers and future researchers are also presented at the end of this article.

酒店网站感知质量与在线预订意向关系研究:以网络使用经验为调节变量

摘要

本研究探讨了消费者酒店网站感知质量对在线预订意向的影响机制。基于动态视角, 本研究以隐私, 安全性和消费者感知风险作为自变量, 在线预订意向为因变量, 提出假设并建立模型。此外, 本研究认为消费者的网络使用经验是一种动态的学习过程, 因此, 本研究假设消费者的网络使用经验会调节消费者网站质量感知与预订意向之间的因果关系。通过分析大样本调查数据, 我们发现网站质量的三个维度对消费者预订意向均具有显著影响, 其中网站可用性对预订意向的影响程度最高。此外, 消费者的日均和年均上网经历均会调节感知质量对预订意向的影响。在文章末尾, 本研究提出了相关实践建议以及研究展望。

Introduction

Information communication technologies (ICTs), particularly the Internet, have revolutionized business modes and operations in tourism and hospitality industries (Law, Qi, & Buhalis, 2010). Amongst various tourism-related sectors, hotels have the most use for the Internet. Specifically, the Internet allows hotels to adopt a portfolio of distribution channels, from direct selling channels (e.g. toll-free numbers and hotel websites) to outsourced parties (e.g. online travel agencies [OTAs] and traditional travel agencies) (O'Connor & Frew, 2002; Xu, He, & Hua, 2015). As a natural extension of offline marketing efforts, the Internet offers various marketing tools, including websites, advertising banners, social networks and online videos (Pozniak, 2015). Hence, modern hotels have launched their own websites with booking channels to encourage direct selling, decrease their distribution cost, increase their control over price dispersion and prevent brand erosion (Morosan & Jeong, 2008).

Given the importance of websites, considerable academic efforts have been exerted to examine website utilization in various hotel operations (e.g. Law & Chen, 2012; Law & Hsu, 2006). Although existing research has aided in understanding website utilization, the dynamic aspects of websites have been overlooked. More specifically, after years of development, hotel websites have evolved from a mere electronic brochure to a transactional and relational platform (Law & Wong, 2010). Currently, hotel websites can process online transactions in real time (Tse, 2013). However, virtual communities magnify the threat of online vendors' opportunistic behaviors such as misuse of personal information and credit card fraud (Shen & Chiou, 2010). Hence, to argue that the financial security and privacy of websites are as important as website usability and functionality in influencing consumers' behavioral intentions and actual behaviors is reasonable. Therefore, we hypothesize elements of security and privacy which also exist in hotel website quality. Moreover, we examine the impacts of website quality on consumers' hotel booking behavior as our first research objective.

Furthermore, after approximately three decades since the launch of commercial Internet applications in the early 1990s (Law et al., 2010), the Internet has subsequently become an intrinsic part of people's lives (Das & Sahoo, 2011). Based on the power law of practice, Johnson, Bellman, and Lohse (2003) have suggested that learning is important in virtual environments wherein future behaviors could further reinforce initial practices. Likewise, Lehto, O'Leary, and Morrison (2004) have mentioned that consumer behaviors are partially influenced by people's past experiences which will help offset perceived risks and uncertainties. Therefore, experiences and prior knowledge of Internet usage influence consumers' perceptions, attitudes and behaviors in various virtual communities (Blake, Neuendorf, & Valdiserri, 2003). However, only few studies in the hospitality context have specifically considered customers' Internet experience as a moderating variable. Thus, the second objective of this study is to identify the moderating effect of consumers' Internet experiences.

Conceptual framework and hypothesis development

Hotel website quality

To serve targeted markets better, hotels must have a more in-depth understanding of website quality, which is a crucial determinant of e-commerce success (Kim & Niehm, 2009). Defined as the 'overall excellence or effectiveness [of a website] in delivering intended messages to its audience and viewers' (Jeong, Oh, & Gregoire, 2003, p. 162), website quality has been repeatedly regarded as a multi-dimensional concept. However, particular dimensions may vary relative to the research objectives. Loiacono, Watson, and Goodhue (2002) conceptualized usefulness, ease of use, entertainment and complimentary relationship as the underlying dimensions of website quality which work under the framework of the widely adopted technology acceptance model. Likewise, Kim and Niehm (2009) have stated that website quality should be interpreted from the aspects of information, security, ease of use, enjoyment and service quality.

Following research streams from other disciplines whilst considering the particularities of tourism and hospitality industries, scholars have contributed to website utilization literature from a relatively novel perspective. As one of the earliest studies concerning this topic, Au Yeung and Law (2004) have found that when consumers' perceptions are considered, website quality can be divided into two aspects: system and information quality. The former aspect involves website usability, whereas the latter focuses on functionality. Specifically, website usability pertains 'to what extent a website is efficient and enjoyable for its products/services being promoted', whereas website functionality refers to 'the degree of information provision about the website's services/products' (Au Yeung & Law, 2004, p. 309). This dual-dimension conceptualization is repeatedly adopted by subsequent researchers. Following this dual-dimension framework, Bai, Law, and Wen (2008) have empirically investigated the effects of these two dimensions on the purchase intentions of Chinese Internet users. Kim, Ma, and Kim (2006) have defined website quality as constituting information that needs satisfaction, service performance and reputation, convenience, price benefits, technological inclination and safety which determine the purchase intentions of customers by examining 12 hotels in Beijing, China. However, Kim et al. (2006) have considered purchase intentions, instead of re-purchase intentions or actual purchase behaviors of existing customers, as a dependent variable. Moreover, Liu and Zhang (2014) have comparatively examined factors affecting customers' selection of online booking channels (OTA vs. hotel websites). The results of the comparison show that OTAs perform better than hotel websites in two out of three selected aspects, except for website quality.

However, this widely adopted dual-dimension framework overlooks the dynamic nature of website utilization in the hotel industry. Booking a room online usually requires consumers to provide their personal and financial information, such as IDs and credit card numbers. Therefore, transactions conducted on hotel websites normally require consumers to provide their personal information and usually involve high ticket prices that entail higher risks in terms of finance and privacy. Researchers have emphasized the critical roles of Internet security in consumers' decision-making (e.g. Lang, 2000), whereas several research efforts could be highlighted in examining the antecedents of privacy and security (e.g. Lee & Cranage, 2011) and their influence on trust (Escobar-Rodíguez & Carvajal-Trujillo, 2013; Kim, Chung, & Lee, 2011).

Law and Hsu (2006) have empirically found elements of hotel websites that can impress consumers in different ways. These various website dimensions will then have varying influences on consumers' behavioral intentions (Law & Hsu, 2006). Except for the study of Bai et al. (2008), a few studies have simultaneously examined the effects of individual website dimensions on online booking intentions. However, Bai et al. (2008), have failed to consider security and privacy features. O'Connor (2007) has analyzed the privacy practices of hotel websites, offering outlined information on the hotel usage of customer data. A follow-up study has revealed that hotels in the US are the most ethical users of customers' personal data (O'Connor, 2008). Therefore, an intriguing and practically important question is raised: how do Internet users consider the effects of privacy and security features in their decision-making? This study aims to provide answers to this question by proposing three compositions of hotel website quality, namely, functionality, usability and privacy and security, and by empirically investigating the indicative ability of these dimensions to Internet users' booking intentions.

Online booking intentions

Understanding behavioral intentions of consumers is important because their actions are a function of their intentions (Grewal, Krishnan, Baker, & Borin, 1998). Around five decades ago, scholars found that measures of behavioral intentions were, to some extent, superior in understanding the psychology of consumers because actual behaviors could be influenced by other stimuli, such as discounts and coupons, instead of by genuine preferences (Day, 1969). The accessibility to data of behavioral intentions also contributes to the widespread adoption of consumers' intention measures that have been regarded as a 'routine application in consumer research investigations' (Kalwani & Silk, 1982, p. 243).

Previous studies in the hospitality field have examined numerous specific behavioral intentions, including consumers' online booking intentions. In today's competitive market, increases in room bookings performed online, such as in websites of hotels, have numerous benefits including lower costs (Wong & Law, 2005), non-existing physical and geographical barriers (Li, Li, He, Ward, & Davies, 2011) and reduced dependence on intermediaries (Starkov, 2002). Therefore, understanding consumers' booking intentions has increasingly become necessary. Moreover, such knowledge certainly helps increase the effectiveness of marketing activities aimed at boosting online sales.

The connection amongst the quality of hotel websites, hotels' key online distribution channels and online booking intentions has gained extensive attention from the academia. Jeong et al. (2003) have indicated that website quality can predict customer satisfaction with online information, which determines customers' online behavioral intentions. Law and Hsu (2006) have emphasized the importance of website quality in travelers' search for high-quality accommodations during their trip planning stage. More recently, Wang, Chan, and Pan (2015) have used Singapore as a case example wherein they looked into the impact of mass media on tourists' intention to travel.

Consumers' internet experiences

Investigations on consumers' decisions in an online environment have revealed that the consumer's Internet experience is crucial in influencing the attitudes, perceptions and behaviors of other consumers. Generally, users with more extensive Internet experience possess the skills and confidence to use the Internet for a broader range of activities, from communication to entertainment (Citrin, Sprott, Silverman, & Stem, 2000). Nysveen and Pedersen (2004) have suggested that the moderating effects of users' general experience with Internet should be considered to investigate the effectiveness of the website features efficiently. Liang and Huang (1998) have observed that consumers' concerns vary based on their experience with the web. Specifically, inexperienced users are concerned about asset specificity and uncertainty of the product and process, whereas experienced users are only bothered by the latter. Bruner and Kumar (2000) have designed an experiment wherein the results suggest that Internet experience is as important as the website design and that both significantly influence the hierarchy of effects in web advertising.

Other researchers go beyond the concept of Internet experience and use proxies for the discussion. Yoon (2002) has used two personal variables, namely, familiarity and prior satisfaction with e-commerce to represent Internet experience, which precede perceived consumer trust and satisfaction. In the tourism context, Law (2009) has found that online purchase experiences determine whether online buyers are for or against the disintermediation of hotel reservations. Accordingly, studies investigating consumer behavioral intentions in the online context must also consider Internet experience.

Consistent with the studies of Chang and Chen (2008) and Nysveen and Pedersen (2004), Internet experience in the present study pertains to users' experience with websites in general rather than with a specific website. A number of studies have repeatedly concluded that users with significant experiences in certain products are more likely to adopt new related products (e.g. Citrin et al., 2000; Gefen, Karahanna, & Straub, 2003; Ward & Lee, 2000). This conclusion is logical because experienced users are equipped with sufficient knowledge to judge the quality of products/services. Furthermore, heavy Internet users are prone to use the Internet as a shopping platform. From the data collected from a survey of university students, Citrin et al. (2000) have empirically supported the proposed positive relationship between Internet usage and online shopping intentions.

Hypothesis development

Websites have become the main communication channels between consumers and organizations (Sharp, 2002). The marketing effectiveness of a website in delivering product/service-related messages and in constructing images is dependent on its design (Baloglu & Pekcan, 2006). In the tourism and hospitality contexts, travelers usually search for relevant information prior to embarking on their trip. Therefore, the usefulness of websites as marketing tools is relative to their web content. Meanwhile, previous literature also emphasizes the importance of information quality to company performance and business profitability (Mukhopadhyay, Kekre, & Kalathur, 1995). Chung and Law (2003) have identified a vast discrepancy amongst hotels in using their own websites as a marketing tool. Then, they have concluded that good management of online information in websites can bring marketing competitiveness to hotels (Chung & Law, 2003). Similarly, Wong and Law (2005) have empirically supported the viewpoint that the quality of online information is a principal motivator for travelers to book rooms via hotel websites. The results of another empirical study conducted by Bai et al. (2008) have also supported the proposed positive relationship between website information and customer satisfaction. This relationship ultimately determines purchase intentions.

Whilst acknowledging the critical roles of information presented on Internet, hotel marketers must also focus on the aspect of ease of use. Previous studies, such as Murphy, Forrest, Wotring, and Brymer (1996), have shown that providing customers with the easiest and most rewarding access to relevant information is as important as the content in the marketing strategy of differentiation. Moreover, the Internet has become a transaction platform that requires consumers to provide information such as credit card numbers and other personal information. To assure consumers that their private information are discreetly used and protected, online sellers present explicit statements, including privacy and security statements, on their websites. Palmer, Bailey, and Faraj (2000) have found that the use of trusted third parties and privacy statements can increase consumers' confidence on websites for business purposes. Therefore, to understand the online behavior of customers, Nysveen and Pedersen (2004) have suggested consumers' Internet experiences be used as a moderating variable in examining the performance of e-commerce sites.

Based on the above discussions, the following hypotheses have been formulated:

H1: Consumers' perceptions on website usability positively affect their online booking intentions.

H2: Consumers' perceptions on website functionality positively affect their online booking intentions.

H3: Consumers' perceptions on privacy and security positively affect their online booking intentions.

H4(a): The effects of website usability on online booking intentions are greater (fewer) for consumers with more (less) Internet experience.

H4(b): The effects of website functionality on online booking intentions are greater (fewer) for consumers with more (less) Internet experience.

H4(c): The effects of privacy and security on online booking intentions will be greater (fewer) for consumers with more (less) Internet experience.

As shown in Figure 1, these six hypotheses comprise the conceptual framework of this study.

Methodology

Measurement development

A questionnaire survey was employed to obtain empirical data on responses that would approve or disapprove the proposed inter-variable relationships above. The questionnaire development process started with the literature review for an initial list of measurement items. The current study mainly referred to Au Yeung and Law (2004), Chung and Law (2003), Law and Hsu (2006) and Bai et al. (2008), in which scales were empirically verified as statistically reliable and valid. The reexamination of the measurement scales from previous studies, particularly those from attitude studies, could increase their explanatory power (Hair, Black, Babin, Anderson, & Tatham, 2010; Sirakaya, Teye, & Sönmez, 2002).

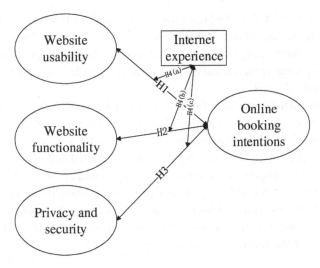

Figure 1. Conceptual framework of the study.

The scales we referred to were not targeted at Chinese Internet users. Thus, we conducted additional in-depth interviews and two online surveys to refine the measures obtained in the literature. The respondents were four hotel marketing practitioners and eight experienced Internet users who were also well-informed travelers. The interviews mainly aimed at reviewing literature-based measurement items in terms of retention and deletion. Particularly, certain interviewees emphasized the necessity of including information on privacy policy relating to the collection, usage, storage and disclosure of customers' personal data and secured online payment system. This study followed suggestions from the interview participants and added items for privacy and security, all of which were retained as measures of the privacy and security dimension in the final model.

The willingness of consumers to book their rooms online was recorded to measure their online booking intentions. Previous literature also used the behavioral willingness of consumers to examine their online purchase intentions (e.g. Wu & Liu, 2007). Similarly, the present study used behavioral willingness in measuring the online booking intentions of consumers. The recommendation of Sheppard, Hartwick, and Warshaw (1988) was also considered in which the specific timeframe was included to assess intention using estimated performance. All items were measured using a seven-point Likert scale, ranging from 1 (strongly disagree) to 7 (strongly agree). A seven-point Likert scale is more sensitive and more reliable than a five-point Likert scale (Cummins & Gullone, 2000). More importantly, increasing the number of choices can better capture the differences in the participants' responses (Preston & Colman, 2000).

In measuring Internet experience, the present study followed the method of Morosan and Jeong (2008), who asked respondents to specify the number of hours they spent daily on surfing and browsing the Internet. Ward and Lee (2000) mentioned that consumers with more years of Internet experience were more efficient in searching for information online. To explore the determinants of e-satisfaction and purchase intentions of Chinese online consumers, Kim et al. (2006) used the yearly length of Internet use to differentiate experienced from inexperienced Internet users. Therefore, this study also asked the respondents about their yearly Internet usage. Likewise, the initial questionnaire solicited information on demographic characteristics, namely, gender, age, education level and monthly disposable income.

Given that the participants were from Mainland China, the questionnaire was translated into simplified Chinese by a native Mandarin speaker specializing on the English language. Afterward, a Ph.D. student in Marketing, who was also fluent in English, translated the questionnaire back to English. The back-translated version was compared with the initial questionnaire to minimize language-related errors. Before the pilot test, a pretest was conducted amongst a group of tourism and hospitality graduate students and a total of 11 Chinese Internet users. Minor revisions on the ambiguous wording in the questionnaire were subsequently implemented. For example, 'time frame of 12 months' replaced the term, 'in the near future'.

Pilot test

This study focused on Internet users. Therefore, conducting online surveys was appropriate. We commissioned a survey company, Sojump (URL: www.sojump.com), for data collection during the pilot test and main survey. At the pilot test stage, a total of 422 valid questionnaires were collected. The pilot test aimed to diagnose problems on the proposed measurement scales. An exploratory factor analysis was then conducted using SPSS 20. The results of the analysis are presented in Table 1. Factor loadings and eigenvalues were used to delete/retain certain items. Items with factor loadings equal to or larger than 0.5 were included, and factors with eigenvalues equal to or larger than 1 were considered significant (Hair et al., 2010).

As expected, a three-factor solution for hotel website quality was generated. Specifically, six items were loaded on the first factor of website quality, namely, 'website usability', which pertains to the efforts of consumers in navigating a website. The factor loadings of these six measures ranged from 0.59 to 0.808, which explained more than 60% of the variances. Five other items were loaded on the second factor, namely, 'website functionality', which is related to the information presented on a website. These items explained more than 50% of the variances and had factor loadings ranging from 0.591 to 0.736. The remaining three items were loaded on the third factor, namely, 'security and privacy', which explained 70% of the variances. The proposed four items of online booking intentions were loaded on a single factor, and more than 70% of the variances were explained. The factor loadings ranged from 0.775 to 0.875, which exceeded the cutoff value of 0.5.

The reliability of each individual scale was further examined for their item-to-total correlations. That is, the relationship of an item to the total score and Cronbach's alpha values. Table 1 shows that all traits have relatively high item-to-total correlations ranging from 0.444 to 0.755. These estimates exceeded the cutoff value of 0.25 that was used in previous studies (e.g. Kusluvan & Kusluvan, 2000) to assess scale reliability. All Cronbach's alpha values were higher than the cutoff point of 0.6 (Hair et al., 2010), indicating the satisfactory internal consistency of the multi-item scales in assessing the variables of interest.

Table 1. Summary of measurement scales.

Measurement items	Factor loadings	Item-to-total correlations	Eigenvalues	Cronbach's alpha
Hotel website usability			3.738	0.876
U1 Clear language	0.740	0.740		
U2 Easily understandable information	0.779	0.742		
U3 User-friendly layout	0.808	0.643		
U4 well-organized information	0.798	0.751		
U5 Graphics matched with texts	0.590	0.605		
U6 Simple website navigation (e.g. menu or site map)	0.628	0.619		
Hotel website functionality			2.542	0.753
F1 Hotel reservation information	0.591	0.444		
F2 Hotel facilities information	0.729	0.529		
F3 Information of promotions/special offers	0.586	0.509		
F4 Price information of hotel rooms	0.736	0.607		
F5 Information of destinations where the hotels are located	0.650	0.525		
Security and privacy			2.116	0.787
SP1 Privacy policy relating to customers' personal data	0.832	0.561		
SP2 Information on a secured online payment system	0.727	0.679		
SP3 Information on third-party recognition	0.710	0.648		
Online booking intentions			2.822	0.861
OPI1 I will likely book hotel rooms from hotel websites in the next 12 months	0.775	0.623		
OPI2 I will possibly book hotel rooms from hotel websites in the next 12 months	0.837	0.706		
OPI3 I am willing to book hotel rooms from hotel websites	0.875	0.755		
OPI4 I plan to book hotel rooms from hotel websites	0.869	0.746		

KMO = 0.914, Chi-square = 2566.803,
Bartlett's Test of Sphericity: df = 91, Sig. = 0.000;
Total variance explained = 61.028
Rotation Method: Varimax with Kaiser Normalization. Rotation converged in 5 iterations.

After securing the reliability of measurement scales, the main survey was conducted on the same online platform, Sojump. The respondents in the pilot test were excluded from the main survey to ensure research rigor. A total of 842 questionnaires were collected. Additionally, the data obtained from the survey underwent hierarchical regression analysis to achieve a clear explanation on the existence of moderator effects (Arnold & Evans, 1979). Prior to regression analysis, AMOS 20.0 was used to verify the reliability and validity of the proposed measurement models. Detailed results of the data analysis are presented in the subsequent sections.

Data analysis results

Sample profiles

Table 2 presents the demographic profile of the respondents in the main survey. Approximately 47.1% of the participants were males. Moreover, almost half of these respondents were aged from 26 to 35 years old. More than 80% were university graduates, and more than 40% earned over CNY 6,000 per month (USD 1 = CNY 6.19) (Travelex, 2015). Overall, the respondents in this study were generally young, middle-aged, earning a satisfactory income and had a decent educational background.

Table 2. Demographic profiles of respondents.

Demographic characteristics	Frequency	Percentage (%)
Gender		
Male	397	47.1
Female	445	52.9
Age		
Below 18 years old	2	0.24
18–25 years old	251	29.81
26–35 years old	403	47.86
36–45 years old	149	17.70
46–55 years old	32	3.80
56 – 65 years old	5	0.59
Education		
Below secondary/high school	3	0.4
Completed secondary/high school	64	7.6
Completed college/university diploma/degree	710	84.3
Completed postgraduate degree	65	7.7
Average monthly income (CNY)		
3,000 or below	118	14.01
3,001–6,000	346	41.09
6,001–9,000	200	23.75
9,001–12,000	104	12.35
12,001 or above	38	4.51
No salary/refused to answer	36	4.28

Reliability and validity tests

Confirmatory factor analysis was performed using AMOS 20.0 software to verify construct validity. The results of the analysis are presented in Tables 3 and 4. Construct validity refers to 'the extent to which an operationalisation of a construct actually measures what it purports to measure' (John & Reve, 1982, p. 520). Construct validity can be examined using three criteria, namely, reliability, convergent validity and discriminant validity. The reliability test verifies the extent to which an instrument is reliable and remains consistent in various contexts (Nunnally, 1978). The composite reliability ranged between 0.752 and 0.880; indicating adequate reliability.

This study further examined convergent and discriminant validities. Convergent validity tests the extent to which the items that measure the same construct are correlated, whereas discriminant validity tests verify inter-variable correlations (Anderson & Gerbing, 1988). Convergent validity is ensured if the factor loadings and average variance extracted (AVE) are larger than the 0.5 threshold (Hair et al., 2010). Table 3 shows that all factor loadings and AVE values are close to or larger than 0.5, thus suggesting a statistically acceptable convergent validity. To ensure satisfactory discriminant validity, inter-construct correlations should be lower than 0.85 (Kline, 2005). Following the suggestion from Chin (1998), this study went further to examine discriminant validity by comparing the square root of the AVE of each variable to the correlation coefficients of the specific construct with any other constructs. The results in Table 4 show that the square roots of AVE estimates are greater than corresponding correlations, thereby indicating acceptable discriminant validity. Table 5 shows that the correlations between two random variables are below the cutoff values. The relatively low correlations at below the critical value of 0.75 further confirmed the absence of the multicollinearity problem amongst the independent variables (Tsui, Ashford, Clair, & Xin, 1995).

Table 3. Validity and reliability tests of measurement models.

Measurement items	Factor loadings	AVE	Composite reliability
Website usability		**0.550**	**0.880**
U1 Clear language	0.757		
U2 Easily understandable information	0.766		
U3 User-friendly layout	0.755		
U4 well-organized information	0.818		
U5 Graphics matched with texts	0.686		
U6 Simple website navigations (e.g. menu or site map)	0.657		
Website functionality		**0.380**	**0.752**
F1 Hotel reservation information	0.640		
F2 Hotel facilities information	0.678		
F3 Information of promotions/special offers	0.552		
F4 Price information of hotel rooms	0.604		
F5 Information of destinations where the hotels are located	0.599		
Security and privacy		**0.574**	**0.797**
SP1 Privacy policy relating to customers' personal data	0.567		
SP2 Information on a secured online payment system	0.806		
SP3 Information on third-party recognition	0.867		
Online booking intentions		**0.511**	**0.799**
OBI1 I will likely book hotel rooms from hotel websites in the next 12 months	0.498		
OBI2 I will possibly book hotel rooms from hotel websites in the next 12 months	0.588		
OBI3 I am willing to book hotel rooms from hotel websites	0.846		
OBI4 I plan to book hotel rooms from hotel websites	0.856		

$\chi^2(df) = 418.572$ (73); RMR = 0.055; GFI = 0.935; NFI = 0.922; CFI = 0.935; TLI = 0.918; RMSEA = 0.075

Table 4. Correlation coefficients among variables.

	Mean	S.D.	WU	WF	PS	OBI
Website usability (WU)	5.86	0.71	**0.74**			
Website functionality (WF)	5.56	0.84	0.56**	**0.62**		
Privacy and security (PS)	5.88	0.98	0.47**	0.55**	**0.76**	
Online booking intentions (OBI)	5.23	0.73	0.36**	0.30**	0.25**	**0.71**

** denotes that the correlation is significant at the 0.01 level (two-tailed). Diagonal values (in bold) are the square roots of AVEs.

After securing sale reliability and validity, hierarchical regression was adopted to test the hypotheses. Cohen and Cohen (1983) suggested that the interaction variables should be integrated into the models after the addition of corresponding elements to differentiate the main effects from the interaction effects. Accordingly, a three-step regression was conducted to investigate the effects of website quality on online booking intentions and the moderating roles of daily and yearly Internet usage in these relationships. Prior to regression analysis, the continuous moderator variables were centered to reduce multicollinearity and to provide unbiased parameter estimates (Aiken & West, 1991).

Previous studies discussed the effects of demographic factors on consumers' online behaviors (e.g. Keaveney & Parthasarathy, 2001; Li, Kuo, & Rusell, 1999; Wu, 2003). Therefore, demographic characteristics (i.e. gender, age, educational background and monthly disposable salary) were treated as control variables and introduced into the regression model in the first step. The main effects of three independent variables (i.e. website usability, website functionality and privacy and security) and two moderating variables (i.e. daily/yearly Internet experience) were then tested in the second step. In the

Table 5. Results of multiple regression tests.

	IED		IEY		VIF	
	Model 1	Model 2	Model 3	Model 4	IED	IEY
Gender	−0.002	−0.008	0.001	−0.006	1.084	1.072
Age	−0.033	−0.027	−0.027	−0.028	1.076	1.145
Education	−0.046	−0.024	−0.036	−0.045	1.070	1.082
Salary	0.011	0.010	0.010	0.008	1.076	1.078
WU	0.204***	0.210***	0.187***	0.191***	1.017	1.016
IED	0.008	0.007			1.016	
IEY			−0.002	−0.002		1.118
WU * IED		0.036**			1.017	
WU * IEY				0.027**		1.005
					Durbin–Watson	
R^2	0.043	0.052	0.042	0.053	1.910	2.046
ΔR^2	0.042	0.009	0.041	0.011		
F-value	6.213	6.560	6.104	6.694		

	IED		IEY		VIF	
	Model 7	Model 8	Model 9	Model 10	IED	IEY
Gender	−0.044	−0.043	−0.040	−0.042	1.090	1.081
Age	0.028	0.026	0.028	0.028	1.080	1.153
Education	−0.052	−0.049	−0.045	−0.044	1.063	1.080
Salary	0.007	0.008	0.007	0.007	1.078	1.077
WF	0.284***	0.284***	0.259***	0.261***	1.032	1.031
IED	0.001	0.001			1.021	
IEY			−0.002	−0.002		1.117
WF * IED		0.013			1.005	
WF * IEY				0.006		1.005
					Durbin–Watson	
R^2	0.079	0.081	0.079	0.080	1.905	1.958
ΔR^2	0.079	0.001	0.078	0.001		
F-value	12.015	10.484	11.954	10.305		

	IED		IEY		VIF	
	Model 11	Model 12	Model 13	Model 14	IED	IEY
Gender	−0.017	−0.018	−0.011	−0.012	1.088	1.075
Age	−0.012	−0.011	−0.009	−0.011	1.065	1.139
Education	−0.032	−0.032	−0.024	−0.024	1.063	1.083
Salary	0.015	0.015	0.013	0.013	1.074	1.076
PS	0.164***	0.164***	0.149***	0.154***	1.009	1.026
IED	0.010	0.011			1.019	
IEY			−0.001	−0.002		1.119
PS * IED		−0.011			1.003	
PS * IEY				0.011		1.021
					Durbin–Watson	
R^2	0.028	0.029	0.027	0.029	1.948	1.951
ΔR^2	0.027	0.001	0.026	0.002		
F-value	4.015	3.545	3.890	3.524		

** denotes $p \leq 0.01$, whereas *** denotes $p \leq 0.001$. WU is abbreviated for website usability, WF is for website functionality, PS is for privacy and security, IED is for daily Internet experience and IEY is for yearly Internet experience.

third step, all independent variables, moderating variables and the interactions between the predictors and moderating variables were included in the model. The regression results are presented in Table 5.

Models 1, 2 and 3 evaluate daily Internet usage, whereas Models 4, 5 and 6 evaluate yearly Internet usage. The last two columns report the scores of the variance inflation factors (VIF). The VIF examines the extent to which the non-orthogonality amongst the independent and moderator variables inflates the standard errors. In the models, the VIF estimates ranged from 1.003 to 1.153 which were well below the recommended cutoff value of 10 (Neter, Wasserman, & Kutner, 1985). Therefore, this study was free of multicollinearity problems. Autocorrelation was then tested using Durbin–Watson statistics. A Durbin–Watson value that is close to 0 indicates a strong positive correlation, whereas a value of 4 indicates a strong negative correlation (Durbin & Watson, 1971). Table 5 shows that the Durbin–Watson values of all models range from 1.905 to 1.954, indicating the absence of autocorrelation.

Main effects of independent and moderator variables

Prior to examining the main effects of independent and moderator variables, the effects of the designated control variables, which were statistically insignificant, were determined. After including website usability and daily Internet usage, the explanatory power of the regression model significantly increased ($F = 6.213$, $p \leq 0.001$). The same positive changes were observed when yearly Internet experience was considered ($F = 6.104$, $p \leq 0.001$). The main effects of website usability on consumers' booking intentions in the models were positively significant ($ß = 0.204, 0.187$, $p \leq 0.001$), thus supporting H1. The introduction of website functionality and daily Internet usage into the model also significantly increased the explanatory ability of the regression model ($F = 12.015$, $p \leq 0.001$). The model further improved when website functionality and yearly Internet usage were included ($F = 11.954$, $p \leq 0.001$). The regression results indicated that website functionality with regression coefficients of 0.284 and 0.259 that were considered significant at 0.001 level was a strong predictor of online booking intentions. Therefore, H2 is statistically supported. As expected, privacy and security also significantly influenced consumers' intention to book rooms via the Internet ($ß = 0.164, 0.149$, $p \leq 0.001$). The inclusion of privacy, security and Internet experience increased the explanatory power of the model ($F = 4.105, 3.890$). These changes were significant at 0.001 level. Therefore, H3 is empirically supported.

Moderating effects of internet experience on the relationship between website quality and online booking intentions

Regarding the moderating role of Internet experience, which was operationalized as daily and yearly Internet usage, the sign and significance of $ß$ coefficients were used to test the proposed hypotheses. The inclusion of the interaction effect of website usability and daily Internet usage increased the predictive power of the former, which was statistically significant at 0.001. The moderating effect of yearly Internet usage was also significant. Its inclusion increased not only the explanatory power of the model but also the predictive ability of website usability ($\Delta R^2 = 0.011$, $\Delta ß = 0.004$, $p \leq 0.001$). Therefore, H4(a) is empirically supported.

Another series of hierarchical regression was conducted to test the hypothesis concerning website functionality and consumers' Internet experiences. The interaction variable of website functionality and Internet experience (i.e. daily and yearly Internet usage) slightly increased the explanatory power of the model and the predictive ability of website functionality. However, such marginal changes were not statistically significant. The influence of privacy and security of online booking intentions increased after considering the moderating effect of Internet experience. However, the coefficients of the interaction variables were not significant. Therefore, H4(b) and H4(c) are not statistically supported.

Further statistically significant interactions were observed via post-hoc plotting. By following Aiken and West (1991), the significant interaction between Internet experience and website usability was re-computed into high and low values which corresponded to one standard deviation above and below the mean. These two values represented the conditional value, which referred to the specific value of the moderator in which the regression of Y on X was considered (Darlington, 1990, as cited in Aiken & West, 1991). Simple regressions were then performed for website usability on online booking intentions, the conditional value of the moderator and website usability (conditional moderator interaction for high and low moderator values). Figures 2 and 3 demonstrate the regression pattern of online booking intentions on website usability features relative to the levels of daily and yearly Internet usage.

Discussion and conclusions

Conclusions

As a supplement to existing literature, this study considers the dynamic nature of website development and customer market by conceptualizing website quality as three-dimensional and by considering the roles of customers' Internet experiences. The analysis results empirically support the proposed hypotheses. Amongst these dimensions, website usability has the strongest influence on the respondents' purchase intentions. This finding has important implications for website design. Hence, efforts should be devoted to increase website usability, which enables easy access to desired information. This proposal is especially important in today's market where consumers live in an era of information explosion. Pedro Colaco, President and CEO of GuestCentric, has commented that Internet

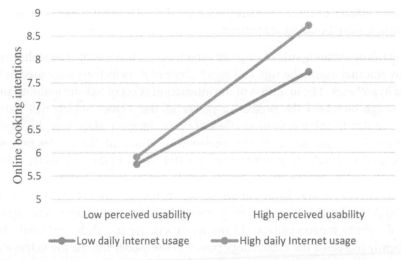

Figure 2. Moderating effect of daily internet usage on the relationship between website usability and online booking intentions.

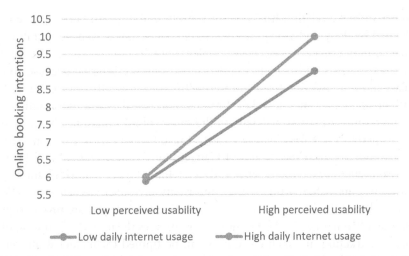

Figure 3. Moderating effect of yearly internet usage on the relationship between website usability and online booking intentions.

users usually spend 5 to 10 seconds exploring a website (Tnooz, 2013). Hence, hoteliers should be informed about the core and complementary functions of hotel websites as information and sales channels. Moreover, hotel websites should have a user-friendly design in which customers can easily locate navigation buttons and use the reservation system.

Website functionality, which pertains to information presented on websites, is also of considerable importance. On the one hand, this finding can be attributed to the inherent information-intensive nature of the hotel industry. On the other hand, non-hotel-owned websites have a few means to acquire information related to a specific feature, such as available facilities. The famous notion of 'content is king' (McCarthy, 1995, as cited in Hernández, JiméNez, & Martín, 2009, p. 364) remains applicable in this context. Therefore, hoteliers should be more discreet in presenting quality information on their websites, especially exclusive detailed information. For example, a three-star or higher rated hotel is expected to have a fitness center. However, information on the types and quantity of sports equipment may be more exclusive to the hotels themselves. Therefore, hoteliers must update their websites with the latest information, such as new product/service promotions and renovations. This finding is specifically crucial for themed hotels that target customers from small niche markets because detailed information on these hotels can only be obtained from their websites.

This study also identifies the significant role of security and privacy in improving the purchase intentions of consumers. This feature brings benefits and challenges to hoteliers. Hotel-owned websites have been well-recognized by the respondents as transaction tools with the potential of becoming effective e-commerce tools. However, the respondents are also aware of the potential risks involved in Internet transactions. Therefore, addressing these concerns on online transactions, including the reliability of third-party security seals (e.g. Paypal or Alipay) and privacy statements, must be prioritized.

An interesting discovery of this study is the moderating effect of Internet experiences on consumers' attitudes toward hotel websites. Amongst the three sets of inter-variable correlations, only the relationship between website usability and booking intention can be moderated by daily and yearly Internet usage. Particularly, website usability is more influential amongst experienced users, which may be attributed to the benefits of decreased search costs and higher confidence in using the Internet because consumers accumulate more knowledge from the web (Zhu & Zhang, 2010). Over time, Internet users with greater experience and skills become more familiar with information delivery styles and pay more attention to details on the source of information, whereas those who may lack experience are less likely to verify the information they obtain. This result extends the findings from the studies of Flanagin and Metzger (2000) and Lehto, Kim, and Morrison (2006) based on the elaboration likelihood model, in which Internet users' experiences, to some extent, explain users' information verification behaviors. Web users who have mastered the necessary skills in navigating the Internet are prone to purchase online frequently (George, 2002). This finding reinforces the underlying notion of online relationship marketing in which customers can be trained (Schneider & Bowen, 2010) and that the cognitive loyalty program could be actualized (Oliver, 1999). Operationally, a navigation scheme that can be quickly understood by visitors and has various personalized elements can foster habitual practices. Such mechanism is based on the power law of practice wherein the cognitive lock-in can then be implemented (Johnson et al., 2003).

Theoretical and practical implications

This study is of critical significance to hoteliers in China where computers are primarily used in reserving hotel rooms and purchasing airline tickets, whereas the new modes of search engines and mobile applications merely serve as complementary distribution channels (iResearch, 2013). However, most of the online room reservations in the country are conducted via OTAs, which pose potential risks to hotels. OTAs in China occasionally go into a price war with one another. However, hotels mainly suffer from squeezed margins and deterioration of service quality. In addition, overreliance on OTAs provides these agencies with more bargaining power in their negotiations with hotels about commissions. To encourage more direct sales from their own websites, Chinese hoteliers should exert additional efforts in refining their websites as an effective marketing strategy. Moreover, given that the bank credit system in China is less advanced than that in Western countries, the adoption of a mixed payment system, that is, integrating online and offline payment means, may lower potential financial risks. Likewise, Ma, Buhalis, and Song (2003) have recommended a combination of online e-commerce and offline operations to Chinese hoteliers to remove the barriers of e-commerce in the hotel industry.

This study contributes to online hotel marketing literature in several aspects. The analysis reveals that website usability is the most important factor amongst the three proposed dimensions. However, this finding is in contrast to that of Kim et al. (2006), which highlights product and service information as the most influential to purchase intentions. Such discrepancy may be credited to the evolving nature of the market. Hotel websites in China have developed into distribution channels of information and sales with increasing emphasis on privacy and security issues. Moreover, Internet users increasingly acquire certain Internet skills, form certain habits of use and demonstrate the function of experience-based cognitive costs in consumer choice (Murray & Häubl, 2007). This study empirically verifies such argument, thus complementing the findings of Kim et al. (2006)

who have found that hotel website dimensions have an Internet experience-based influence on purchase intentions. However, Kim et al. (2006) have simply differentiated experienced from inexperienced Internet users according to their yes/no responses to the question on whether they had Internet experience. Therefore, the present study has methodologically increased the rigor of the research design by including two self-reported questions and by performing a multiple regression analysis for the survey data.

Limitations and future research

This study has several limitations. Firstly, online surveys have certain shortcomings, such as coverage bias and impersonal responses (Hung & Law, 2011), which may affect the persuasiveness of the findings. Secondly, the respondents have been asked to indicate their booking intentions instead of their actual purchase, which may have been overstated. Thirdly, this study does not differentiate users who have actually booked rooms through hotel websites from those who have used alternative channels. The findings of this study imply that respondents who have booked from hotel-owned websites may behave differently.

Aside from addressing the abovementioned limitations, the findings of this work may be extended in several directions. Firstly, the empirically identified moderating role of Internet experience implies the cognitive lock-in in virtual environments, which pinpoints the skill-based loyalty program. However, such a topic is beyond the current research objective. Nevertheless, studies focusing on skill-based loyalty programs are of practical value to hotel practitioners because habits-based loyalty involves high switching costs which can deny easy duplication by competitors. Secondly, this research verifies privacy and security as an additional website dimension. Interface elements carry divergent weights on varying website categories, such as travel agencies and destination websites. Future researchers may examine whether the inclusion of such dimension is a phenomenon beyond the discussed website types. Lastly, Internet experience is a dynamic concept that changes over time. Therefore, future researchers may adopt a chronological angle to identify the variations in consumer attitudes and behaviors.

Disclosure statement

No potential conflict of interest was reported by the authors.

Funding

This research was sponsored by the National Natural Science Foundation of China (grant No. 71802179) and the Education Department of Zhejiang Province, China (Project No. Y201636043).

ORCID

Rob Law ⓘ http://orcid.org/0000-0001-7199-3757

References

Aiken, L. S., & West, S. G. (1991). *Multiple regression testing and interpreting interactions.* Newbury Park, CA: Sage Publications.

Anderson, J. C., & Gerbing, D. W. (1988). Structural equation modelling in practice: A review and recommended two-step approach. *Psychological Bulletin, 103*(3), 411–423.

Arnold, H. J., & Evans, M. G. (1979). Testing multiplicative models does not require ratio scales. *Organizational Behavior and Human Performance, 24*(1), 41–59.

Au Yeung, T., & Law, R. (2004). Extending the modified heuristic usability evaluation technique to chain and independent hotel websites. *International Journal of Hospitality Management, 23*(3), 307–313.

Bai, B., Law, R., & Wen, I. (2008). The impact of website quality on customer satisfaction and purchase intentions: Evidence from Chinese online visitors. *International Journal of Hospitality Management, 27*(3), 391–402.

Baloglu, S., & Pekcan, Y. A. (2006). The website design and internet site marketing practices of upscale and luxury hotels in Turkey. *Tourism Management, 27*(1), 171–176.

Blake, B. F., Neuendorf, K. A., & Valdiserri, C. M. (2003). Innovativeness and variety of internet shopping. *Internet Research, 13*(3), 156–169.

Bruner, G., & Kumar, A. (2000). Web commercials and advertising hierarchy-of-effects. *Journal of Advertising Research, 40*(1), 35–42.

Chang, H. H., & Chen, S. W. (2008). The impact of customer interface quality, satisfaction and switching costs on e-loyalty: Internet experience as a moderator. *Computers in Human Behavior, 24*(6), 2927–2944.

Chin, W. (1998). The partial least squares approach to structural equation modeling. In G. A. Marcoulides (Ed.), *Modern methods for business research* (pp. 295–336). Mahwah, NJ: Lawrence Erlbaum.

Chung, T., & Law, R. (2003). Developing a performance indicator for hotel websites. *International Journal of Hospitality Management, 22*(1), 119–125.

Citrin, V. A., Sprott, D. E., Silverman, S. N., & Stem, D. E. (2000). Adoption of internet shopping: The role of consumer innovativeness. *Industrial Management & Data Systems, 100*(7), 294–300.

Cohen, J., & Cohen, P. (1983). *Applied multiple regression/correlation analysis for the behavioral sciences.* Hilldale, NJ: Lawrence Erlbaum Associates.

Cummins, R. A., & Gullone, E. (2000). *Why we should not use 5-point likert scales: The case for subjective quality of life measurement.* Retrieved from http://www.deakin.edu.au/research/acqol/iwbg/correspondence/2002/Cummins_Gullone_2000_Likert_Scales.doc

Das, B., & Sahoo, J. S. (2011). Social networking sites–A critical analysis of its impact on personal and social life. *International Journal of Business and Social Science, 2*(14), 222–228.

Day, G. S. (1969). A two-dimensional concept of brand loyalty. *Journal of Advertising Research, 9*(3), 29–35.

Durbin, J., & Watson, G. S. (1971). Testing for serial correlation in least squares regression. *Biometrika, 58*(1), 1–19.

Escobar-Rodíguez, T., & Carvajal-Trujillo, E. (2013). An evaluation of Spanish hotel websites: Informational vs. relational strategies. *International Journal of Hospitality Management, 33*, 228–239.

Flanagin, A. J., & Metzger, M. J. (2000). Perceptions of Internet information credibility. *Journalism & Mass Communication Quarterly, 77*(3), 515–540.

Gefen, D., Karahanna, E., & Straub, D. W. (2003). Inexperience and experience with online stores: The importance of TAM and trust. *IEEE Transactions on Engineering Management, 50*(3), 307–321.

George, J. F. (2002). Influences on the intent to make Internet purchases. *Internet Research, 12*(2), 165–180.

Grewal, D., Krishnan, R., Baker, J., & Borin, N. (1998). The effect of store name, brand name and price discounts on consumers' evaluations and purchase intentions. *Journal of Retailing, 74*(3), 331–352.

Hair, J. F., Black, W. C., Babin, B. J., Anderson, R. E., & Tatham, R. L. (2010). *Multivariate data analysis* (6th ed.). Upper Saddle River, NJ: Prentice Hall.

Hernández, B., JiméNez, J., & Martín, M. J. (2009). Key website factors in e-business strategy. *International Journal of Information Management, 29*(5), 362–371.

Hung, K., & Law, R. (2011). An overview of Internet-based surveys in hospitality and tourism journals. *Tourism Management, 32*(4), 717–724.

iResearch. (2013). *China online travel market dramatically grows 29.0% in 2013*. Retrieved from http://www.iresearchchina.com/views/4837.html

Jeong, M., Oh, H., & Gregoire, M. (2003). Conceptualizing web site quality and its consequences in the lodging industry. *International Journal of Hospitality Management, 22*(2), 161–175.

John, G., & Reve, T. (1982). The reliability and validity of key informant data from dyadic relationships in marketing channels. *Journal of Marketing Research, 19*(4), 517–524.

Johnson, E. J., Bellman, S., & Lohse, G. L. (2003). Cognitive lock-in and the power law of practice. *Journal of Marketing, 67*(2), 62–75.

Kalwani, M. U., & Silk, A. J. (1982). On the reliability and predictive validity of purchase intention measures. *Marketing Science, 3*(1), 243–285.

Keaveney, S. M., & Parthasarathy, M. (2001). Customer switching behavior in online services: An exploratory study of the role of selected attitudinal, behavioral, and demographic factors. *Journal of the Academy of Marketing Science, 29*(4), 374–390.

Kim, H., & Niehm, L. S. (2009). The impact of website quality on information quality, value, and loyalty intentions in apparel retailing. *Journal of Interactive Marketing, 23*(3), 221–233.

Kim, M. J., Chung, N., & Lee, C. L. (2011). The effect of perceived trust on electronic commerce: Shopping online for tourism products and services in South Korea. *Tourism Management, 32* (2), 256–265.

Kim, W. G., Ma, X., & Kim, D. J. (2006). Determinants of Chinese hotel customers' e-satisfaction and purchase intentions. *Tourism Management, 27*(5), 890–900.

Kline, R. B. (2005). *Principles and practice of structural equation modeling* (2nd ed.). New York: The Guilford Press.

Kusluvan, S., & Kusluvan, Z. (2000). Perceptions and attitudes of undergraduate tourism students towards working in the tourism industry in Turkey. *Tourism Management, 21*(3), 251–269.

Lang, T. C. (2000). The effect of the internet on travel consumer purchasing behaviour and implications for travel agencies. *Journal of Vacation Marketing, 6*(4), 368–385.

Law, R. (2009). Disintermediation of hotel reservations: The perception of different groups of online buyers in Hong Kong. *International Journal of Contemporary Hospitality Management, 21*(6), 766–772.

Law, R., & Chen, S. Z. (2012). Representation of destination cultural factors on hotel websites: Content analysis of Beijing hotel websites. *Asia Pacific Journal of Tourism Research, 17*(2), 210–229.

Law, R., & Hsu, C. H. (2006). Importance of hotel website dimensions and attributes: Perceptions of online browsers and online purchasers. *Journal of Hospitality & Tourism Research*, *30*(3), 295–312.

Law, R., Qi, S., & Buhalis, D. (2010). Progress in tourism management: A review of website evaluation in tourism research. *Tourism Management*, *31*(3), 297–313.

Law, R., & Wong, R. (2010). Analysing room rates and terms and conditions for the online booking of hotel rooms. *Asia Pacific Journal of Tourism Research*, *15*(1), 43–56.

Lee, C. H., & Cranage, D. A. (2011). Personalization-privacy paradox: The effects of personalization and privacy assurance on customer responses to travel web sites. *Tourism Management*, *32* (5), 987–994.

Lehto, X. Y., Kim, D. Y., & Morrison, A. M. (2006). The effect of prior destination experience on online information search behaviour. *Tourism and Hospitality Research*, *6*(2), 160–178.

Lehto, X. Y., O'Leary, J. T., & Morrison, A. M. (2004). The effect of prior experience on vacation behavior. *Annals of Tourism Research*, *31*(4), 801–818.

Li, H., Kuo, C., & Rusell, M. G. (1999). The impact of perceived channel utilities, shopping orientations, and demographics on the consumer's online buying behavior. *Journal of Computer-Mediated Communication*, *5*(2). doi:10.1111/j.1083-6101.1999.tb00336.x

Li, S., Li, J. Z., He, H., Ward, P., & Davies, B. J. (2011). WebDigital: A web-based hybrid intelligent knowledge automation system for developing digital marketing strategies. *Expert Systems with Applications*, *38*(8), 10606–10613.

Liang, T. P., & Huang, J. S. (1998). An empirical study on consumer acceptance of products in electronic markets: A transaction cost model. *Decision Support Systems*, *24*(1), 29–43.

Liu, J. N. K., & Zhang, E. Y. (2014). An investigation of factors affecting customer selection of online hotel booking channels. *International Journal of Hospitality Management*, *39*, 71–83.

Loiacono, E. T., Watson, R. T., & Goodhue, D. L. (2002). WebQual: A measure of website quality. *Marketing Theory and Applications*, *13*(3), 432–438.

Ma, J. X., Buhalis, D., & Song, H. (2003). ICTs and internet adoption in China's tourism industry. *International Journal of Information Management*, *23*(6), 451–467.

Morosan, C., & Jeong, M. (2008). Users' perceptions of two types of hotel reservation web sites. *International Journal of Hospitality Management*, *27*(2), 284–292.

Mukhopadhyay, T., Kekre, S., & Kalathur, S. (1995). Business value of information technology: A study of electronic data interchange. *MIS Quarterly*, *19*(2), 137–156.

Murphy, J., Forrest, E. J., Wotring, C. E., & Brymer, R. A. (1996). Hotel management and marketing on the internet: An analysis of sites and features. *Cornell Hotel and Restaurant Administration Quarterly*, *37*(3), 70–82.

Murray, K. B., & Häubl, G. (2007). Explaining cognitive lock-in: The role of skill-based habits of use in consumer choice. *Journal of Consumer Research*, *34*(1), 77–88.

Neter, J., Wasserman, W., & Kutner, M. H. (1985). *Applied linear statistical models: Regression, analysis of variance and experimental designs*. Homewood, IL: Irwin.

Nunnally, J. (1978). *Psychometric methods*. New York: McGraw-Hill.

Nysveen, H., & Pedersen, P. E. (2004). An exploratory study of customers' perception of company web sites offering various interactive applications: Moderating effects of customers' internet experience. *Decision Support Systems*, *37*(1), 137–150.

O'Connor, P. (2007). Online consumer privacy: An analysis of hotel company behavior. *Cornell Hospitality Quarterly*, *48*(2), 183–200.

O'Connor, P. (2008). E-mail marketing by international hotel chains: An industry practices update. *Cornell Hospitality Quarterly*, *49*(1), 42–52.

O'Connor, P., & Frew, A. J. (2002). The future of hotel electronic distribution: Expert and industry perspectives. *Cornell Hotel and Restaurant Administration Quarterly*, *43*(3), 33–45.

Oliver, R. L. (1999). Whence consumer loyalty? *Journal of Marketing*, *63*, 33–44.

Palmer, J. W., Bailey, J. P., & Faraj, S. (2000). The role of intermediaries in the development of trust on the WWW: The use and prominence of trusted third parties and privacy statements. *Journal of Computer-Mediated Communication*, *5*(3). doi:10.1111/j.1083-6101.2000.tb00342.x

Pozniak, L. (2015). Unregulated markets and Internet financial communication: Qualitative and quantitative approaches. *Review of Business & Finance Studies*, 6(1), 109–120.

Preston, C. C., & Colman, A. M. (2000). Optimal number of response categories in rating scales: Reliability, validity, discriminating power, and respondent preferences. *ActaPsychologica*, 104 (1), 1–15.

Schneider, B., & Bowen, D. E. (2010). Winning the service game. In P. P. Maglio, C. A. Kieliszewski, & J. C. Sphohrer (Eds.), *Handbook of service science* (pp. 31–59). New York: Springer US.

Sharp, L. (2002). Positive response action: The ultimate goal of website communication. *Journal of Communication Management*, 6(1), 41–52.

Shen, C. C., & Chiou, J. S. (2010). The impact of perceived ease of use on Internet service adoption: The moderating effects of temporal distance and perceived risk. *Computers in Human Behavior*, 26(1), 42–50.

Sheppard, B. H., Hartwick, J., & Warshaw, P. R. (1988). The theory of reasoned action: A meta-analysis of past research with recommendations for modifications and future research. *Journal of Consumer Research*, 15(3), 325–343.

Sirakaya, E., Teye, V., & Sönmez, S. (2002). Understanding residents' support for tourism development in the central region of Ghana. *Journal of Travel Research*, 41(1), 57–67.

Starkov, M. (2002). *Brand erosion or how not to market your hotel on the web*. Retrieved from http://www.hotel-online.com/News/PR2002_2nd/Apr02_BrandErosion.html

Tnooz. (2013). *Hotel websites: Tips for a multi-device and info-hungry world (full of impatient consumers)*. Retrieved from http://www.tnooz.com/article/hotel-websites-tips-for-a-multi-device-and-info-hungry-world-full-of-impatient-consumers/#sthash.axywqWsT.dpuf

Travelex. (2015). *Online currency converter*. Retrieved from http://www.travelex.com.hk/HK/Currency-Converter-EN/

Tse, T. S. (2013). The marketing role of the Internet in launching a hotel: The case of Hotel Icon. *Journal of Hospitality Marketing & Management*, 22(8), 895–908.

Tsui, A. S., Ashford, S. J., Clair, L. S., & Xin, K. R. (1995). Dealing with discrepant expectations: Response strategies and managerial effectiveness. *Academy of Management Journal*, 38(6), 1515–1543.

Wang, D., Chan, H., & Pan, S. (2015). The impacts of mass media on organic destination image: A case study of Singapore. *Asia Pacific Journal of Tourism Research*, 20(8), 860–874.

Ward, M. R., & Lee, M. J. (2000). Internet shopping, consumer search and product branding. *Journal of Product & Brand Management*, 9(1), 6–20.

Wong, J., & Law, R. (2005). Analysing the intention to purchase on hotel websites: A study of travellers to Hong Kong. *International Journal of Hospitality Management*, 24(3), 311–329.

Wu, J., & Liu, D. (2007). The effects of trust and enjoyment on intention to play online games. *Journal of Electronic Commerce Research*, 8(2), 128–140.

Wu, S. I. (2003). The relationship between consumer characteristics and attitude toward online shopping. *Marketing Intelligence & Planning*, 21(1), 37–44.

Xu, L., He, P., & Hua, Z. (2015). A new form for a hotel to collaborate with a third-party website: Setting online-exclusive-rooms. *Asia Pacific Journal of Tourism Research*, 20(6), 635–655.

Yoon, S. J. (2002). The antecedents and consequences of trust in online-purchase decisions. *Journal of Interactive Marketing*, 16(2), 47–63.

Zhu, F., & Zhang, X. (2010). Impact of online consumer reviews on sales: The moderating role of product and consumer characteristics. *Journal of Marketing*, 74(2), 133–148.

Social Media Comments about Hotel Robots

Hio Nam Io and Chang Boon Lee

ABSTRACT

The Henn-na Hotel in Japan has employed robots for its operations since 2015. In January 2019, the hotel announced it had fired half its robotic workforce. This news generated many comments on social media. The purpose of this study is to analyze the comments to inform researchers and practitioners about people's reactions to this news. Based on topic modeling techniques, the results show the comments focus on three topics: (1) The difficulty of using robots to replace human services, (2) The robot embodiment, and (3) The apprehension about job replacement. Reviews of the associated comments indicate there is skepticism about the robots' abilities to replace human services. However, there is also apprehension about job losses when robots become more capable of taking over the jobs. With regards to the robot embodiment, there are low sentiments for the female humanoid at the front desk as it was perceived as 'scary' and 'horrible'. The comments suggest the hotel to: (1) upgrade its technology, (2) improve the appearance of the female robot, and (3) address people's concerns regarding job losses. The study discusses the implications of the results.

社交媒体对酒店机器人的评论

摘要

从2015年起,日本的海茵娜酒店就开始使用机器人进行运营。2019年1月,酒店宣布解雇了一半的机器人员工。这新闻在社交媒体上引起了许多评论。本研究的目的是通过对相关评论的分析使研究人员和酒店从业者了解人们对这一新闻的反应。基于主题模型技术,结果显示,评论集中在三个主题上:(1)使用机器人代替人类服务的困难,(2)机器人的呈现形式,及(3)对工作被取代的担忧。回顾相关的评论表明,人们对机器人取代人类服务的能力持怀疑态度。然而,也有人担心,当机器人在未来变得更有能力接管工作时,人类便会失业。关于机器人的呈现形式,评论的感情显示低落,因为前台放置的女性人形机器被认为是恐怖和吓人。评论表示酒店应:(1)升级其技术,(2)改善女性机器人的外观,以及 (3)解决人们对失业的担忧。该研究讨论了结果的含义。

Introduction

Traditionally, robots are used in an industrial setting to perform repetitive tasks with high precision and minimal downtime (Arai et al., 2010). Recent improvements in artificial intelligence (AI) have enabled robots to perform complex tasks, and they can now be used even to man service operations (Barrett et al., 2015). Robots have a more demanding role in a service setting as they need to understand and interpret the users' requirements and solve their problems. There are also other issues about using robots because users may feel uneasy or anxious when they interact with a robot, as compared to a person (Nomura et al., 2006). The use of service robots is still in its early stage (Wirtz et al., 2018). Researchers and practitioners are keen to find out how people perceive service robots so that they can improve the acceptance and use of these robots.

The hospitality industry is just beginning to use robots in its operations. The industry uses different kinds of service robots. For example, *Sacarino* is a robot that serves hotel guests by providing information about hotel services. It can also accompany guests through the hotel spaces (Zalama et al., 2014). *Karotz* is another robot that interacts orally with tourists and provides information and recommendations about hotels and tourism activities (Nieto et al., 2014). The robots working in hotels have different serving capabilities and positioning. Some are virtual, while others can move and interact with the customers physically. The technology giants have been actively developing service robots for the hospitality industry. IBM has collaborated with Hilton to develop a concierge robot (Statt, 2016) and Alibaba has also developed AliGenie, a personal assistant that is able to run unmanned hotels (Jia et al., 2018).

The Henn-na Hotel in Japan is the first in the world that used human-like robots to serve its guests (Alexis, 2017). Two well-known robots in Henn-na Hotel are the female humanoid robot and the dinosaur robot. They work at the front desk to answer queries and perform check-in for the guests. The other robots that work in the hotel include a car-like robot that transport luggage to the guest rooms, a robot that works in the cloakroom, and the robot cleaners (Pierce, 2015). Recently, the hotel announced that it had fired half its robotic workforce (Hertzfeld, 2019). According to reports about the dismissal, some customers complained they were awoken in the middle of the night because the in-room assistant mistook the customers' snores as commands and kept asking the customers to repeat their requests (Ryall, 2019). Some customers also complained that the robots could not understand or answer their queries.

Robots are a novel innovation that are not widely available. Few studies have determined whether people are happy with robots serving them. If for some reasons people do not have good sentiments about robots, then it will be difficult to introduce this type of technology innovation in the hotel's operations. People may not have the experience of staying at a robot hotel, but they may have gathered some impressions about robots from reading articles or viewing videos. Analyzing comments in social media is useful because we can understand people's perceptions, which can affect their attitudes and behaviors (Ajzen & Fishbein, 2005). Furthermore, people's comments on social media can influence others as well. For example, comments on social media can affect potential guests in their pre-travel decision to stay at a hotel (Varkaris & Neuhofer, 2017).

Given the background about service robots in the hotel industry, it is useful to determine how people perceive the use of hotel robots. The research question for this study is 'What are people's perceptions and sentiments about hotel robots?' To answer this question, this study analyzed the comments at the Weibo microblogging website about the dismissal of robots at Henn-na Hotel. The results derived from this study can help to inform researchers and practitioners about people's reactions to the use of hotel robots. They can provide insights on how hotels can better manage the use of robots for their operations.

This paper proceeds as follows. The next section provides related work on the use of robots in hotels, the classification of robots, prior research on hotel robots, and perceptions of robots. Then the research method explains how this study was conducted. This is followed by a presentation of the results and a discussion of the findings. The paper ends with the limitations of the results.

Related work

Use of robots in hotels

The development of AI technologies in recent years has facilitated the adoptions of robots in hotels. It has empowered practitioners to work alongside robots to reduce the repetitive tasks performed by human staff (Tung & Law, 2017). Two important streams of AI development – namely, natural language processing and computer vision, have contributed to the performance of robots. These developments enable robots to understand human languages and sense their environment. Robots can now provide meaningful responses to users' requests and they can move and position themselves at the required locations (Saeedi et al., 2016). Some robots can interact directly with the customers, such as performing guests' check-in, delivering requested items to the rooms, offering information to guests, as well as providing concierge services (S. Ivanov et al., 2017). Other robots can perform automation tasks, such as cloth handling (Hata et al., 2008) and cooking (Bollini et al., 2013).

Classification of robots

There are various ways to classify robots. They can be classified into 3 types based on their presence. They are the copresent robots, telepresent robots, and virtual agents (Li, 2015). Copresent robots are 'physically embodied as well as physically present in the user space'. Telepresent robots are 'physically embodied in the real world, but the interaction is mediated using a computer monitor, television or projector screen'. Virtual agents are those that 'have similar appearance and behavior to a robot but are digitally embodied'. Many experiments have been conducted to compare the benefits of using different forms of robots. Most of the work indicate that physically present robots have greater influence than telepresent robots. For example, Lee et al. (2006) show that people have more positive evaluations in interacting with a physically embodied social agent than a disembodied one. The results of an experimental study conducted by Wainer et al. (2006) also suggest that physically embodied robots are more favorable than virtual ones in the context for therapy robots.

Robots can also be classified based on their morphology. Morphology is defined as 'the shape of its body and limbs, as well as the type and placement of sensors and effectors' (Pfeifer et al., 2007). Anthropomorphic robots, also known as humanoid robots, are mimicking human being's appearance or behavior. Sophia, the first robot with a Saudi Arabian citizenship, is an example of an anthropomorphic robot (Weller, 2017). The female human-like robot in Henn-na Hotel is also an anthropomorphic robot. On the other hand, robots that look like living creatures, such as cats or dogs are called zoomorphic robots. The nabaztag robot is an example of a zoomorphic robot. It has a cute appearance and looks like a rabbit (Hoffmann & Krämer, 2013). The robot dinosaur in Henn-na Hotel is another example of a zoomorphic robot. Other morphologies include those that are caricatured and functional. Caricatured robots are those that do not resemble living things, such as basketball robots, and functional robots are designed based on its original functions, such as meal delivery robots (Fong et al., 2003).

Researchers have compared how different morphologies affect the user perceptions of the robots. There are two notable research areas regarding morphologies. The first indicates that anthropomorphic robots will lead users to have higher expectations (Nowak & Biocca, 2003). According to some researchers, anthropomorphic robots offer more natural and effective interactions compared to their less human-like counterparts (Duffy, 2003). The human-like features of these robots can help to facilitate the formation of rapport and empathy with the users and therefore the users are likely to have more trust and higher acceptance when interacting with these robots (Strait et al., 2017). The users would expect more human intelligence when they find more anthropomorphic features on the robots.

The second research area is related to the uncanny valley theory (Mori et al., 2012). The theory indicates that people are averse to highly human-like features. The uncanny valley theory predicts that as nonrealistic robots become increasingly human-like, people would like them more. However, once robots start to become highly human-like, people would find them eerie and disturbing. The relationship between the robots' perceived human likeness and their likability is therefore nonlinear. The theory implies that any kind of human-likeness manipulation will lead to experienced negative affinity at close-to-realistic levels. Researchers have provided a number of explanations for the uncanny valley theory (Rosenthal-Von Der Pütten & Krämer, 2014). Some explanations attribute the uncanny valley theory to conflicting perception cues while others relate to biological and cultural aspects of survival instincts. Wang et al. (2015) have also proposed a dehumanization hypothesis to explain the uncanny phenomenon.

The two areas of research about morphologies have led to deeper explorations. Kim et al. (2019) conducted four experiments and found that anthropomorphism of service robots increase psychological warmth but decreases attitude or liking. The researchers suggested that the appearances and behaviors of robots should not be too human-like to avoid negative attitudes toward them. They also urge managers and researchers to collaborate to determine the optimal level of anthropomorphism.

Prior research on hotel robots

There are only a handful of prior studies about hotel robots as hotels are just beginning to employ robots in their operations. A study by Tussyadiah and Park (2018) aimed to understand consumers' evaluation of hotel service robots and their effects on adoption intention. The study focused on check-in robot and room-delivery robot. Part of the study required participants to answer an online survey based on watching a video about the robots. The study found that factors such as anthropomorphism, perceived intelligence, and perceived safety were positively related to the acceptance of hotel service robots.

Another study by Tung and Au (2018) was based on customers' encounters with hotel robots. The study used 329 reviews in TripAdvisor, Agoda, Yelp, and Booking.com to evaluate the experiences with robotics in four hotels (Yotel New York, Aloft Cupertino, Henn-na Hotel Japan and Marriott Residence Inn LAX). They based their evaluation criteria on five dimensions of user experiences derived from prior research on human-robot interactions. The five dimensions are embodiment, emotion, human-oriented perception, feeling of security, and co-experience. The main results of the study highlight the importance of robotic embodiment and human-oriented perceptions on consumer experiences. In terms of robotic embodiment, the study found that users experienced discrepancies between an anthropomorphic robot that is structurally similar to a human, but failed to perform human-based tasks such as check-in for customers. This resulted in negative guest experiences. In terms of the robot's human-oriented perceptions, many users found the robots could not engage the users with the current technology. They could not recognize voices and physical gestures and they have limited language ability. These limitations arouse users' frustration and disappointment.

S. Ivanov et al. (2018) investigated young Russian adult attitudes toward the potential use of robots in the hospitality industry. The study was based on data gathered from a 2016–2017 survey among 260 participants. Among the results, they show that respondents were indifferent toward the appearance of robots, but they preferred to be served by human employees. Women were found to be less positive than men toward service robots. Also, the respondents considered three groups of activities are most acceptable areas for robotization, namely: (1) logistics/transporting goods, (2) information provision about the hotel, and (3) processing payments through the automated teller machines and point of sale terminals.

There is also a recent study about the use of human-like robots in Henn-na Hotel (Yu, 2020). The study aimed to uncover public perceptions regarding robots as frontline employees. It analyzed comments on the YouTube platform about robots at Henn-na Hotel. The study coded the comments based on dimensions in the Godspeed scale, which is a scale used to measure user perceptions of robots (Bartneck et al., 2009). The main results of the study found that the perceptions of human-like robots tend to be negative.

It should be noted that Yu's (2020) study excluded comments from China because Youtube was not accessible in China. As the Chinese form a large proportion of the tourist market in Japan (Hurst, 2019), the comments among Chinese people are valuable. The current study, which is based on comments contributed by the Weibo users, analyzed how Chinese people felt about the robots and their reactions to the robots' retrenchment. Also noteworthy is that the research method used in this study is different from that in Yu (2020). As will be explained in the 'Research method' section, this study used a topic modeling software to conduct the analysis rather than perform manual coding. A sentiment analysis software was also used to determine the sentiments of the comments.

Perceptions of robots

Perception is the process by which organisms interpret and organize sensation to produce a meaningful experience of the world (Lindsay & Norman, 1977). Every person perceives the world differently and whatever that is perceived is not necessarily the same as what it really is. Perceptions are affected by the perceiver, the object of perception, and the environment.

In this research, perceptions about hotel robots were gathered from comments at a Chinese social media website. The comments were based on what people know about robots or their personal experience at Henn-na Hotel. People may not have access to robots and due to the rapid improvements in technology, people could have different perceptions regarding robots' capabilities (Cha et al., 2015). It is useful to identify people's perceptions because they can help to understand human behavior. For example, the technology acceptance model (TAM) has established that it is people's perceptions regarding the usefulness and ease of use of technology that contribute to their acceptance and usage of technology (Davis, 1989). Many studies have provided empirical support for the TAM (Adams et al., 1992). A number of studies have also extended the TAM by considering other factors that may affect technology adoption. Among them, Van der Heijden (2004) has added perceived enjoyment to show that perceived enjoyment also affects the adoption of hedonic systems.

As service robots replace human employees, people have expectations that robots would fulfill the roles of the human servers. Stock and Merkle (2017) used the role theory (Solomon et al., 1985) to propose that a service robot should not only be useful and easy to use, but it should also be able to relate to the users during a service encounter. The researchers included a relational component comprising elements such as benevolence and understanding to explain the adoption of service robots.

There are many articles that warn about robots displacing jobs (Titcomb, 2015). A McKinsey report has forecasted that one-fifth of the global work force could lose their jobs by 2030 (Manyika et al., 2017). A large-scale study conducted across 27 countries in the European Union also showed that public opinions regarding robots exhibited a marked negative trend between 2012 and 2017, due possibly to the fear of robots replacing jobs (Gnambs & Appel, 2019). Other studies have shown that the threat of perceived job insecurity is increasing due to the use of robots at the workplace (Nam, 2019). Granulo et al. (2019) urged researchers to find out more about the psychological reactions of workers who are displaced by robots so that appropriate support programmes can be tailored to the unemployed.

Regarding job replacement, Huang and Rust (2018) theory of AI job replacement could provide a useful reference. The AI job replacement theory specifies four intelligences required for service tasks – mechanical, analytical, intuitive, and empathetic – and it lays the way organizations should decide between humans and machines for accomplishing those tasks. Currently, technology can be used for mechanical and analytical tasks. Eventually, however, AI can possibly perform higher intelligence tasks and it could present a threat to human employment.

Research method

Weibo is one of the most popular microblogging websites in China (Wang, 2017). News about the dismissal of robots at Henn-na Hotel had generated many discussions among Chinese netizens on the Weibo website. The hashtag, '#日本酒店解雇半数机器人#' (A Japanese hotel fired half its robotic workforce) was among the top 50 hottest trending topics in Weibo for 15 days, from 16 January 2019 (the day news about the robot dismissal was published) to 30 January 2019. This study based the data collection period during these 15 days. There were 43 posts about the robot dismissal news, and they were accompanied by a video that showed the robots in Henn-na hotel. A web crawler called 'GooSeeker' (https://www.gooseeker.com/) was used to crawl the comments under these 43 posts. After data pre-processing, such as removing duplicate comments from the same user and those with non-related comments, there were totally 1,401 valid comments available for analysis.

This study used topic modeling and sentiment analysis to analyze the comments. Topic modeling is a statistical technique that is used to extract a list of keywords from a set of documents and cluster the frequently used keywords into specific groups. Eickhoff and Neuss (2017) introduced topic modeling for research in Information Systems and other managerial disciplines. The LDAvis package has been developed to help researchers visualize and interpret topic modeling results from mining large corpus (Chuang et al., 2012). This study used LDAvis to perform topic modeling analysis for the comments. The visual results from LDAvis provide a 'global view of the topics (and how they differ from each other) while at the same time allowing for a deep inspection of the terms most highly associated with each individual topic' (Sievert & Shirley, 2014). The inter-topic distance map generated by LDAvis can help to answer questions such as 'How prevalent is each topic?' and 'How do the topics relate to each other?' The map plots the topics as circles in a two-dimensional plane whose centers are determined by computing the distance between topics, and the areas of the circles represent each topic's overall prevalence. The map can help to guide the optimal number of clusters to be used for topic modeling.

Sentiment analysis was also conducted on the data. Sentiment analysis is a natural language processing method for tracking the mood about a product or topic (Pak & Paroubek, 2010). Depending on the data to be analyzed, different tools can be used to conduct sentiment analysis. In this study, the BosonNLP (https://www.bosonnlp.com/) is used to perform sentiment analysis as this is an industry-leading tool used to perform the analysis involving Chinese data (Ying et al., 2017). The tool will return a sentiment score ranging from 0 to 1 for each comment. When the sentiment score is close to 0, it means the comment has a negative sentiment. When the score is close to 1, it has a positive sentiment. The scores enable a quick feel of the data. After obtaining the sentiment scores, further analyzes were conducted to review the results generated by the software. Human reviews of the comments can help to provide understanding of the context for the sentiments and they can yield further insights. For example, reviewing the comments can help to identify the reasons for extreme sentiments or why there is a mixture sentiments in a topic. Figure 1 shows the research process for this study.

Results

As the number of comments available for topic modeling was not considered very large (n = 1,401), this study analyzed the data by setting the number of topics to three, four, five, and six. Figure 2 shows the results using different number of topics. The results indicate there were topic diffusion when the number of topics was set at four, five, and six, as the circles in the inter-topic distance maps were very close or they over-lapped one

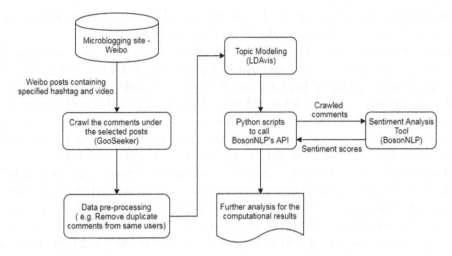

Figure 1. Research process.

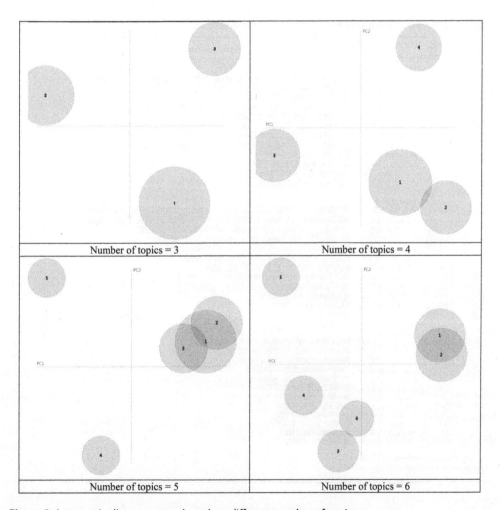

Figure 2. Inter-topic distance maps based on different number of topics.

another. The best result was obtained when the analysis was based on three topics as the map shows three large, distinct, and non-overlapping circles.

Table 1 shows the details of the LDAvis clustering results based on three topics. The right side of the table shows the terms that are highly associated with each topic as well as their frequency distribution. The frequency distribution includes the overall frequency as well as the frequency within the selected topic. The table shows that while topics #1 and #3 share some common terms such as 'service' and 'job', each topic also has a number of terms that are almost unique. For example, the nearly unique terms in topic #1 include 'now', while those in topic #3 include 'in the future', 'next time', and 'then'.

Based on the terms in the topics and their associated comments, the study identified an appropriate topic for each cluster. The researchers discussed the titles of the topics to avoid individual bias. The titles are: (1) The difficulty of using robots to replace human services, (2) The robot embodiment, and (3) The apprehension about job replacement. A point to note is that the topic modeling results do not indicate which topic a comment belongs to. The terms that are associated with one topic can appear in another topic, but

Table 1. Top frequently used terms and their sentiment scores.

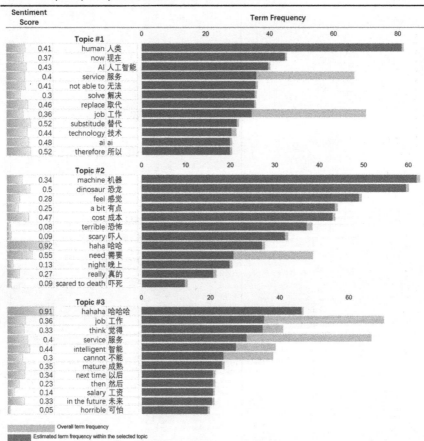

the contexts of the terms may vary across topics. The description of the topics and their related comments are presented in the next few subsections.

With regards to sentiment analysis, the results found that among the 1,401 comments, 891 (64%) have sentiment scores below 0.5. An analysis of the scores show that there are several comments with extreme sentiments. Those with low scores pertain mostly to comments about the female humanoid and the apprehension of job replacements, while those with high scores relate to the happiness that the robots were retrenched. Table 1 includes the average sentiment score for the comments containing the terms in the extracted topics.

Topic #1: The difficulty of using robots to replace human services

The comments related to this topic said that services provided by human staff cannot be easily replaced by robots because the interactions provided by the robots are very different from those of the human staff. For example, there are comments like *'Service is a kind of thing that cannot be replaced by robots'* and *'Robots are still not a substitute for humans'*. The comments point out that robots are not able to have emotions and human touch like a human being. Also, when users interact with robots, they always compare the experience between robots and human staff, such as *'In the service industry, robots cannot replace people, there is a big difference in the interactions and feelings'* and *'How to replace the warmth from a human?'*

The comments show that the frontline robots in the hotel may not replace the experience provided by a human employee as the robots cannot perform like a human being. In the case of industrial robots, they are just required to implement the tasks accurately and efficiently. For service robots, however, they are required to understand the feelings of the customers and give appropriate responses. For instance, one comment mentioned the need for personalization is very important in the hotel industry. Sometimes, even human staff cannot fulfill the customer's personalized request. So, it is even more difficult for the robots to do it. A related comment said that ' ... *robots cannot undertake the role of the hotel service, which is a highly demanding field'*.

Another term associated with this topic is 'not able to'. The use of this term is mainly related to situations when robots cannot solve problems for customers, and therefore, they need help from human staff. The comments from one writer who had stayed at Henn-na Hotel said the robot cannot solve his/her problems and so s/he had to be attended by a human staff. Another writer who had also stayed at the hotel commented that the robot was not easy to use.

When customers treat robots as normal hotel staff, they will ask questions and expect the robot to respond like a human being. If robots cannot respond correctly or create more inconvenience for customers, customers may have negative sentiments for the robots. One comment said, *'When it relates to thinking, the robot is not able to solve the problem'*.

In addition, the term 'technology' also appears frequently in this topic. The comments associated with this term explained why the performance of robots employed in Henn-na Hotel cannot satisfy its operations. As Henn-na Hotel started using robots sometime in 2015, the technologies the hotel adopted may not have kept up-to-date over the years. It

Table 2. Comments related to Topic #1 (The difficulty of using robots to replace human services).

Data exemplar	Sentiment score
Service is a kind of thing that still cannot be replaced by robots. (服务这种东西 … 机器人还是无法取代的)	0.24
Robots are still not a substitute for humans. (机器人还是无法替代人类)	0.45
In the service industry, robots cannot replace people, there is a big difference in the interactions and feelings. (服务业, 机器人无法代替人的, 交流感觉差太远了)	0.12
How to replace the warmth from a human? (人的温度带来的温情怎么代替)	0.46
With the current intelligent technology, robots cannot undertake the role of the hotel service, which is a highly demanding field. Many people are made dizzy by the guests, how can robots handle them? (目前的智能技术, 机器人根本无法承担酒店服务这种个性化要求很高的领域, 很多人都被住客搞的头昏脑涨呢, 何况机器人)	0.08
When it relates to thinking, the robot is not able to solve the problem. (涉及到思考的问题的话 机器人是无法解决的)	0.02
No matter how good the machine is, there is no human touch. It is never as warm as the greetings from living people. (机器再好也没有人情味, 始终不及活生生的人的问候来得温暖)	0.21
When we went to Japan in August this year, we lived in this hotel. It was a chain. At that time, we lived in Asakusa Bridge. The service was really worrying. The robot is a gimmick. I was exhausted after checked in. Other problems are not able to be solved by the robot. When we wanted to ask for some information, we had to call the human staff in the office, really troublesome. (今年8月去日本的时候住过这家酒店, 是连锁, 当时我们住在浅草桥店, 服务真心是堪忧, 机器人就是个噱头, 累死人才能办完入住, 别的问题也无法解决, 问个信息都得call在办公室的服务员出来, 真心麻烦)	0.14
I have lived this hotel once, the robot is really not easy to use, problems need to be solved by human staff. (住过这个一次, 机器人的确不好用, 让人来解决的)	0.10
It is still early to replace human (想要取代人类还早着)	0.10
Technology innovation is very important if you want to invest in robots. (要想投入机器人, 技术更新是很重要的保障啊)	0.45
The technology didn't keep updated. (是技术没跟上时代吧)	0.30
If the technology is not mature, don't put it into the market too early. (技术不成熟就不要太早投入市场啊)	0.08

also explained why customers had to ask the human staff for help in some situations. Examples of comments related to technology include: *'Technology innovation is very important if you want to invest in robots'*, *'The technology didn't keep updated'* and *'If the technology is not mature, don't put it into the market too early'*.

Table 2 shows examples of comments related to topic #1. As shown on the table, most comments under this topic have low sentiments. They are mostly skepticism and negativities about using robots to substitute for human services.

Topic #2: The robot embodiment

Topic #2 refers to the physical embodiment of the robot. Within the context of this topic, the word 'dinosaur' refers to the robot with a dinosaur embodiment in Henn-na Hotel. Although most of the comments complained that the robot dinosaur was quite 'horrible' or 'scary' such as *'That dinosaur is quite scary'* and *'The dinosaur really wouldn't scare the children?'*, there are also a few positive comments, such as *'The dinosaur is so cute'* and *'The dinosaur wearing a hat is so cute'*.

Table 3. Selected comments related to Topic #2 (The robot embodiment).

Data exemplar	Sentiment score
That dinosaur is quite scary (那个恐龙挺吓人的)	0.16
The dinosaur really wouldn't scare the children? (那恐龙真的不会吓到小朋友吗)	0.08
The dinosaur is so cute (恐龙好可爱)	0.95
The dinosaur wearing a hat is so cute (那只恐龙戴个帽子好可爱)	0.96
That female robot is so scary (那个女机器人好吓人)	0.03
I think the female robot is very horrible, won't the people living there feel scared? (我觉得那个机器'女人'好可怕啊, 他们住着看见她不害怕吗?)	0.02
I don't dare to live in such a hotel at night. (晚上一个人不敢住这样的酒店)	0.13
Too scary, especially at night (太吓人了, 特别是晚上)	0.07
I dare not go out at night (晚上都不敢出门)	0.02
Why do they use such an ugly robot? It is scary. (为什么要用这样难看的机器人看着好吓人)	0.03
I feel a little horrible to live in such a hotel. (感觉住在这样的酒店有点恐怖)	0.06

To further analyze if there is a difference between how people perceived the female robot and the robot dinosaur in the hotel, this study extracted the comments related to the female robot and then performed sentiment analysis for the related comments. There are 19 comments that are related to the female robot, and the average sentiment score is 0.23, which is relatively low or negative compared to the word 'dinosaur' which has a sentiment score of 0.50. Comments related to the female robot include: *'That female robot is so scary'*, *'Why do they use such an ugly robot?'*, and *'I think the female robot is very horrible, won't the people living there feel scared?'* Interestingly, there are quite a few comments about the female robot at night. The comments reveal that people are afraid of meeting the female robot in the hotel at night, such as *'I don't dare to live in such a hotel at night'*, *'Too scary, especially at night'* and *'I dare not go out at night'*.

Table 3 shows examples of comments related to topic #2. The table shows the sentiment scores for the comments about the robot embodiment are generally negative except for a few related to the dinosaur.

Topic #3: The apprehension about job replacement

Table 1 shows that the terms that are almost unique to topic #3 include 'hahaha', 'in the future', 'next time', and 'then'. The theme for topic #3 is related to the concerns about job replacement in the future. Some comments indicate that it is fortunate the hotel robots had been fired as they were not able to replace the human servers: *'Human still has advantages, hahaha'* and *'Robots still can't replace human's brain, it can be a danger if they can, hahaha'*. The use of 'hahaha' in the comments indicate positive sentiment or happiness.

Although the comments on topic #1 (the difficulty of using robots to replace human services) have indicated that human services are difficult to replace, there are also those who feel that robots will eventually replace human services in the future. The comments

Table 4. Selected comments related to Topic #3 (Apprehension about job replacement).

Data exemplar	Sentiment score
Human still has advantages, hahahahaha (人还是有优势的啊, 哈哈哈哈哈)	0.99
Robots still can't replace human's brain, it can be a danger if they can, hahahahahaha (还不能取代大脑思维, 能取代了人类就危险了, 哈哈哈哈哈哈)	0.87
It's just that the technology is not mature enough, and robots will replace humans in the future. (只是技术不够成熟而已, 以后只会机器人代替人。)	0.46
Artificial intelligence is getting more and more powerful, many people will lose their jobs. (人工智能越来越发达, 会很多人没工作的)	0.37
If the robot can replace human's jobs in the future, will we be unemployed? (如果以后机器人可以代替人工作的话, 那我们不是失业了吗)	0.14
It's getting harder to find work in the future (以后工作越来越难找)	0.14
It is difficult to find a stable job these years! (这年头找一份稳定的工作难呐！)	0.13
I really cannot believe that you dare to let AI replace the labor work under the current population in China. (我还真不信, 中国现在的人口, 你敢让AI替代劳动工作)	0.11
I really don't know how to find a job after the robots are developed better in the future. (真不知道以后发达了还怎么找工作。)	0.09
It is not easy to find a job now. (现在找工作也不容易了。)	0.02

that contain the words 'in the future' have a relatively low average sentiment score of 0.34. Examples of related comments include: *'It's just that the technology is not mature enough, and robots will replace humans in the future'*, *'If the robot can replace human's jobs in the future, will we be unemployed?'* and *'I really don't know how to find a job after the robots are developed better in the future'*. The comments show that people are worried about the future when robots take over the employees' jobs. They are concened with the uncertainty that robots will bring. They feel threatened about their job security. Table 4 shows examples of comments related to topic #3.

Discussion

Topic #1 discussion

Topic #1 shows that there were people who were skeptical about hotel robots because they felt that the robots cannot replace human services. A comment from one who had used the robots at Henn-na Hotel said that the robots were unable to solve his/her problems, such as completing the check-in process. The comment said that the robots were not useful. Other comments also said that the robots had difficulty understanding their requests. They had to seek help from hotel staff and this led to inconveniences. There were explicit and implicit comments that hotel robots need to be useful and easy to use. When robots were able to perform tasks such as completing check-in for customers or when they could solve the customers' problems, the customers felt pleased. Their sentiments indicate they were likely to use the robots again. On the other hand, when the interactions between the robots and the customers need human intervention, they were an indication that the robots were problematic and difficult to use. In these cases, customers were unlikely to use the robots again. The comments about the usefulness and ease of use of hotel robots were consistent with the propositions in the TAM, which states that perceived usefulness and perceived ease of use are two important criteria that are positively related to technology adoption (Davis, 1989).

People also expect service robots to show feelings and emotions as they are taking over the roles of human employees. According to the comments, these qualitites are not displayed by the frontline robots at Henn-na Hotel. The perceptions were that the hotel had not been keeping up with technology and therefore it should upgrade its technology accordingly.

Topic #2 discussion

Regarding the embodiment of the robots, there are both positive and negative comments for the dinosaur robot but no compliments for the female robot. The comments said that the female humanoid robot was horrible, ugly, and scary. In a prior study about the robots at Henna-na Hotel, Yu (2020) found that the comments in Youtube tend to be negative when it comes to any discussion about the human-like robot. The results of this study are consistent with those in Yu (2020), and they indicate that the hotel should seek to improve the appearance of the female robot so that customers will not feel uncomfortable with it.

The results of the current study also indicate that the use of the anthropomorphic robot is less favorable than the zoomorphic robot. Almost all the comments about the female robot are negative with a low average sentiment score. On the other hand, some comments say the dinosaur robot is cute. These findings seem to suggest that when robots are more humanoid, users have higher expectations about them (Nowak & Biocca, 2003). Also, based on the uncanny valley theory, it is possible that people feel scared about the female humanoid because it appeared to resemble too much like a human (Mori et al., 2012).

Topic #3 discussion

The comments about the apprehension of using hotel robots relate to the possibility that the robots may provide better services in the future and as a result, people will be replaced in their jobs. The issue about job losses or technological unemployment is a serious concern. They reflect similar feelings about the use of robots in the society as a whole, and not just in the hotel industry. China has recently become very concerned about job losses and unemployment, as these could potentially lead to social unrest and riots (He, 2020). Management has to allay people's fears about robots. People need to be convinced how the issue of job losses will be addressed.

Based on the AI job replacement theory (Huang & Rust, 2018), employers should consider replacing tasks rather than jobs. Robots should only replace those tasks that they are capable of performing. Tasks that robots cannot perform, such as showing feelings and emotions, should be retained for human workers, at least for the moment. This can help to allieviate the fear of unemployment. It can also help the adoption of hotel robots because when users find that robots are able to do the tasks without human intervention, i.e., they are useful and easy to use, people will use them (Davis, 1989). On the other hand, when robots have added roles that are beyond their capability, people may not use them because the tasks that people want the robots to do never get done.

Organizations should also explore other ways to lessen people's fear about being replaced by robots. Employers and educational institutions should make plans to help workers learn new skills so that people are not made redundant at the workplace.

Overall discussion

There are three significant findings in this research. First, the results show that people's expectations of hotel robots were higher than those for industrial robots. Industrial robots are required to perform standard and repetitive tasks only, whereas hotel robots need to be able to solve all the customers' problems. People not only expect hotel robots to be useful and easy to use. They also want robots to work like a human by showing feelings and emotions. They felt that hotel robots were not up to their mark yet. Technically, therefore, there was room for hotel robots to improve.

Second, the results show that the appearance of the female robot can be better as people felt that it was ugly and they were afraid of it. People had low sentiments for the female robot. The appearance of the robot is therefore very important and robot developers should devote attention to this. Third, people were happy to see the robots go. They were concerned about their job security as robots could potentially take over their jobs and they could become jobless. As mentioned earlier, organizations need to address issues related to job losses.

Overall, the results indicate that there are many areas where hotel robots can improve. Robot developers should make the robots useful and easy to use. They should improve the robots' appearance, and have them show feelings and emotions. However, robot developers should take note of the uncanny valley theory. To reiterate, the theory posits that the relationship between the robots' perceived human likeness and their likability is nonlinear (Mori et al., 2012). When robots become too much like humans, people can have an errie feeling about them. Robot developers should optimize the robots' behavior and appearance such that they are not highly human-like so as to avoid negative attitudes toward them.

Conclusion

There are very few studies about the perceptions and sentiments of hotel robots in the literature (S. Ivanov et al., 2019). According to the authors' knowledge, this is the possibly the first study that focused on the perceptions and sentiments of hotel robots among the Chinese social media users. There are two broad contributions from the results of this research. First, from the research perspective, the use of computational techniques such as topic modeling and sentiment analysis has helped to analyze a large number of comments from the social media. In this study, topic modeling summarized people's perceptions of hotel robots into three topics. The first topic shows that people were skeptical because of the difficulty of using robots to replace human services. The second topic indicates that people were scared of the female humanoid at Henn-na Hotel, and the third topic is related to people's apprehension about being replaced by robots. Sentiment analysis has also provided a broad indication of how people felt about hotel robots. Low sentiments were associated with the appearance of the female humanoid and the concern that employees could be replaced by robots in the future. High sentiments were associated with the happiness that people felt because the robots had been retrenched.

The second broad contribution of this research is based on the practical perspective. The results of this study suggest that robot developers should upgrade its technology so that the robots can operate better. The robots should be easy to use and not cause trouble to the users. Better still, they should show feelings and emotions. The appearance of the humanoid is also important. Improvements to the female robot should be optimized such that its behavior and appearance should not be highly human-like in order to avoid people having negative attitudes toward it. Finally, as people are worried about job losses and unemployment, there should be more engagements related to these issues. There should also be training plans to help workers cope with learning new skills so that they can have better job security.

There are several limitations for the results of this study. First, the comments for this study were obtained from several Weibo posts that included a video about the hotel robots. As the video was attached to the news about the robot dismissal, it could have affected people's perceptions of the robots. Second, the comments were collected from the Weibo website and they were based on a specific hashtag. Future studies can make use of other public Chinese datasets and related hashtags. These can help to validate the generalizability of the results. Third, even though using computational methods such as topic modeling and sentiment analysis have the advantage of providing consistent results, they have some limitations related to the actual understanding of the data. In Table 1 for example, the terms 未来 and 以后 have similar meaning as 'in the future'. Their frequencies might be grouped together to provide greater clarity and reliability of the results. The use of more advanced tools that can better understand the human language can help to minimize this limitation.

To conclude, the results of this study contribute to the tourism literature by providing an overview of people's perceptions and sentiments about hotel robots. The results help to keep researchers and practitioners informed about how the Chinese social media users reacted to the dismissal of hotel robots. The results show that people expected the hotel robots to work like a human. They expected the robots to be useful and easy to use, and that they should show feelings and emotions. People were skeptical about the ability of the current technologies to fulfill these expectations, however. They were happy about the dismissal of the robots as it means that people were better than the robots and that people would be able to retain their jobs. Neverthelss, people were fearful because robots can potentially take over their jobs in the future.

Disclosure statement

No potential conflict of interest was reported by the authors.

Funding

This work was supported by the Universityof Macau [MYRG 2018-00118-FBA].

References

Adams, D. A., Nelson, R. R., & Todd, P. A. (1992). Perceived usefulness, ease of use, and usage of information technology: A replication. *MIS Quarterly, 16*(2), 227–247. https://doi.org/10.2307/249577

Ajzen, I., & Fishbein, M. (2005). The influence of attitudes on behavior. In D. Albarracin, B. T. Johnson, & M. P. Zanna (Eds.), *The handbook of attitudes* (pp. 173–221). Lawrence Erlbaum Associates.

Alexis, P. (2017). R-Tourism: Introducing the potential impact of robotics and service automation in tourism. *Ovidius University Annals: Economic Sciences Series, 17*(1), 211–216. http://stec.univ-ovidius.ro/html/anale/RO/2017/Section-III/16.pdf

Arai, T., Kato, R., & Fujita, M. (2010). Assessment of operator stress induced by robot collaboration in assembly. *CIRP Annals, 59*(1), 5–8. https://doi.org/10.1016/j.cirp.2010.03.043

Barrett, M., Davidson, E., Prabhu, J., & Vargo, S. L. (2015). Service innovation in the digital age: Key contributions and future directions. *MIS Quarterly, 39*(1), 135–154. https://doi.org/10.25300/MISQ/2015/39:1.03

Bartneck, C., Kulić, D., Croft, E., & Zoghbi, S. (2009). Measurement instruments for the anthropomorphism, animacy, likeability, perceived intelligence, and perceived safety of robots. *International Journal of Social Robotics, 1*(1), 71–81. https://doi.org/10.1007/s12369-008-0001-3

Bollini, M., Tellex, S., Thompson, T., Roy, N., & Rus, D. (2013). Interpreting and executing recipes with a cooking robot. In J. P. Desai, G. Dudek, O. Khatib, & V. Kumar (Eds.), *Experimental robotics* (pp. 481–495). Springer.

Cha, E., Dragan, A. D., & Srinivasa, S. S. (2015). Perceived robot capability. In *Proceedings of the 24th IEEE International Symposium on Robot and Human Interactive Communication (RO-MAN)* (pp. 541–548). IEEE.

Chuang, J., Ramage, D., Manning, C., & Heer, J. (2012). Interpretation and trust: Designing model-driven visualizations for text analysis. In *Proceedings of the SIGCHI Conference on Human Factors in Computing Systems* (pp. 443–452). ACM.

Davis, F. D. (1989). Perceived usefulness, perceived ease of use, and user acceptance of information technology. *MIS Quarterly, 13*(3), 319–340. https://doi.org/10.2307/249008

Duffy, B. R. (2003). Anthropomorphism and the social robot. *Robotics and Autonomous Systems, 42*(3–4), 177–190. https://doi.org/10.1016/S0921-8890(02)00374-3

Eickhoff, M., & Neuss, N. (2017). Topic modelling methodology: Its use in information systems and other managerial disciplines. In *Proceedings of the 25th European Conference on Information Systems (ECIS)* (pp.1327–1347). Guimarães.

Fong, T., Nourbakhsh, I., & Dautenhahn, K. (2003). A survey of socially interactive robots. *Robotics and Autonomous Systems, 42*(3–4), 143–166. https://doi.org/10.1016/S0921-8890(02)00372-X

Gnambs, T., & Appel, M. (2019). Are robots becoming unpopular? Changes in attitudes towards autonomous robotic systems in Europe. *Computers in Human Behavior, 93*, 53–61. https://doi.org/10.1016/j.chb.2018.11.045

Granulo, A., Fuchs, C., & Puntoni, S. (2019). Psychological reactions to human versus robotic job replacement. *Nature Human Behaviour, 3*(10), 1062–1069. https://doi.org/10.1038/s41562-019-0670-y

Hata, S., Hiroyasu, T., Hayashi, J. I., Hojoh, H., & Hamada, T. (2008). Robot system for cloth handling. In *2008 34th Annual Conference of IEEE Industrial Electronics* (pp. 3449–3454). IEEE.

He, L. (2020, January 13). China is really worried about unemployment. *CNN Business.* https://edition.cnn.com/2020/01/13/economy/china-2020-economy/index.html

Hertzfeld, E. (2019). *Japan's Henn na Hotel fires half its robot workforce.* Questex LLC. https://www.hotelmanagement.net/tech/japan-s-henn-na-hotel-fires-half-its-robot-workforce

Hoffmann, L., & Krämer, N. C. (2013). Investigating the effects of physical and virtual embodiment in task-oriented and conversational contexts. *International Journal of Human-Computer Studies, 71*(7–8), 763–774. https://doi.org/10.1016/j.ijhcs.2013.04.007

Huang, M. H., & Rust, R. T. (2018). Artificial intelligence in service. *Journal of Service Research, 21*(2), 155–172. https://doi.org/10.1177/1094670517752459

Hurst, D. (2019). *Amid thaw, Japan is seeing boom in Chinese tourist.* James Pach. https://thediplomat.com/2019/03/amid-thaw-japan-is-seeing-a-boom-in-chinese-tourists

Ivanov, S., Gretzel, U., Berezina, K., Sigala, M., & Webster, C. (2019). Progress on robotics in hospitality and tourism: A review of the literature. *Journal of Hospitality and Tourism Technology, 10*(4), 489–521. https://doi.org/10.1108/JHTT-08-2018-0087

Ivanov, S., Webster, C., & Berezina, K. (2017). Adoption of robots and service automation by tourism and hospitality companies. *Revista Turismo & Desenvolvimento, 27*(28), 1501–1517. https://ssrn.com/abstract=2964308

Ivanov, S., Webster, C., & Garenko, A. (2018). Young Russian adults' attitudes towards the potential use of robots in hotels. *Technology in Society, 55*, 24–32. https://doi.org/10.1016/j.techsoc.2018.06.004

Jia, K., Kenney, M., Mattila, J., & Seppala, T. (2018). The application of artificial intelligence at Chinese digital platform giants: Baidu, Alibaba and Tencent. In *ETLA reports* (pp. 81).

Kim, S. Y., Schmitt, B. H., & Thalmann, N. M. (2019). Eliza in the uncanny valley: Anthropomorphizing consumer robots increases their perceived warmth but decreases liking. In *Marketing letters* (Vol. 30(01): 1–12).

Lee, K. M., Jung, Y., Kim, J., & Kim, S. R. (2006). Are physically embodied social agents better than disembodied social agents? The effects of physical embodiment, tactile interaction, and people's loneliness in human–robot interaction. *International Journal of Human-computer Studies, 64*(10), 962–973. https://doi.org/10.1016/j.ijhcs.2006.05.002

Li, J. (2015). The benefit of being physically present: A survey of experimental works comparing copresent robots, telepresent robots and virtual agents. *International Journal of Human-Computer Studies, 77*, 23–37. https://doi.org/10.1016/j.ijhcs.2015.01.001

Lindsay, P. H., & Norman, D. A. (1977). *Human information processing: An introduction to psychology.* Academic Press.

Manyika, J., Lund, S., Chui, M., Bughin, J., Woetzel, J., Batra, P., Ko, R., & Sanghvi, S. (2017, November). What the future of work will mean for jobs, skills, and wages. *McKinsey Quarterly.* https://www.mckinsey.com/~/media/mckinsey/featured%20insights/future%20of%20organiza tions/what%20the%20future%20of%20work%20will%20mean%20for%20jobs%20skills%20and %20wages/mgi%20jobs%20lost-jobs%20gained_report_december%202017.ashx

Mori, M., MacDorman, K. F., & Kageki, N. (2012). The uncanny valley [from the field]. *IEEE Robotics & Automation Magazine, 19*(2), 98–100.

Nam, T. (2019). Technology usage, expected job sustainability, and perceived job insecurity. *Technological Forecasting and Social Change, 138*(1), 155–165. https://doi.org/10.1016/j.techfore.2018.08.017

Nieto, D., Quesada-Arencibia, A., García, C. R., & Moreno-Díaz, R. (2014, December). A social robot in a tourist environment. In R. Hervás, S. Lee, C. Nugent, & J. Bravo (Eds.), *Ubiquitous computing and ambient intelligence: Personalisation and user adapted services* (pp. 21–24). Springer.

Nomura, T., Suzuki, T., Kanda, T., & Kato, K. (2006). Measurement of negative attitudes toward robots. *Interaction Studies, 7*(3), 437–454. https://doi.org/10.1075/is.7.3.14nom

Nowak, K. L., & Biocca, F. (2003). The effect of the agency and anthropomorphism on users' sense of telepresence, copresence, and social presence in virtual environments. *Presence: Teleoperators & Virtual Environments, 12*(5), 481–494. https://doi.org/10.1162/105474603322761289

Pak, A., & Paroubek, P. (2010). Twitter as a corpus for sentiment analysis and opinion mining. In *LREC 2010, Seventh International Conference on Language Resources and Evaluation* (pp. 1320–1326).

Pfeifer, R., Lungarella, M., & Iida, F. (2007). Self-organization, embodiment, and biologically inspired robotics. *Science, 318*(5853), 1088–1093. https://doi.org/10.1126/science.1145803

Pierce, A. (2015). A hotel staffed by robots. *Tech Directions, 75*(2), 8–9. http://www.technologyto day.us/columnPDF/A_Hotel_Staffed_by_Robots.pdf

Rosenthal-Von Der Pütten, A. M., & Krämer, N. C. (2014). How design characteristics of robots determine evaluation and uncanny valley related responses. *Computers in Human Behavior, 36*, 422–439. https://doi.org/10.1016/j.chb.2014.03.066

Ryall, J. (2019). *AI fail: Japan's Henn-na Hotel dumps 'annoying' robot staff, hires humans.*South China Morning Post. https://www.scmp.com/news/asia/east-asia/article/2182295/ai-fail-japans -henn-na-hotel-dumps-annoying-robot-staff-hires

Saeedi, S., Trentini, M., Seto, M., & Li, H. (2016). Multiple-robot simultaneous localization and mapping: A review. *Journal of Field Robotics, 33*(1), 3–46. https://doi.org/10.1002/rob.21620

Sievert, C., & Shirley, K. (2014). A method for visualizing and interpreting topics. In *Proceedings of the Workshop on Interactive Language Learning, Visualization, and Interfaces* (pp. 63–70). ACL.

Solomon, M. R., Surprenant, C., Czepiel, J. A., & Gutman, E. G. (1985). A role theory perspective on dyadic interactions: The service encounter. *Journal of Marketing, 49*(1), 99–111. https://doi. org/10.1177/002224298504900110

Statt, N. (2016). *Hilton and IBM built a Watson-powered concierge robot.* Vox Media. https://www. theverge.com/2016/3/9/11180418/hilton-ibm-connie-robot-watson-hotel-concierge

Stock, R. M., & Merkle, M. (2017). A service robot acceptance model: User acceptance of humanoid robots during service encounters. In *2017 IEEE International Conference on Pervasive Computing and Communications Workshops (PerCom Workshops)* (pp. 339–344). IEEE.

Strait, M. K., Aguillon, C., Contreras, V., & Garcia, N. (2017). The public's perception of human-like robots: Online social commentary reflects an appearance-based uncanny valley, a general fear of a "Technology takeover", and the unabashed sexualization of female-gendered robots. In *Proceedings of the 26th IEEE International Symposium on Robot and Human Interactive Communication (RO-MAN)* (pp. 1418–1423). IEEE.

Titcomb, J. (2015). *Should humans fear the rise of the machine?.* Telegraph. https://www.telegraph. co.uk/technology/news/11837157/Should-humans-fear-the-rise-of-the-machine.html

Tung, V. W. S., & Au, N. (2018). Exploring customer experiences with robotics in hospitality. *International Journal of Contemporary Hospitality Management, 30*(7), 2680–2697. https://doi. org/10.1108/IJCHM-06-2017-0322

Tung, V. W. S., & Law, R. (2017). The potential for tourism and hospitality experience research in human-robot interactions. *International Journal of Contemporary Hospitality Management, 29* (10), 2498–2513. https://doi.org/10.1108/IJCHM-09-2016-0520

Tussyadiah, I. P., & Park, S. (2018). Consumer evaluation of hotel service robots. In B. Stangl & J. Pesonen (Eds.), *Information and communication technologies in tourism 2018* (pp. 308–320). Springer.

Van der Heijden, H. (2004). User acceptance of hedonic information systems. *MIS Quarterly, 28* (4), 695–704. https://doi.org/10.2307/25148660

Varkaris, E., & Neuhofer, B. (2017). The influence of social media on the consumers' hotel decision journey. *Journal of Hospitality and Tourism Technology, 8*(1), 101–118. https://doi.org/10.1108/ JHTT-09-2016-0058

Wainer, J., Feil-Seifer, D. J., Shell, D. A., & Mataric, M. J. (2006). The role of physical embodiment in human-robot interaction. In *Proceedings of the 15th IEEE International Symposium on Robot and Human Interactive Communication (RO-MAN)* (pp. 117–122). IEEE.

Wang, S., Lilienfeld, S. O., & Rochat, P. (2015). The uncanny valley: Existence and explanations. *Review of General Psychology, 19*(4), 393–407. https://doi.org/10.1037/gpr0000056

Wang, Y. (2017). *The rise of Weibo: Lessons Twitter can learn from Chinese upstart.* Forbes. https://www.forbes.com/sites/ywang/2017/06/06/the-rise-of-weibo-lessons-twitter-can-learn-from-chinese-upstart/#4bf1d3ba20b0

Weller, C. (2017). *Meet the first-ever robot citizen — A humanoid named Sophia that once said it would 'destroy humans'.* https://www.businessinsider.com/meet-the-first-robot-citizen-sophia-animatronic-humanoid-2017-10

Wirtz, J., Patterson, P. G., Kunz, W. H., Gruber, T., Lu, V. N., Paluch, S., & Martins, A. (2018). Brave new world: Service robots in the frontline. *Journal of Service Management, 29*(5), 907–931. https://doi.org/10.1108/JOSM-04-2018-0119

Ying, K., Jingchang, P., & Minglei, W. (2017). Research on sentiment analysis of Micro-blog's topic based on TextRank's abstract. In *Proceedings of the 2017 International Conference on Information Technology* (pp. 86–90). ACM.

Yu, C. E. (2020). Humanlike robots as employees in the hotel industry: Thematic content analysis of online reviews. *Journal of Hospitality Marketing & Management, 29*(1), 22–38. https://doi.org/10.1080/19368623.2019.1592733

Zalama, E., García-Bermejo, J. G., Marcos, S., Domínguez, S., Feliz, R., Pinillos, R., & López, J. (2014). Sacarino, a service robot in a hotel environment. In M. Armada, A. Sanfeliu, & M. Ferre (Eds.), *ROBOT2013: First Iberian Robotics Conference. Advances in Intelligent Systems and Computing* (pp. 3–14). Springer.

Index

Page numbers in **bold** refer to tables and those in *italic* refer to figures.

Abdullah, J. 82–3, **83**
accessibility indicators 9, 18, **18**
Ahluwalia, R. 66
Aiken, L. S. 109, 112
Amaro, S. 42, 53, 54
AMOS 20.0 software 107, 108
anthropomorphic/humanoid robots 122–4, 133
ArcGIS: HSR and expressway 13; network analysis 2–3; OD cost matrix tool 14
artificial intelligence (AI) 120–1, **132**
Au, N. 46, 101, 124
autocorrelation 111, 124
Au Yeung, T. 101, 104
average variance extracted (AVE) 48, 49, 90, 108
aviation, travel transportation mode 9–15, 17–20
Ayeh, J. K. 46

Bai, B. 101, 103, 104
Bailey, J. P. 104
Bakewell, C. 29
Barbaro-Forleo, G. 65
Becker-Olsen, K. 62, 74
Beijing–Guangzhou HSR line 12, 17
Beijing–Shanghai HSR line 10, 12, 17, 20
Bellman, S. 100
Berezina, K. 124
Bergeron, J. 65
Bhattacharya, C. 61–2, 66
Bigné, J. E. 85–6
Bijmolt, T. 65
Blodgett, J. G. **26**, 28
Bonilla-Priego, M. J. 62
Bonnafous, A. 10
BosonNLP, sentiment analysis 126
brand engagement: brand-based processes 66; conceptual framework 66, *67*; description 65; new and repeat customers 66; self-enhancement concept 66
Brock, J. L. 67
Brown, G. 84
Bruinsma, F. 10
Bruner, G. 103
Brymer, R. A. 103
Buhalis, D. 42, 44, 45, 114

Burnkrant, R. 66
Business for Social Responsibility (2006) 63

Cai, L. A. 3
Cao, J. 10
caricatured robots 123
Carroll, A. 63
Chang, H. H. 2, 103
Chang, Y. H. 63
Chan, H. 102
check-in for customers 121, 124, 132
Chen, C. -L. 10
Chen, S. W. 103
Chen, Y. 5, 86, 91
Cheung, D. 65
Chinese millennials: Generation Y 42; lack of siblings 43; leisure travel 43; little emperors/empresses 42–3; 80s and 90s 42
Chin, W. 108
Chung, C. D. 5, 44, 45, 101, 103, 104
Chung, T. 103, 104
Chu, R. 30, 67
Citrin, V. A. 102, 103
club spa 26
Cohen, E. 85
Cohen, J. 109
Cohen, P. 109
comparative fit index (CFI) 48, 70, **109**
composite reliability (CR) 48, 89, **90**, 108, **109**
confirmatory factor analysis (CFA) 48, **49**
construct validity 108
consumers' internet experiences 100, 102–4, 111
consumers' perceptions 100, 101, 104
consumer survey: hypotheses testing 71, *72*; measurement model 70, **72**; respondent profiles 70, **71**
contour measure 10, 11
convergent validity 48, 89, 108, **109**
copresent robots 122
corporate brand association 64
corporate philanthropy activities 64
corporate social responsibility (CSR) initiatives 4–5; communicated hotel brands 62; consumers' brand engagement 65–6;

domains 63; Facebook 62; frequency of hotels' on facebook 68, **69**; Hong Kong case study 62–3; hotel context 62; properties' investments 73–4; public engagement and relationship building 73; social media's role 73; tourism and hospitality 63–4; *see also* consumer survey
Creyer, E. 65
cruise ship spa 26
customer satisfaction 63, 68, **69**, **72**, 81, 92–4, 102, 103; expectancy-disconfirmation framework 84; perceived discrepancy 85; tourist 85; tourist consumption 85

daily accessibility (DA) 10, 11
day spa 26, 27, 30
Del Bosque, I. R. 64, 86, 87
destination image (DI) 2, 5, 85–7, 89–93
destination spa 26
detachment-recovery, autonomy, mastery, meaning, and affiliation (DRAMMA) 84
Diener, E. 82, 84, 87
discriminant validity **49**, 108, **109**
Duarte, P. 42, 53, 54
Dunford, M. 10
Durbin–Watson statistics 111
Du, S. 66

Eickhoff, M. 126
Ekmekcioglu, C. 83
Emmons, R. A. 87
engagement in mobile technology 60; conceptual model **47**, **52**; defined 46; measurements 48–9, **49**; procedures 47–8; TAM 46; utilitarian, hedonic functions 46
environmental CSR (ESCR) 63, 65, 66, 68, **69**, 70–5, **72**

Fan, A. 3
Fang, Z. 10
Faraj, S. 104
Federal Statistical Office (FSO) 87
Feil-Seifer, D. J. 122
Ferrell, O. C. 65
Filep, S. 84, 93
Flanagin, A. J. 114
Fong, L. H. N. 2
Font, X. 62, 63
Forrest, E. J. 103
frequency distribution 128
Fritz, C. 83

Gao, L. 5
Gao, Y. 3
Garmendia, M. 10
Gilbert, D. 82–3
Givoni, M. 10
Godspeed scale 124
Gómez, G. 10
González, R. 10
Goodhue, D. L. 100–1

GooSeeker, web crawler 126
Gregoire, M. 102
Gretzel, U. 53, 124
Griffin, S. 87
gross domestic product (GDP) 82
Growth from Knowledge (GFK) 43
Guix, M. 62
Guiyang–Guangzhou HSR line 12
Gutiérrez, J. 10, 20

happiness: customer satisfaction 84–5; effects of vacation 82–3; and life satisfaction 82; spillover effects 84; and tourist experiences 83–4; *see also* life satisfaction (LS)
Harbin–Dalian HSR line 12
Hartwick, J. 105
Haytko, D. L. 29
hedonic function 44–7, 49–52, 54, 60
Henderson, J. 64
The Henn-na Hotel in Japan: classification of robots 122–3; difficulty of using robots 129–30, **130**; human-like robots 121; inter-topic distance maps *127*; job replacement 131–2, **132**; perception process 124–5; prior research, hotel robots 123–4; research method 125–6, *127*; research questions 121–2; robot embodiment 130–1, **131**; social media 121; use of robots 122; *see also* life satisfaction (LS)
Henriques, C. 53
high-speed rail (HSR) 2–3; accessibility measurement 11–13, *13*; China 11; China's High-Speed Rail Network construcion 10; destination accessibility 9; indicators 11; Jiangsu Province 11; Madrid–Barcelona–French border high-speed line 10; quantitative methods 10; transportation mode selection 13–14, *14*, **15**; *see also* market potential methods
Hills, P. 65
Hinesly, M. D. 52
Holcomb, J. L. 62, 64, 68
Hong Kong case study *see* corporate social responsibility (CSR) initiatives
Hong Kongers 27, 30
Hong Kong Hotels Association (HKHA) 24–5
Hosany, S. 84
hotel-owned websites 113, 115
hotel spas: ambience 28; attributes of selection **26**; awakening of senses 26; branded/generic products 27; classification 26; experience of 26; facilities of 28; females for promotion 27; health service providers 25; incentives 34; managers 34; millennial consumers 28–9; mobile technology 30; olfactory cues 35; respondents' behavioral intention 30; selective attributes, millennials 30, **32**; servicescape 35; skin care products and herbal supplements 26; socio-demographic characteristics, respondents 30–1, **31**; therapists 27; *see also* spa attributes
hotel website quality: defined 100; functionality 101; IDs and credit

card numbers 101; technology acceptance model 101

Howat, G. 84

Hsiao, S.-L. 84

Hsu, C. H. 101, 102, 104

Huang, J. S. 102

Huang, M. H. 125

independent and moderator variables 110, 111

information communication technologies (ICTs): consumers' internet experiences 102–3; hotel website quality 100–2; marketing effectiveness 103–4; measurement development 104–6, *105*; offline marketing efforts 100; online booking intentions 102; pilot test 106–7, **107**; reliability and validity tests 108–11; sample profiles 107, **108**; tourism and hospitality industries 99; website usability and functionality 100

International Spa Association (2017) 25

Ivanov, S. 124

Iyer, R. 34

Jenkins, O. H. 87

Jeong, M. 102, 105

Jiangsu Province 11

Jiao, J. 10

Jin, F. 10

Johnson, E. J. 100

Joppe, M. 29

Jung, S. 63

Jung, Y. 122

Kang, K. H. 63

Karotz robot 121

Kim, B. 63

Kim, D. J. 48, 101, 106, 114, 115

Kim, D. Y. 52, 114

Kim, H. 101

Kim, J. H. 63, 122

Kim, S. R. 122

Kim, S. Y. 123

Kim, W. G. 101, 106, 114, 115

Kim, Y. H. 48

King, L. 82

Kirk, D. 64

Kumar, A. 103

Lalicic, L. 46

Lam, L. W. 2

Lam, L. Y. J. 3

Laroche, M. 65

Larsen, R. J. 87

Law, R. 2, 46, 101–4

LDAvis package 126, 128

Lee, K. M. 122

Lee, M. J. 105

Lehto, X. Y. 100, 114

leisure mobility: demographic and personal information 49, **50**; mediation test

analysis 51; multiple regression analyses 50, **51**; Net Generation and digital natives 42; non-work related trips 42; tourism destinations 42; *see also* Chinese millennials; leisure travel; mobile technology

leisure travel 3–4, 43–54, **60**; *see also* mobile technology

Leung, D. 5

Leung, T. C. H. 63

Levinson, D. M. 10

Liang, T. P. 102

Liang, Y. 10, 20

life satisfaction (LS) 86; customer satisfaction to tourist satisfaction 84–5; effects of vacation on happiness 82–3; happiness and consumer evaluation 82; spillover effects 84; tourist experiences and happiness 83–4; on tourist satisfaction 89–90, **90**

Lilienfeld, S. O. 123

lipstick effect phenomenon 25

Li, Q. 10

Li, R. 86, 91

Little, J. 36

Liu, J. N. K. 101

Liu, M. T. C. 67

Liu, X. C. 10

Liu, Y. 10–11

Li, X. 2

logistics/transporting goods 124

Lohse, G. L. 100

Loiacono, E. T. 100–1

López, E. 10

Lu, S. 10

Lynch, P. 64

Lynes, J. 63

Lyubomirsky, S. 82

Maignan, I. 65

Mainland Chinese 27, 48

Ma, J. X. 114

Mao, L. 10–11

Marchand, M. A. 83

market potential methods 2–3, 9–12, *16*, 16–18, *17*, **18**, *20*

Marktl, W. 83

Martín, H. S. 86, 87

Masson, S. 10

Mataric, M. J. 122

Matteucci, X. 84, 93

Ma, X. 101, 106, 114, 115

medical spa 26

Menerault, P. 10

Merkle, M. 125

Metzger, M. J. 114

millennial consumers: baby boomers 28; consumption 28; digital generation and technologically savvy 29; fickle loyalties 29; Generation Y 28; hotel spa-goers 30; internet, influence of 30; social media influence 29; mineral spring spa 26

Mitchell, V. W. 29
mobile technology 42, 43; communication 45; entertainments 45; functions of 44; Mafengwo app 45; mobile apps utilization 45; mobility and portability 44; stages of travel 44; travelers 44–5; travel experience 45–6; wireless networks and appliances 43
mobility 41–2
Monzón, A. 10
Morosan, C. 100, 105
morphology of robots 122
Morrison, A. M. 52, 100, 114
Murphy, J. 103
Murray, K. B. 64

nabaztag robot 123
Nawijn, J. 83
negative affect 81–3, 85–7, 89, **90, 91,** 92
Neuss, N. 126
Newman, D. B. 84
Niehm, L. S. 100, 101
Niu, Y. 11, 20
Noble, S. M. 29
non-vacationers 82–3
normed fit index (NFI) 48
Nunnally, J. C. 48, 89, 108
Nysveen, H. 102–4

O'Connor, P. 100–2
Oh, H. 102
Okumus, F. 62, 64
O'Leary, J. T. 100
online booking intentions 101, 102, 104–6, **107,** 109, 111–13
online surveys 105, 106, 115, 123
online travel agencies (OTAs) 100, 101, 114
O'Regan, M. 2
Organization for Economic Co-operation and Development (OECD) 87
Ortega, E. 10

Pacheco, R. 62
Palmer, J. W. 104
Pan, S. 2, 102
Park, J. 52
Park, K. S. 27
Park, S. 123
partial least squares SEM (PLS-SEM) 88
Pavot, W. 87
Pearce, P. L. 2
Pedersen, P. E. 102–4
perception process 27, 62, 63, 85, 87, 93, 100, 101, 124–5
Petiot, R. 10
Phillips, J. 29
'pop-up and go' scheme 34–5
positive affect (PA) 47, 51, 66, 73, 81, 83, 86, 89–93, 104
Potential Values (PV) 10
privacy and security 100–2, 104–6, 109–15

processing payments 124
PROCESS Model One 33

Qian, J. 11, 20
Qualtrics screening process 31, 48, 67

Reisenwitz, T. H 34
Reisinger, Y. 27, 46
reliability 12, 32, 48, 68, 70–1, 89, **90,** 106–8, **109,** 113, 135
Remedios, P. 26
resort or hotel spa 26
Ricks, J. M. 64
Rietveld, P. 10, 12
robot embodiment 124, 128, 130–1, **131**
robots: industrial setting 120–1; researchers and practitioners 121; service robots 121; service setting 121; *see also* The Henn-na Hotel in Japan
Rochat, P. 123
root mean square error of approximation (RMSEA) 48
Ross, W. 65
Rothwell, M. 29
Rust, R. T. 125
Ryan, C. 2

Sánchez, J. 86
Sánchez-Mateos, H. S. M. 10
Sánchez, M. I. 64, 86
Schkade, D. 82
Schmitt, B. H. 123
security and privacy 100–2, 104–7, 109–15
Sen, S. 66
sentiment analysis, natural language processing method 126
servicescape 35–6
Shanghai–Kunming HSR line 12
Shaw, S. L. 10
Sheldon, K. M. 82
Shell, D. A. 122
Sheppard, B. H. 105
Shi, G. C. 67
Shi, J. 3
Sigala, M. 124
Silverman, S. N. 103
Simmons, C. 62, 74
Singh, J. 64
Snell, R. S. 63
social function 3, 43–52, 54, 60
societal CSR (SCSR) 5, 63, 64, 66, 68–71, 73, 74
Song, H. 114
Sonnentag, S. 81–3, 93
Sophia robot 122
spa attributes: floodlight analysis 33; process output **33**
Spiekermann, K. 10
Sprott, D. E. 103
stakeholders' CSR (StCSR) 66, 68, 70; benefits of 65; defined 63, 64; firm's 65

Statistical Package for Social Sciences (SPSS) 31
Stem, D. E. 103
Stock, R. M. 125
Strauss-Blasche, G. 83–4
structural equation modeling (SEM) approach 88
Sun, C. 10–11
Sun, M. 2

Taiwanese 27, 63
Tao, R. 10
Tay, L. 84
technology acceptance model (TAM) 46, 101, 125, 133
technology and chinese tourists research (2000–2020): journals 1, 2; leading tourism journals 1–2, 4; research themes and subject networks 1, 3
telepresent robots 122
Terry, M. 27
Thalmann, N. M. 123
topic modeling technique 124, 126, 128, 134, 135
Torres, A. 65
tourist destination choice 9
tourist satisfaction (TS): composite reliability 89; conceptual model 86; customer satisfaction 81; data and measurement 87–8; effects of affect **91**, 91–2, *92*; effects of vacation on happiness 82–3; *ex-ante* life satisfaction 81; expectancy-disconfirmation framework 81; research design 87; respondent profiles 88, *89*; sociodemographic of respondents **89**; structural equation modeling (SEM) approach 88; vacation 81; *see also* happiness; life satisfaction (LS)
Traditional Chinese Medicine (TCM) 27
traditional travel agencies 100
Tribo, J. 65
Tsaur, S.-H. 84
Tung, V. W. S. 124
Tussyadiah, I. P. 53, 123
Tzschentke, N. 64

uncanny valley theory 123, 133, 134
United Nations World Tourism Organization (UNWTO) 43
Unnava, H. 66
Upchurch, R. S. 64
Ureña, J. M. 10
utilitarian function 44, 46, 47, 60

vacationers 83
Van der Heijden, H. 125
variance inflation factors (VIF) 32, 110–11
Veenhoven, R. 83
Verhoef, P. 65

Vickerman, R. W. 10
Vingerhoets, A. J. 83
virtual agents 122
visiting spas, Hong Kong hotels: lipstick effect phenomenon 25; local consumers 25; service quality and preferences 25; urban residents 24; *see also* hotel spas
Vogel, C. M. 64
Voigt, C. 84

Wachter, K. 48
Wainer, J. 122
Wakefield, K. L. **26**, 28
Wang, D. 11, 20, 102
Wang, J. 10
Wang, L. 10–11
Wang, S. 123
Wang, Y. 10
Ward, M. R. 105
Warshaw, P. R. 105
Watson, R. T. 100–1
website functionality 101, 104–7, 109–13, 113
website quality and online booking intentions 111–12, *112*, *113*
website usability 100, 101, 104–7, 109–14, *112*, *113*
Webster, C. 124
Wegener, M. 10
Weibo, microblogging websites 121, 125–6
weighted average travel time (WATT) 10, 11
Weismayer, C. 46
Welford, R. 65
Weng, J. 2
Wen, I. 101, 103, 104
West, S. G. 112
Wong, I. A. 67
Wong, J. 103
World Youth Student and Educational Travel Confederation (WYSETC) 43
Wotring, C. E. 103
Wu, D. 10, 20
Wuhan–Guangzhou HSR line 12
Wu, M. Y. 2
Wu, W. 10, 20

Yeh, C. H. 63, 84
Yoon, S. J. 103
Young, A. M. 52
Yu, C. E. 124, 133

Zach, F. J. 53
Zhang, E. Y. 101
Zhu, X. 2
zoomorphic robots 122–3, 133